DIES BOREALES.

DIES BOREALES;

OR

CHRISTOPHER UNDER CANVASS.

BY

PROFESSOR JOHN WILSON,

AUTHOR OF "NOCTES AMBROSIANÆ," "RECREATIONS OF CHRISTOPHER NORTH," &c. &c.

PHILADELPHIA:

A. HART, LATE CAREY AND HART.

1850.

PHILADELPHIA:
T. K. AND P. G. COLLINS, PRINTERS.

DIES BOREALES.

No. I.

CHRISTOPHER UNDER CANVASS.

Scene—*Cladich, Lochawe-side.*

Time—*Sunrise.*

North—Buller—Seward.

North. "Under the opening eyelids of the Morn!" Me-feels, Amici, at this moment, the charm of that Impersonation. Slowly awaking from sleep—scarcely conscious of her where-abouts—bewildered by the beauty of the revelation, nor recognizing her beloved lochs and mountains—visionary and nameless all as if an uncertain prolongation of her Summer's Night's dream.

Seward. I was not going to speak, my dear sir.

North. And now she is broad awake. She sees the heaven and the earth, nor thinks, God bless her, that 'tis herself that beautifies them!

Seward. Twenty years since I stood on this knoll, honored sir, by your side—twenty years to a day—and now the same perfect peace possesses me—mysterious return—as if all the intervening time slid away—and this were not a renewed but a continuous happiness.

North. And let it slide away into the still recesses of Memory—the Present has its privileges—and they may be blamelessly, wisely, virtuously enjoyed—and without irreverence to the sanctity of the Past. Let it slide away—but not into oblivion—no danger, no fear of oblivion—even joys will return on their wings of gossamer;—sorrows may be buried, but they are immortal.

Seward. I see not the slightest change on this Grove of Sycamores. Twenty years tell not on boles that have for centuries been in their prime. Yes—that one a little way down—and that one still farther off—*have* grown, and those striplings, then but saplings, may now be called Trees.

Buller. I never heard such a noise.

North. A cigar in your mouth at four o'clock in the morning! Well—well.

Buller. There, my dear sir, keep me in countenance with a Manilla.

North. The Herb! You have high authority—Spenser's for "noise."

Buller. I said noise—because it is a noise. Why the hum of bees overhead is absolutely like soft sustained thunder, and yet no bees visible in the umbrage. The sound is like that of one single bee, and he must be a giant. Ay—there I see a few working like mad—and I guess there must be myriads. The Grove must be full of bees' nests.

North. Not one. Hundreds of smokes are stealing up from hidden or apparent cottages—for the region is not unpopulous, and not a garden without its hives—and early risers though we be, the *matutinæ apes* are still before us, and so are the birds.

Buller. They, too, are making a noise. Who says a shilfa

cannot sing? Of the fifty now "pouring his throat," as the poet well says, I defy you to tell which sings best. That splendid fellow on the birch-tree top—or yonder gorgeous tyke on the yellow oak—or——

North. "In shadiest covert hid" the leader of the chorus that thrills the many-nested underwood with connubial bliss.

Seward. Not till this moment heard I the waterfall.

Buller. You did, though, all along—a felt accompaniment.

North. I know few glens more beautiful than Cladich-Cleugh!

Buller. Pardon me, sir, if I do not attempt that name.

North. How mellifluous!—Cladich-Cleugh!

Buller. Great is the power of gutturals.

North. It is not inaccessible. But you must skirt it till you reach the meadow where the cattle are beginning to browse. And then threading your way through a coppice, where you are almost sure to see a roe, you come down upon a series of little pools, in such weather as this so clear that you can count the trouts; and then the verdurous walls begin to rise on either side and right before you; and you begin to feel that the beauty is becoming magnificence, for the pools are now black, and the stems are old, and the cliffs intercept the sky, and there are caves, and that waterfall has dominion in the gloom, and there is sublimity in the sounding solitude.

Buller. Cladick-Cloock.

North. A miserable failure.

Buller. Cladig-Cloog.

North. Worser and worser.

Seward. Any footpath, sir?

North. Yes—for the roe and the goat.

Buller. And the man of the Crutch.

North. Good. But I speak of days when the Crutch was in its tree-bole——

Buller. As the Apollo was in its marble block.

North. Not so good. But, believe me, gentlemen, I have done it with the Crutch.

Seward. Ay, sir, and could do it again.

North. No. But you two are yet boys—on the sunny side of fifty—and I leave you, Seward, to act the guide to Buller up Cladich-Cleugh.

Buller. Pray, Mr. North, what may be the name of that sheet of water?

North. In Scotland we call it LOCH-AWE.

Buller. I am so happy—sir—that I talk nonsense.

North. Much nonsense may you talk.

Buller. Twas a foolish question—but you know, sir, that by some strange fatality or another I have been three times called away from Scotland without having seen *Loch-Awe.*

North. Make good use of your eyes now, sirrah, and you will remember it all the days of your life. That is Cruachan—no usurper he—by divine right a king. The sun is up, and there is motion in the clouds. Saw you ever such shadows? How majestically they stalk! And now how beautifully they glide! And now see you that broad black forest, half-way up the mountain?

Buller. I do.

North. You are sure you do.

Buller. I am.

North. You are mistaken. It is no broad black forest—it is mere gloom—shadow that in a minute will pass away, though now seeming steadfast as the woods.

Buller. I could swear it is a forest.

North. Swear not at all. Shut your eyes. Open them. Where now your wood?

Buller. Most extraordinary ocular deception.

North. Quite common. Yet no poet has described it.

See again. The same forest a mile off. No need of trees—sun and cloud make our visionary mountains sylvan: and the grandest visions are ever those that are transitory—ask your soul.

Buller. Your Manilla is out, my dear sir. There is the case.

North. Caught like a cricketer. You must ascend Cruachan. "This morning gives us promise of a glorious day;" you cannot do better than take time by the forelock, and be off now. Say the word—and I will myself row you over the Loch. No need of a guide: inclining to the left for an hour or two after you have cleared yonder real timber and sap wood—and then for an hour or two to the right—and then for another hour or two straight forwards—and then you will see the highest of the three peaks within an hour or two's walk of you—and thus, by mid-day, find yourself seated on the summit.

Buller. Seated on the summit.

North. Not too long, for the air is often very sharp at that altitude—and so rare, that I have heard tell of people fainting.

Buller. I am occasionally troubled with a palpitation of the heart—

North. Pooh, nonsense. Only the stomach.

Buller. And occasionally with a determination of blood to the head—

North. Pooh, nonsense. Only the stomach. Take a calker every two hours on your way up—and I warrant both heart and head—

Buller. Not to-day. It looks cloudy.

North. Why, I don't much care though I should accompany you—

Buller. I knew you would offer to do so, and I feel the delicacy of putting a decided negative on the proposal. Let us defer it till to morrow. For my sake, my dear sir, if not for your own, do not think of it; it will be no disappointment to me to remain with you here—and I shudder at the thought of your fainting on the summit. Be advised, my dear sir, be advised—

North. Well, then, be it so—I am not obstinate; but such another day for the ascent there may not be during the summer. On just such a day I made the ascent some half-century ago. I took it from Tyanuilt—having walked that morning from Dalmally, some dozen miles, for a breathing on level ground, before facing the steepish shoulder that roughens into Loch Etive. The fox-hunter from Gleno gave me his company with his hounds and terriers nearly half-way up, and after killing some cubs we parted—not without a tinful of the creature at the Fairies' Well—

Buller. A tinful of the creature at the Fairies' Well!

North. Yea—a tinful of the creature at the Fairies' Well. Now I am a total abstinent.

Buller. A total abstinent!

North. By heavens! he echoes me. Pleasant, but mournful to the soul is the memory of joys that are past! A tinful of the unchristened creature to the health of the Silent People. Oh! Buller, there are no Silent People now.

Buller. In your company, sir, I am always willing to be a listener.

North. Well, on I flew as on wings.

Buller. What! Up Cruachan?

North. On feet, then, if you will; but the feet of a deer.

Buller. On all-fours?

North. Yes—sometimes on all-fours. On all-fours, like a frog in his prime, clearing tiny obstructions with a spang. On all-fours, like an ourang-outang, who, in difficult places, brings his arms into play. On all-fours, like the—

Buller. I cry you mercy.

North. Without palpitation of the heart; without determination of blood to the head; without panting; without dizziness; with merely a slight acceleration of the breath, and now and then something like a gasp after a run to a knowe which we foresaw as a momentary resting-place—we felt that we were conquering Cruachan! Lovely level places, like platforms—level as if water had formed them, flowing up just so far continually, and then ebbing back to some unimaginable sea—awaited our arrival, that on them we might lie down, and from beds of state survey our empire, for our empire it was felt to be, far away into the lowlands, with many a hill between—many a hill, that, in its own neighborhood, is believed to be a mountain—just as many a man of moderate mental dimensions is believed by those who live beneath his shade to be of the first order of magnitude, and with funeral honors is interred.

Buller. Well for him that he is a hill at all—eminent on a flat, or among humbler undulations. All is comparative.

North. Just so. From a site on a mountain's side—far from the summit—the ascender hath sometimes a sublimer—often a lovelier vision—than from its most commanding peak. Yet still he has the feeling of ascension—stifle that, and the discontent of insufficiency dwarfs and darkens all that lies below.

Buller. Words to the wise.

North. We fear to ascend higher lest we should lose what we comprehend: yet we will ascend higher, though we know the clouds are gathering, and we are already enveloped in mist. But there were no clouds—no mist on that day—and the secret top of Cruachan was clear as a good man's conscience, and the whole world below like a promised land.

Buller. Let us go—let us go—let us go.

North. All knowledge, my dear boy, may be likened to

stupendous ranges of mountain—clear and clouded, smooth and precipitous; and you or I in youth assail them in joy and pride of soul, not blind, but blindfolded often, and ignorant of their inclination; so that we often are met by a beetling cliff with its cataract, and must keep ascending and descending, ignorant of our whereabouts, and summit-seeking in vain. Yet all the while are we glorified. In maturer mind, when experience is like an instinct, we ascertain levels without a theodolite, and know assuredly where dwell the peaks. We know how to ascend—sideways or right on; we know which are midway heights; we can walk in mist and cloud as surely as in light, and we learn to know the Inaccessible.

Buller. I fear you will fatigue yourself—

North. Or another image. You sail down a stream, my good Buller, which widens as it flows, and will lead through inland seas—or lochs—down to the mighty ocean; what that is I need not say: you sail down it, sometimes with hoisted sail—sometimes with oars—on a quest or mission all undefined; but often anchoring where no need is, and leaping ashore, and engaging in pursuits or pastimes forbidden or vain —*with the natives*—

Buller. The natives!

North. Nay—adopting their dress—though dress it be none at all—and becoming one of themselves—naturalized; forgetting your mission clean out of mind! Fishing and hunting with the natives—

Buller. Whom?

North. The natives—when you ought to have been pursuing your voyage on—on—on. Such are youth's pastimes all. But you had not deserted—not you: and you return of your own accord to this ship.

Buller. What ship?

North. The ship of life—leaving some to lament you, who

knew you only as a jolly mariner, who was bound afar! They believed that you had drawn up your pinnace for ever on that shore, in that lovely little haven, among weeds and palms—unknowing that you would relaunch her some day soon, and, bounding in her over the billows, rejoin your ship, waiting for you in the offing, and revisit the simple natives no more!

Buller. Methinks I understand now your mysterious meaning.

North. You do. But where was I?

Buller. Ascending Cruachan, and near the summit.

North. On the summit. Not a whit tired—not a bit fatigued; strong as ten—active as twenty ownselves on the flat—divinely drunk on draughts of ether—happier a thousand times, greater and more glorious, than Jupiter, with all his gods, enthroned on Olympus.

Buller. Moderately speaking.

North. In imagination I hear him barking now as he barked then—a sharp, short, savage, angry, and hungry bark—

Buller. What? A dog? A Fox?

North. No—no—no. An Eagle—the Golden Eagle from Ben-Slarive, known—no mistaking him—to generations of Shepherds for a hundred years.

Buller. Do you see him?

North. Now I do. I see his eyes—for he came—he comes sughing close by me—and there he shoots up in terror a thousand feet into the sky.

Buller. I did not know the bird was so timid—

North. He is not timid—he is bold; but an Eagle does not like to come all at once within ten yards of an unexpected man—any more than you would like suddenly to face a ghost.

Buller. What brought him there?

North. Wings nine feet wide.

Buller. Has he no sense of smell?

North. What do you mean, sir?

Buller. No offence.

North. He has. But we have not always all our senses about us, Buller, nor our wits either—he had been somewhat scared, a league up Glen Etive, by the Huntsman of Gleno—the scent of powder was in his nostrils; but fury follows fear, and in a minute I heard his bark again—as now I hear it—on the highway to Benlura.

Buller. He must have had enormous talons.

North. My hand is none of the smallest—

Buller. God bless you, my dear sir—give me a grasp.

North. There.

Buller. Oh! thumbikins!

North. And one of his son's talons—whom I shot—was twice the length of mine; his yellow knobby loof at least as broad—and his leg like my wrist. He killed a man. Knocked him down a precipice, like a cannon-ball. He had the credit of it all over the country—but I believe his wife did the business, for she was half-again as big as himself; and no devil like a she-devil fighting for her imp.

Buller. Did you ever rob an Eyrie, sir?

North. Did you ever rob a lion's den? No, no, Buller. I never—except on duty—placed my life in danger. I have been in many dangerous-looking places among the Mountains, but a cautious activity ruled all my movements. I scanned my cliff before I scaled him—and as for jumping chasms—though I had a spring in me—I looked imaginatively down the abyss, and then sensibly turned its flank where it leaned on the greensward, and the liberated streamlet might be forded, without swimming, by the silly sheep.

Buller. And are all those stories lies?

North. All. I have sometimes swam a loch or a river in my clothes, but never except when they lay in my way, or when I was on an angling excursion; and what danger could there possibly be in doing that?

Buller. You might have taken the Cramp, sir.

North. And the Cramp might have taken me—but neither of us ever did—and a man, with a short neck or a long one, might as well shun the streets in perpetual fear of apoplexy as a good swimmer evade water in dread of being drowned. As for swimming in my clothes, had I left them on the hither, how should I have looked on the thither side?

Seward. No man, in such circumstances, could, with any satisfaction to himself, have pursued his journey, even through the most lonesome places.

Buller. Describe the view from the summit.

North. I have no descriptive power, but, even though I had, I know better than that. Why, between Cruachan and Buchail-Etive lie hundreds on hundreds of mountains of the first, second, and third order, and, for a while at first, your eyes are so bewildered that you cannot see any one in particular; yet, in your astonishment, have a strange vision of them all, and might think they were interchanging places, shouldering one another off into altering shapes in the uncertain region, did not the awful stillness assure you that there they had all stood in their places since the Creation, and would stand till the day of doom.

Buller. You have no descriptive power!

North. All at once dominion is given you over the Whole. You gradually see Order in what seemed a Chaos; you understand the character of the Region—its formation—for you are a Geologist, else you have no business, no right there; and you know where the valleys are singing for joy, though you hear them not—where there is provision for the cattle on a hundred hills—where are the cottages of Christian men on the green braes sheltered by the mountains, and where may stand, beneath the granite rocks out of which it was built, the not unfrequent House of God.

Buller. To-morrow we shall attend Divine Service—

North. At Dalmally.

Buller. I long ago learned to like the ritual of the Kirk. I should like to believe in a high-minded, purified Calvinist, who could embrace, in his brotherly heart, a high-minded, purified English Bishop, with all his Episcopacy.

North. And why should he not, if he can recognize the Divine Spirit flowing through the two sets of sensible demonstrations? He can; unless the constitution of the Anglican Christian Religion wars, either by its dogmas or by its ecclesiastical ordinances, against his essential intelligence of Christianity.

Buller. And who shall say it does?

North. Many say it, not I.

Buller. And you are wise and good.

North. Many thousands, and hundreds of thousands, wiser and better. I can easily suppose a mind, strong in thought, warm in feeling, of an imagination susceptible and creative, by magnanimity, study, and experience of the world, disengaged from all sectarian tenets, yet holding the absolute conviction of religion, and contemplating, with reverence and tenderness, many different ways of expression which this inmost spiritual disposition has produced or put on—having a firmest holding on to Christianity as pure, holy, august, divine, true, beyond all other modes of religion upon the earth—partly from intuition of its essential fitness to our nature, partly from intense gratitude, partly, perhaps, from the original entwining of it with his own faculties, thoughts, feelings, history, being. Well, he looks with affectionate admiration upon the Scottish, with affectionate admiration on the English Church, old affection agreeing with new affection; and I can imagine in *him* as much generosity required to love his own Church, the Presbyterian, as yours the

Episcopalian, and that, Latitudinarian as he may be called, he loves them both. For myself, you know how I love England, all that belongs to her, all that makes her what she is; scarcely more—surely not less—Scotland. The ground of the Scottish Form is the overbearing consciousness that religion is immediately between man and his Maker. All hallowing of things outward is to that consciousness a placing of such earthly things as interpositions and separating intermediates in that interval unavoidable between the Finite and the Infinite, but which should remain blank and clear for the immediate communications of the Worshipper and the Worshipped.

Buller. I believe, sir, you are a Presbyterian?

North. He that worships in spirit and in truth cannot endure, cannot imagine, that anything but his own sin shall stand betwixt him and God.

Buller. *That,* until it be in some way or another extinguished, shall and must.

North. True as Holy Writ. But intervening saints, images, and elaborate rituals, the contrivance of human wit—all these the fire of the Spirit has consumed, and consumes.

Buller. The fire of the Presbyterian spirit?

North. Add history. War and persecution have afforded an element of human hate for strengthening the sternness——

Buller. Of Presbyterian Scotland.

North. Drop that word, for I more than doubt if you understand it.

Buller. I beg pardon, sir.

North. The Scottish service, Mr. Buller, comprehends Prayer, Praise, Doctrine, all three necessary verbal acts amongst Christians met, but each in utmost simplicity.

Buller. Episcopalian as I am, that simplicity I have felt to be most affecting.

North. The Praise, which unites the voices of the congregation, must be written. The Prayer, which is the burning towards God of the soul of the Shepherd upon the behalf of the Flock, and upon his own, must be unwritten, unpremeditated, else it is not prayer. Can the heart ever want fitting words? The teaching must be to the utmost, forethought, at some time or at another, as to the Matter. The Teacher must have secured his intelligence of the Matter ere he opens his mouth. But the Form, which is of expediency only, he may very loosely have considered. That is the Theory.

Buller. Often liable in practice, I should fear, to sad abuse.

North. May be so. But it presumes that capable men, full of zeal, and sincerity, and love—fervent servants and careful shepherds—have been chosen, under higher guidance. It supposes the holy fire of the new-born Reformation, of the newly-regenerated Church——

Buller. Kirk.

North. Of the newly-regenerated Church, to continue undamped, inextinguishable.

Buller. And is it so?

North. The Fact answers to the Theory more or less. The original Thought—simplicity of worship—is to the utmost expressed, when the chased Covenanters are met on the greensward, between the hillside and the brawling brook, under the colored or uncolored sky. Understand that, when their descendants meet within walls and beneath roofs, they *would* worship after the manner of their hunted ancestors.

Buller. I wish I were better read than I am in the history of Scotland, civil and ecclesiastic.

North. I wish you were. I say, then, my excellent friend, that the Ritual and whole ordering of the Scottish Church is moulded upon, or issues out of, the human spirit kindling in conscious communication of the Divine Spirit. The power of the Infinite—that is, the Sense of Infinitude, of Eternity—reigns there; and the Sense is the inmost soul of the sustaining contact with Omnipotence, and self-consciousness intense, and elation of Divine favor personally vouchsafed, and joy of anticipated everlasting bliss, and triumph over Satan, death, and hell, and immeasurable desire to win souls to the King of the Worlds.

Buller. In England we are, I am ashamed to say it, ill informed on——

North. In Scotland we are, I am ashamed to say it, ill informed on——

Buller. But go on, sir.

North. What place is there for Forms of any kind in the presence of these immense overpowering realities? For Forms, Buller, are of the Imagination; the Faculty that inhales and lives by the Unreal. But some concession to the humanity of our nature intrudes. Imagination may be subordinated, subjugated, but will not, may not, forego all its rights. Therefore, forms and hallowing associations enter.

Buller. Into all Worship.

North. Form, too, is in part, Necessary Order.

Buller. Perhaps, sir, you may be not unwilling to say a few words of our Ritual.

North. I tremble to speak of your Ritual; for it appears to me as bearing on its front an excellence which might be found incompatible with religious truth and sincerity.

Buller. I confess that I hardly understand you, sir.

North. The Liturgy looks to be that which the old Churches are, the Work of a Fine Art.

Buller. You do not urge that as an objection to it, I trust, sir?

North. A Poetical sensibility, a wakeful, just, delicate, simple Taste, seem to have ruled over the composition of each Prayer, and the ordering of the whole Service.

Buller. You do not urge that as an objection to it, I trust, sir?

North. I am not urging objections, sir. I seldom—never, indeed—urge objections to anything. I desire only to place all things in their true light.

Buller. Don't frown, sir—smile. Enough.

North. The whole composition of the Service is copious and various. Human Supplication, the lifting up of the hands of the creature, knowing his own weakness, dependence, lapses, and liability to slip—man's own part, dictated by his own experience of himself—is the basis. Readings from the Old and New Volume of the Written Word are ingrafted, as if God audibly spoke in his own House; the Authoritative added to the Supplicatory.

Buller. Finely true. We Church of England men love you, Mr. North—we do indeed.

North. The hymns of the sweet Singer of Israel, in literal translation, adopted as a holier inspired language of the heart.

Buller. These, sir, are surely three powerful elements of a Ritual Service.

North. Throughout, the People divide the service with the Minister. They have in it their own personal function.

Buller. Then the Homily, sir.

North. Ay, the Homily, which, one might say, interprets between Sunday and the Week—fixes the holiness of the Day in precepts, doctrines, reflections, which may be carried home to guide and nourish.

Buller. Altogether, sir, it seems a meet work of worshippers met in their Christian Land upon the day of rest and aspiration. The Scottish worship might seem to remember the flame and the sword. The persecuted Iconoclasts of two centuries ago, live in their descendants.

North. But the Ritual of England breathes a divine calm.

You think of the people walking through ripening fields on a mild day to their Church door. It is the work of a nation sitting in peace, possessing their land. It is the work of a wealthy nation, that, by dedicating a part of its wealth, consecrates the remainder—that acknowledges the Fountain from which all flows. The prayers are devout, humble, fervent. They are not impassioned. A wonderful temperance and sobriety of discretion; that which, in worldly things, would be called good sense, prevails in them; but you must name it better in things spiritual. The framers evidently bore in mind the continual consciousness of writing for ALL. That is the guiding, tempering, calming spirit that keeps in the Whole one tone—that, and the hallowing, chastening awe which subdues vehemence, even in the asking for the Infinite, by those who have nothing but that which they earnestly ask, and who know that unless they ask infinitely, they ask nothing. In every word, the whole Congregation, the whole nation prays—not the Individual Minister; the officiating Divine Functionary, not the Man. Nor must it be forgotten that the received Version and the Book of Common Prayer—observe the word COMMON, expressing exactly what I affirm—are beautiful by the words; that there is no other such English—simple, touching, apt, venerable, hued as the thoughts are—musical—the most English English that is known—of a Hebraic strength and antiquity, yet lucid and gracious, as if of and for to-day.

Buller. I trust that many Presbyterians sympathize with you in these sentiments.

North. Not many—few. Nor do I say I wish there were more.

Buller. Are you serious, sir?

North. I am. But cannot explain myself now. What are the Three Pillars of the Love of any Church? Innate Religion, Humanity, Imagination. The Scottish worship better satisfies the first principle, that of England the last; the Roman Catholic still more the last—and are not your Cathedrals Roman Catholic? I think that the Scottish and English, better than the Roman Catholic, satisfy the Middle Principle—Humanity—being truer to the highest requisitions of our Nature, and nourish our faculties better, both of Will and Understanding, into their strength and beauty. Yet what divine-minded Roman Catholics there have been, and are, and will be!

Buller. Pause for a moment, sir—here comes Seward.

North. Seward! Is he not with us? Surely he was, an hour or two ago—but I never missed him, your conversation has been so interesting and instructive. Seward! why you are all the world like a drowned rat!

Seward. But I am none, but a stanch Conservative. Would I had had a Protectionist with me to keep me right on the Navigation Laws.

North. What do you mean? What's the matter?

Seward. Why, your description of the Pools in Cladich-Cleugh inspired me with a passion for one of the Naiads.

North. And you have had a ducking?

Seward. I have indeed. Plashed souse, head over heels, into one of the prettiest pools, from a slippery ledge some dozen feet above the sleeping beauty. Were you both deaf that you did not hear me bawl?

North. I have a faint recollection of hearing something bray, but I suppose I thought it came from the Gipsies' Camp.

Buller. Are you wet?

Seward. Come, come, Buller.

Buller. Why so dry?

North. Sair drooket.

Buller. Where's your Tile?

Seward. I hate slang.

Buller. Why, you have lost a shoe, and much delightful conversation.

North. I must say, Seward, that I was hurt by your withdrawing yourself from our Colloquy.

Seward. Sir, you are beginning to get so prosy——

Buller. I insist, Seward, on your making an apology on your knees to our Father for your shocking impiety. I shudder to repeat the word, which you must swallow—P—R—O—S—Y.

Seward. On my knees! Look at them.

North. My dear, dearer, dearest, Mr. Seward, you are bleeding—I fear a fracture. Let me——

Seward. I am not bleeding, only a knap on the knee-pan, sir.

Buller. Not bleeding! Why you must be drenched in blood, your face is so white.

North. A *non-sequitur,* Buller. But from a knap on the knee-pan I have known a man a lamiter for life.

Seward. I lament the loss of my Sketch-Book.

Buller. It is a judgment on you for that Caricature.

North. What caricature?

Buller. Since you will force me to tell it, a caricature of——YOURSELF, sir. I saw him working away at it with a most wicked leer on his face, while you supposed he was taking notes. He held it up to me for a moment, clapped the boards together with the grin of a fiend, and then off to Cladick-Cloock, where he met with Nemesis.

North. Is that a true bill, Mr. Seward?

Seward. On my honor as a gentleman, and my skill as an artist, it is not. It is a most malignant misrepresentation——

Buller. It was indeed.

Seward. It was no caricature. I promised to Mrs. Seward to send her a sketch of the illustrious Mr. North; and finding you in one of the happiest of your many-sided attitudes——

North. The act is to be judged by the intention. You are acquitted of the charge.

Buller. To make a caricature of You, sir, under any circumstances, and for any purpose, would be sufficiently shocking; but HERE AND NOW, and that he might send it to his WIFE, so transcends all previous perpetration of *crimen læsæ majestatis*, that I am beginning to be incredulous of what these eyes beheld—nay, to disbelieve what, if told to any human being, however depraved, would seem to him impossible, even in the mystery of iniquity, and an insane libel on our fallen nature.

Seward. I did my best. Nor am I, sir, without hope that my Sketch-Book may be recovered, and then you will judge for yourself, sir, if it be a caricature. A failure, sir, it assuredly was, for what artist has succeeded with YOU?

North. To the Inn, and put on dry clothes.

Seward. No. What care I about dry or wet clothes! Here let me lie down and bask in this patch of intense sunshine at your feet. Don't stir, sir; the Crutch is not the least in the way.

North. We must be all up and doing—the HOUR and the MEN. The CAVALCADE. Hush! Hark! the Bagpipe! The Cavalcade can't be more than a mile off.

Seward. Why staring thus like a Goshawk, sir?

Buller. I hear nothing. Seward, do you?

Seward. Nothing. And what can he mean by Cavalcade? Yet I believe he has the Second Sight. I have heard it is in the Family.

North. Hear nothing? Then both of you must be deaf. But I forget, we Mountaineers have Fine Ears—your sense of hearing has been educated on the Flat. Not now? "The Campbell's are coming"—that's the march—that's the go—that's the gathering.

Buller. A Horn—a Drum, sure enough—and—and—that incomprehensible mixture of groans and yells must be the Bagpipe.

North. See, yonder they come, over the hill-top, the ninth mile-stone from Inverary! There's the VAN, by the Road-Surveyor lent me for the occasion, drawn by Four Horses. And there's the WAGGON, once the property of the lessee of the Swiss Giantess, a noble unicorn. And there the SIX TENT-CARTS, Two-steeded; and there the TWO BOAT-CARRIAGES, horsed I know not how. But don't you see the bonny BARGES aloft in the air? And Men on horseback—count them—there should be four. You hear the Bagpipe now, surely, "The Campbells are coming." And here is the whole Concern, gentlemen, close at hand, deploying across the Bridge.

Buller. Has he lost his senses at last?

Seward. Have we lost ours? A Cavalcade it is, with a vengeance.

North. One minute past Seven! True to their time within sixty seconds. This way, this way. Here is the Spot, the Centre of the Grove. Bagpipe, Drum and Horn—music all—silence. Silence, I cry—will nobody assist me in crying silence!

Seward and Buller. Silence, silence, silence.

North. Give me the Speaking-Trumpet that I may call silence.

Seward. Stentor may put down the Drum, the Horns, the Fifes, and the Serpent, but the Bagpipe is above him—the Drone is deaf as the sea—the Piper moves in a sphere of his own.

Buller. I don't hear a syllable you are saying—ah! the storm is dead, and now what a BLESSED CALM.

North. Wheel into line—Prepare to—pitch tents.

Enter the Field of the Sycamore Grove on Horseback, ushered by Archy M'Callum, Harry Seward, Marmaduke Buller, Vallance Volusene, Nepos Woodburn. *Van Waggon, Carriages, and Carts, &c., form a Barricade between the Rear of the Grove and the Road to Dalmally.*

Adjutant Archy M'Callum! call the Roll of the Troops.

Adjutant. Peter of the Lodge, Sewer and Seneschal, *Here.* Peterson ditto, Comptroller of the cellars, *Here.* Kit Peterson, tiger there, *Here.* Michael Dods, cook at that place, *Here.* Ben Brawn, maniciple, *Here.* Roderick M'Crimmon, king of the Pipes, *Here.* Pym and stretch, body-men to the young Englishers, *Here, Here.* Tom Moody, huntsman at Under-cliff Hall, North Devon, *Here.* The Cornwall clipper, head game-keeper at Pendragon, *Here.* Billy Balmer of Bowness, Windermere, Commodore, *Here.*

North. Attention! Each man will be held answerable for his subordinates. The roll will be called an hour after sunrise, and an hour before sunset. Men, remember you are under martial law. Camp-master M'Kellar, *Here.* Let the Mid Peak of Cruachan be your pitching point. Old Dee-side tent in the centre, right in Front. Dormitories to the east. To the west the Pavilion. Kitchen range in the rear. Donald Dhu, late Sergeant in the Black Watch, see to the Barricade. The Impediments in your charge. In three hours I command the Encampment to be complete. Admittance to the Field on the Queen's Birth-day. Crowd disperse. Old Boys! What do you think of this? You have often called me a Wizard, a Warlock—no glamour here—'tis real all, and all the Work of the Crutch. Sons, your Fathers! Fathers, your Sons! Your hand, Volusene—and Woodburn, yours.

Seward. Hal, how are you?

Buller. How are you, Marmy?

North. On the stage—in the theatre of fictitious life—such a meeting as this would require explanation, but in the Drama of Real Life, on the Banks of Lochawe, it needs none. Friends of my soul! you will come to understand it all in two minutes' talk with your progeny. Progeny, welcome for your sires' sakes, and your Lady Mothers, and your own, to Lochawe-side. I see you are two Trumps. Volusene, Woodburn, from your faces all well at home. Come, my two old Bucks, let us Three, to be out of the bustle, retire to the Inn. Did you ever see Christopher fling the Crutch? There—I knew it would clear the Sycamore Grove.

SCENE II.—*Interior of the Pavilion.*

TIME—*Two* P. M.

NORTH—SEWARD—BULLER.

Seward. Still at his siesta in his swing-chair. Few faces bear to be looked on asleep.

Buller. Men's faces.

Seward. His bears it well. Awake, it is sometimes too full of expression. And then, how it fluctuates! Perpetual play and interchange as Thought, Feeling, Fancy, Imagination—

Buller. The gay, the grave, the sad, the serious, the pathetic, the humorous, the tragic, the whimsical rules the minute—

"'Tis everything by fits, and nothing long."

Seward. Don't exaggerate. An inapt quotation.

Buller. I was merely carrying on your eulogium of his wide-awake face.

Seward. The prevalent expression is still, the Benign.

Buller. A singular mixture of tenderness and truculence.

Seward. Asleep, it is absolutely saint-like.

Buller. It reminds me of the faces of Chantry's Sleeping Children in Litchfield Cathedral.

Seward. Composure is the word. Composure is mute Harmony.

Buller. It may be so—but you will not deny that his nose is just a minim too long, and his mouth, at this moment, just a minim too open, and the crow-feet——

Seward. Enhance the power of those large drooping eyelids, heavy with meditation, of that high broad forehead, with the lines, not the wrinkles, of age.

Buller. He is much balder than he was on Deeside.

Seward. Or fifty years before. They say that, in youth, the sight of his head of hair once silenced Mirabeau.

Buller. Why, Mirabeau's was black, and my grandmother told me North's was yellow, or rather green, like a star.

North. Your Grandmother, Buller, was the finest woman of her time.

Buller. Sleepers hear. Sometimes a single word from without, reaching the spiritual region, changes by its touch the whole current of their dreams.

North. I once told you that, Buller. At present, I happen to be awake. But surely a man may sit on a swing-chair with his eyes shut, and his mouth open, without incurring the charge of somnolency. Where have you been?

Seward. You told us, sir, not to disturb you till two——

North. But where have you been?

Seward. We have written our dispatches, read our London papers, and had a pull in *gutta percha* to and from Port Sonachan.

North. How does she pull?

Buller. Like a winner. I have written to the builder—

Taylor of Newcastle—to match her against any craft of her keel in the kingdom.

North. Sit down. Where are the Boys?

Seward. Off hours ago to Kilchurn. They have just signalized, "TWO O'CLOCK. 1 SALMO FEROX, lb. 12; 20 YELLOW-FINS, lb. 15; 6 PIKE, lb. 36."

North. And not bad sport, either. They know the dinner hour. Seven sharp.

Seward. They do, and they are not the lads to disregard orders.

North. Four finer fellows are not in Christendom.

Seward. May I presume to ask, sir, what volumes these are lying open on your knees?

North. THE ILIAD, and PARADISE LOST.

Seward. I fear, sir, you may not be disposed to enlighten us, at this hour.

North. But I am disposed to be enlightened. Oxonians, and Double First-Class Men, nor truants since, you will find in me a docile pupil rather than a Teacher. I am no great Grecian.

Buller. But you are, sir; and a fine old Trojan too, methinks! What audacious word has escaped my lips!

North. Epic Poetry! Tell but a Tale, and see Childhood—the harmless, the trustful, the wondering—listen, "all ear;" and so has the wilder and mightier Childhood of Nations listened, trustful, wondering, "all ear," to Tales lofty, profound—*said*, or, as Art grew up, *sung*.

Seward. ΕΠΕ, Say or Tell.

Buller. ΑΕΙΔΕ, Sing.

North. Yes, my lads, these were the received formulas of beseeching with which the Minstrels of Hellas invoked succor of the Divine Muse, when their burning tongue would fit well to the Harp transmitted Tales, fraught with old heroic remembrance, with solemn belief, with oracular wisdom. ΕΠΕ, TELL, ΕΠΟΣ, THE TALE. And when, step after step, the Harp modeling the Verse, and the Verse charming power and beauty, and splendor, and pathos—like a newly-created and newly-creating soul—into its ancestral Tradition—when insensibly the benign Usurper, the Muse, had made the magnificent dream rightly and wholly her own at last. ΕΠΟΣ, THE SUNG TALE. HOMER, to all following ages the chief Master of Eloquence whether in Verse or in Prose, has yet maintained the simplicity of *Telling*.

"For he came beside the swift ships of the Achæans,
Proposing to release his daughter, and bringing immense ransom;
Having in his hand the fillet of the far shooting Apollo,
On the golden rod: and he implored of the Achæans,
And the sons of Atreus, most of all, the two Orders of the People."

These few words of a tongue stately, resplendent, sonorous, and *numerous*, more than ours—and already the near Scamandrian Field feels, and fears, and trembles. MILTON! The world has rolled round, and again round, from the day of that earlier to that of the later Mæonides. All the soul-wealth hoarded n words, which merciful Time held aloft, unsubmerged by the Gothic, by the Ottoman inundation; all the light shrined in the Second, the Intellectual Ark that, divinely built and guided, rode tilting over the tempestuous waste of waters; all the mind, bred and fostered by new Europe, down to within two hundred years of this year that runs: these have put differences between the ILIAD and the PARADISE LOST, in matter and in style, which to state and illustrate would hold me speaking till sunset.

Buller. And us listening.

North. The Fall of Hector and of his Troy! The Fall of Adam and of his World!

Buller. What concise expression! *Multum in parvo,* indeed, Seward.

North. Men and gods mingled in glittering conflict upon the ground that spreads between Ida's foot and the Hellespont! At the foot of the Omnipotent Throne, archangels and angels distracting their native Heaven with arms, and Heaven disburthening her lap of her self-lost sons for the peopling of Hell!

Seward. Hush! Buller, hush!

North. In way of an Episode—yes, an Episode—see the Seventh Book, our Visible Universe willed into being!

Seward. Hush! Buller, hush!

North. For a few risings and settings of yon since-bedimmed Sun, Love and celestial Bliss dwelling amidst the shades and flowers of Eden yet sinless—then from a MORE FATAL APPLE, Discord clashing into and subverting the harmonies of Creation.

> "Sin, and her Shadow, Death; and Misery,
> Death's Harbinger."

The Iliad, indeed!

Seward. I wish you could be persuaded, sir, to give us an edition of Milton.

North. No. I must not take it out of the Doctor's hands. Then, as to Milton's style. If the Christian Theologian must be held bold who has dared to mix the Delivered Writings with his own inventions—bold, too, was he, the heir of the mind that was nursed in the Aristotelian Schools, to unite, as he did, on the other hand, the gait of an understanding accomplished in logic, with the spontaneous and unstudied step of Poetry. The style of Milton, gentlemen, has been praised for simplicity; and it is true that the style of the Paradise Lost has often an austere simplicity; but one sort of it you miss—the proper epic simplicity—that Homeric simplicity of the *Telling.*

Seward. Perhaps, sir, in such a Poem such simplicity could not be.

North. Perhaps not. Homer adds thought to thought, and so builds up. Milton involves thought with thought, and so constructs. Relation is with him argumentative also, and History both Philosophy and Oratory. This was unavoidable. He brought the mind of the latter age to the Form of Composition produced by the primitive time. Again, the style is fitted to the general intention of a Poem essentially didactic and argumentative. Again, the style is personal to himself. He has learnedly availed himself of all antecedent art—minutely availed himself, yet he is no imitator. The style is like no other; it is intensely and completely original. It expresses himself. Lofty, capacious, acute, luminous, thoroughly disciplined, ratiocinative powers wonderfully blend their action with an imagination of the most delicate and profound sensibility to the beautiful, and of a sublimity that no theme can excel.

Seward. Lord Bacon, sir, I believe, has defined Poetry, Feigned History—has he not?

North. He has; and no wonder that he thought much of "Feigned History," for he had a view to Epos and Tragedy, the Iliad and Odyssey, the Attic Theatre, the Æneid, Dante, Ariosto, Tasso, the Romances of Chivalry: moreover, the whole immense Greek Fable, whereof part and parcel remain, but more is perished. Which fables, you know, existed, and were transmitted in Prose—that is, by Oral Tradition in the words of the relator—long before they came into Homeric Verse, or any verse. He saw, Seward, the Memory of Mankind possessed by two kinds of history, both once alike credited. True History which remains True History, and Fabulous History, now acknowledged as Poetry only. It is no wonder that *other* Poetry vanished from importance in his estimation.

Buller. I follow you, sir, with some difficulty.

North. You may with ease. Fabulous History holds place, side by side, with True History, as a rival in dignity, credence, and power, and in peopling the Earth with Persons and Events. For, of a verity, the Personages and Events created by Poesy hold place in our Mind, not in our imagination only, but in our understanding, along with events and personages historically remembered.

Seward. An imposing Parallelism!

North. It is; but does it hold good? And if it does, with what limitations?

Seward. With what limitations, sir?

North. I wish Lord Bacon were here, that I might ask him to explain. Take Homer and Thucydides, the Iliad and the History of the Peloponnesian War. We thus sever, at the widest, the Telling of Calliope from the Telling of Clio, holding each at the height of honor.

Buller. At the widest?

North. Yes; for how far from Thucydides is, at once, the Book of the Games! Look through the Iliad, and see how much and minute picturing of a world with which the Historian had nothing to do! Shall the Historian, in Prose, of the Ten Years' War, stop to describe the Funeral Games of a Patroclus? Yes; if he stop to describe the Burying of every Hero who falls. But the Historian in Prose assumes that a People know their own Manners, and therefore he omits painting their manners to themselves. The Historian in verse assumes the same thing, and, *therefore*, strange to say, he paints the manners! See, then, in the Iliad, how much memorizing of a whole departed scheme of human existence, with which the Prose Historian had nothing to do, the Historian in regulated Metre has had the inspiration and the skill to inweave in the narrative of his ever-advancing Action.

Buller. Would his lordship were with us!

North. Give allt his to—THE HEXAMETER. Remember always, my dear Seward, the shield of Achilles—itself a world in miniature, a compendium of the world.

Seward. Of the Universe.

North. Even so; for Sun, and Moon, and Stars are there, Astronomy and all the learned sisterhood!

Seward. Then to what species of narrative in prose, to one removed at what interval from the history of the Peloponnesian War, belongs that scene of Helen on the Walls of Troy? That scene at the Scæan gate? In the tent of Achilles, where Achilles sits, and Priam kneels?

North. Good. The general difference is obviously this, Publicity almost solely stamps the Thucydidean story—Privacy, more than in equal part, interfused with Publicity, the Homeric. You must allow Publicity and Privacy to signify, besides that which is done in public and in private, that which proceeds of the Public and of the Private will.

Seward. In other words, if I apprehend you aright, the Theme given being some affair of Public moment, Prose tends to gather up the acts of the individual agents, under general aspects, into masses.

North. Just so. Verse, whenever it dare, resolves the mass of action into the individual acts, puts aside the collective doer—the Public, and puts forward individual persons. Glory, I say again, to THE HEXAMETER!

Buller. Glory to the HEXAMETER! The HEXAMETER, like the Queen, has done it all.

North. Or let us return to the Paradise Lost! If the mustering of the Fallen Legions in the First Book—if the Infernal Council held in the Second—if the Angelic Rebellion and Warfare in the Fifth and Sixth—resemble Public History, civil and military, as we commonly speak—if the Seventh Book, relating the Creation by describing the kinds created, be the assumption into Heroic Poetry of Natural History—to what kind of History, I earnestly ask you both, does that scene belong, of Eve's relation of her dream, in the Fifth Book, and Adam's consolation of her uneasiness under its involuntary sin? To what, in the Fourth Book, her own innocent relation of her first impressions upon awaking into Life and Consciousness?

Buller. Ay!—to what kind of History? More easily asked than answered.

North. And Adam's relation to the Affable Archangel of his own suddenly-dawned morning from the night of non-existence, aptly and happily crowned upon the relation made to him by Raphael in the Seventh Book of his own forming under the Omnipotent Hand?

Seward. Simply, I venture to say, sir, to the most interior autobiography—to that confidence of audible words, which flows when the face of a friend sharpens the heart of a man—— and Raphael was Adam's Friend.

North. Seward, you are right. You speak well—as you always do—when you choose. Behold, then, I beseech you, the comprehending power of that little magical band—*Our Accentual Iambic Pentameter.*

Seward. "Glory be with them, and eternal praise,
The Poets who on earth have made us heirs
Of Truth and pure Delight by heavenly lays."

North. Glory to Verse, for its power is great. Man from the garden in Eden, to the purifying by fire of the redeemed Earth—the creation of things visible—Angels Upright and Fallen—and Higher than Angels—all the Regions of Space—Infinitude and Eternity—the Universality of Being—this is the copious matter of the Song. And herein there is place found, proper, distinct, and large, and prominent, for that whispered call to visit, in the freshness of morning, the dropping Myrrh—

to study the opening beauty of the Flowers—to watch the Bee in her sweet labor—which tenderly dissipates from the lids of Eve her ominously-troubled sleep—free room for two tears, which, falling from a woman's eyes, are wiped with her hair—and for two more, which her pitying husband kisses away ere they fall. All these things Verse disposes, and composes, in One Presentment.

Buller. Glory to Verse, for its power is great—glory to *our Accentual Iambic Pentameter.*

North. Let us return to the Iliad. The Iliad is a history told by a mind that is arbiter, to a certain extent only, of its own facts. For Homer takes his decennial War and its Heroes, nay, the tenor of the story too, from long-descended Tradition. To his cotemporary countrymen he appears as a Historian—not feigning, but commemorating and glorifying, transmitted facts.

Seward. Ottfried Müller, asking how far Homer is tied up in his Traditions, ventures to suspect that the names of the Heroes whom Achilles kills, in such or such a fight, are all traditionary.

North. Where, then, is the *Feigned* History? Lord Bacon, Ottfried Müller, and Jacob Bryant, are here not in the main unagreed. "I nothing doubt," says Bacon, "but the Fables, which Homer having received, transmits, had originally a profound and excellent sense, although I greatly doubt if Homer any longer knew that sense."

Buller. What right, may I ask, had Lord Bacon to doubt, and Ottfried Müller to suspect——

North. Smoke your cigar. Ottfried Müller——

Buller. Whew!—poo!

North. Ottfried Müller imagines that there was in Greece a pre-Homeric Age, of which the principal intellectual employment was Myth-making. And Bryant, we know, shocked the opinion of his own day by referring the War of Troy to Mythology. Now, observe, Buller, how there is feigning and feigning—Poet after Poet—and the Poem that comes to us at last is the Poem of Homer; but in truth, of successive ages, ending in Homer——

Seward. Who was then a real living flesh and blood Individual of the human species.

North. That he was——

Seward. And wrote the Iliad.

North. That he did—but how I have hinted rather than told. In the Paradise Lost, the part of Milton is, then, infinitely bolder than Homer's in the Iliad. He is far more of a Creator.

Seward. Can an innermost bond of Unity, sir, be shown for the Iliad?

North. Yes. THE ILIAD IS A TALE OF A WRONG RIGHTED. Zeus, upon the secret top of Olympus, decrees this RIGHTING with his omnipotent Nod. Upon the top of Ida he conducts it. But that is done, and the Fates resume their tenor, Hector falls, and Troy shall fall. That is again the RIGHTING OF A WRONG, done amongst men. This is the broadly-written admonition: "DISCITE JUSTITIAM."

Seward. You are always great, sir, on Homer.

North. Agamemnon, in insolence of self-will, offends Chryses and a God. He refused Chryses—He robs Achilles. In Agamemnon the Insolence of Human Self-will is humbled, first under the hand of Apollo—then of Jupiter—say, altogether, of Heaven. He suffers and submits. And now Achilles, who has no less interest in the Courts of Heaven than Chryses—indeed higher—in over-weening anger fashions out a redress for himself which the Father of Gods and Men grants. And what follows? Agamemnon again suffers and submits. For Achilles—Patroclus' bloody corse! Κειται Πατροκλος—that is the voice that rings! Now he accepts the proffered reconciliation of Agamemnon, before scornfully refused; and in the son of Thetis, too, the insolence of Human Self-will is chastened under the hand of Heaven.

Seward. He suffers, but submits not till Hector lies transfixed—till Twelve noble youths of the Trojans and their Allies have bled on Patroclus' Pyre. And does he submit then? No. For twelve days ever and anon he drags the insensible corse at his horses' heels round that sepulchral earth.

Buller. Mad, if ever a man was.

North. The Gods murmur—and will that the unseemly Revenge cease. Jove sends Thetis to him—and what meeter messenger for minister of mercy than a mother to her son! God-bidden by that voice, he submits—he remits his Revenge. The Human Will, infuriated, bows under the Heavenly.

Seward. Touched by the prayers and the sight of that kneeling gray-haired Father, he has given him back his dead son—and from the ransom a costly pall of honor, to hide the dead son from the father's eyes—and of his own Will and Power Twelve Days' truce: and the days have expired, and the Funeral is performed—and the pyre is burned out—and the mound over the slayer of Patroclus is heaped—and the Iliad is done—and this Moral indelibly writes itself on the heart—the words of Apollo in that Council—

Τλητον γαρ Θυμον Μοιραι Θνητοισιν εδωκαν,

THE FATES HAVE APPOINTED TO MORTALS A SPIRIT THAT SHALL SUBMIT AND ENDURE.

North. Right and good. Τλητον is more than "shall suffer." It is, that shall accept suffering—that shall *bear.*

Seward. Compare this one Verse and the Twenty-four Books, and you have the poetical simplicity and the poetical multiplicity side by side.

Buller. Right and good.

North. Yes, my friends, the teaching of the Iliad is Piety to the Gods—

Seward. Reverence for the rights of Men—

North. A Will humbled, conformed to the Will of Heaven.

Buller. That the Earth is justly governed.

North. Dim foreshadowings, which Milton, I doubt not, discerned and cherished. The Iliad was the natural and spiritual father of the Paradise Lost—

Seward. And the son is greater than the sire.

North. I see in the Iliad the love of Homer to Greece and to humankind. He was a legislator to Greece before Solon and Lycurgus—greater than either—after the manner fabled of Orpheus.

Seward. Sprung from the bosom of heroic life, the Iliad asked heroic listeners.

North. See with what large-hearted love he draws the Men—Hector, and Priam, and Sarpedon—as well as the Woman Andromache—enemies! Can he so paint humanity and not humanize? He humanizes *us*—who have literature and refined Greece and Rome—who have Spenser, and Shakspeare, and Milton—who are Christendom.

Seward. He loves the inferior creatures, and the face of nature.

North. The Iliad has been called a Song of War. I see in it—a Song of Peace. Think of all the fiery Iliad ending in—Reconciled Submission!

Seward. "Murder Impossibility," and believe that there might have been an Iliad or a Paradise Lost in Prose.

North. It could never have been, by human power, *our* Paradise Lost. What would have become of the Seventh Book? This is now occupied with describing the Six Days of Creation. A few verses of the First Chapter of Genesis extended into so many hundred lines. The Book, as it stands, has full poetical reason. First, it has a sufficient motive. It founds the existence of Adam and Eve, which is otherwise not duly led to. The revolted Angels, you know, have fallen, and the Almighty will create a new race of worshippers to supply their place—Mankind.

Seward. For this race that is to be created, a Home is previously to be built—or this World is to be created.

North. I initiated you into Milton nearly thirty years ago, my dear Seward; and I rejoice to find that you still have him by heart. Between the fall of the Angels, and that inhabiting of Paradise by our first parents, which is largely related by Raphael, there would be in the history which the poem undertakes, an unfilled gap and blank without this book. The chain of events which is unrolled would be broken—interrupted—incomplete.

Seward. And, sir, when Raphael has told the Rebellion and Fall of the Angels, Adam, with a natural movement of curiosity, asks of this "Divine Interpreter" how this frame of things began?

North. And Raphael answers by declaring at large the Purpose and the Manner. The Mission of Raphael is to strengthen, if it be practicable, the Human Pair in their obedience. To this end, how apt his discourse, showing how dear they are to the Universal Maker, how eminent in his Universe!

Seward. The causes, then, of the Archangelic Narrative abound. And the personal interest with which the Two Auditors must hear such a revelation of wonders from such a Speaker, and that so intimately concerns themselves, falls nothing short of what Poetry justly requires in relations put into the mouth of the poetical Persons.

North. And can the interest—not now of Raphael's, but

of Milton's "fit audience"—be sustained throughout? The answer is triumphant. The Book is, from beginning to end, a stream of the most beautiful descriptive Poetry that exists. Not, however, mind you, Seward, of stationary description.

Seward. Sir?

North. A proceeding work is described; and the Book is replete and alive with motion—with progress—with action—yes, of action—of an order unusual indeed to the Epos, but unexcelled in dignity—the Creative Action of Deity!

Seward. What should hinder, then, but that this same Seventh Book should have been written in Prose?

North. Why this only—that without Verse it could not have been read! The Verse makes present. You listen with Adam and Eve, and you hear the Archangel. In Prose this illusion could not have been carried through such a subject-matter. The *conditio sine quâ non* of the Book was the ineffable charm of the Description. But what would a series of botanical and zoological descriptions, for instance, have been, in Prose? The *vivida vis* that is in Verse is the quickening spirit of the whole.

Buller. But who doubts it?

North. Lord Bacon said that Poetry—that is, Feigned History—might be worded in Prose. And it may be; but how inadequately is known to Us Three.

Buller. And to all the world.

North. No—nor, to the million who do know it, so well as to Us, nor the reason why. But hear me a moment longer. Wordsworth, in his famous Preface to the Lyrical Ballads, asserts that the language of Prose and the language of Verse differ but in this—that in Verse there is metre—and metre he calls an adjunct. With all reverence, I say that metre is not an adjunct—but vitality and essence; and that verse, in virtue thereof, so transfigures language, that it ceases to be the language of prose as spoken, out of verse, by any of the children of men.

Seward. Remove the metre, and the language will not be the language of Prose ?

North. Not—if you remove the metre only—and leave otherwise the order of the words—the collocation unchanged—and unchanged any one of the two hundred figures of speech, one and all of which are differently presented in the language of Verse from what they are in Prose.

Seward. It must be so.

North. The fountain of Law to Composition in Prose is the Understanding. The fountain of Law to Composition in Verse is the Will.

Seward. ?

North. A discourse in prose resembles a chain. The sentences are the successive links—all holding *to* one another and holding one another. *All is bound.*

Seward. Well?

North. A discourse in verse resembles a billowy sea. The verses are the waves that rise and fall—to our apprehension—each by impulse, life, will of its own. *All is free.*

Seward. Ay. Now your meaning emerges.

North. *E profundis clamavi.* In eloquent prose, the feeling fits itself into the process of the thinking. In true verse, the thinking fits itself into the process of the feeling.

Seward. I perpend.

North. In prose, the general distribution and composition of the matter belong to the reign of Necessity. The order of the parts, and the connection of part with part, are obliged—logically justifiable—say, then, are demonstrable. See an Oration of Demosthenes. In verse, that distribution and composition belong to the reign of Liberty. That order and connection are arbitrary—passionately justifiable—say, then, are delectable. See an Ode of Pindar.

Seward. Publish—publish.

North. In prose the style is last—in verse first; in prose the sense controls the sound—in verse the sound the sense; in prose you speak—in verse you sing; in prose you live in the abstract—in verse in the concrete; in prose you present motions—in verse visions; in prose you expound—in verse you enchant; in prose it is much if now and then you are held in the sphere of the fascinated senses—in verse if of the calm understanding.

Buller. Will you have the goodness, sir, to say all that over again?

North. I have forgot it. The lines in the countenance of Prose are austere. The look is shy, reserved, governed—like the fixed steady lineaments of mountains. The hues that suffuse the face of her sister Verse vary faster than those with which the western or the eastern sky momently reports the progress of the sinking, of the fallen, but not yet lost, of the coming or of the risen sun.

Buller. I have jotted that down, sir.

North. And I hope you will come to understand it. Candidly speaking, 'tis more than I do.

Seward. I do perfectly—and it is as true as beautiful, sir.

Buller. Equally so.

North. I venerate Wordsworth. Wordsworth's poetry stands distinct in the world. That which to other men is an occasional pleasure, or possibly delight, and to other poets an occasional transport, THE SEEING THIS VISIBLE UNIVERSE, is to him—a Life—one Individual Human Life—namely, his Own—traveling its whole journey from the Cradle to the Grave. And that Life—for what else could he do with it?—he has verified—sung. And there is no other such Song. It is a Memorable

Fact of our Civilization—a Memorable Fact in the History of Human Kind—that one perpetual song. Perpetual but infinitely various—as a river of a thousand miles, traversing, from its birthplace in the mountains, diverse regions, wild and inhabited, to the ocean receptacle.

Buller. Confoundedly prosaic at times.

North. He, more than any other true poet, approaches Verse to Prose—never, I believe, or hardly ever, quite blends them.

Buller. Often—often—often, my dear sir.

North. Seldom—seldom—seldom if ever, my dear sir. He tells his Life. His Poems are, of necessity, an Autobiography. The matter of them, then, is his personal reality; but Prose is, all over and properly, the language of Personal Realities. Even with him, however, so peculiarly conditioned, and, as well as I am able to understand his Proposition, against his own Theory of writing, Verse maintains, as by the laws of our insuppressible nature it always will maintain, its sacred Right and indefeasible Prerogative.

To conclude our conversation—

Buller. Or Monologue.

North. Epos is Human History in its magnitude in Verse. In Prose, National History offers itself in parallelism. The coincidence is broad and unquestioned; but on closer inspection, differences great and innumerable spring up and unfold themselves, until at last you might almost persuade yourself that the first striking resemblance deceived you, and that the two species lack analogy, so many other kinds does the Species in Verse embosom, and so escaping are the lines of agreement in the instant in which you attempt fixing them.

Buller. Would that Lord Bacon were here!

North. And thus we are led to a deeper truth. The Metrical Epos imitates History, without doubt, as Lord Bacon says—it borrows thence its mould, not rigorously, but with exceeding bold and free adaptations, as the Iliad unfolds the Ten Years' War in Seven Weeks. But for the Poet, more than another, ALL IS IN ALL.

Seward. Sir?

North. What is the Paradise Lost, ultimately considered?

Buller. Oh!

North. It is, my friends, the arguing in verse of a question in Natural Theology. Whence are Wrong and Pain? Moral and Physical Evil, as we call them, in all their overwhelming extent of complexity sprung? How permitted in the Kingdom of an All-wise and Almighty Love? To this question, concerning the origin of Evil, Milton answers as a Christian Theologian, agreeably to his own understanding of his Religion—so justifying the Universal Government of God, and, in particular, his Government of Man. The Poem is, therefore, Theological, Argumentative, Didactic, in Epic Form. Being in the constitution of his soul a Poet, mightiest of the mighty, the intention is hidden in the Form. The Verse has transformed the matter. Now, then, the Paradise Lost is not history told for itself. But this One Truth, in two answering Propositions, that the Will of Man spontaneously consorting with God's Will is Man's Good, spontaneously dissenting, Man's Evil. This is created into an awful and solemn narrative of a Matter exactly adapted, and long since authoritatively told. But this Truth, springing up in the shape of narrative, will now take its own determination into Events of unsurpassed magnitude, now of the tenderest individuality and minuteness; and all is, hence, in keeping—as one power of life springs up on one spot, in oak-tree, moss, and violet, and the difference of stature, thus understood, gives a deep harmony, so deep and embracing, that none without injury to the whole could be taken away.

Buller. What's all this! Hang that Drone—confound that

Chanter. Burst, thou most unseasonable of Bagpipes! Silence that dreadful Drum. Draw in your Horns—

Seward. Musketry! cannon! huzza! The enemy are storming the Camp. The Delhis bear down on the Pavilion. The life is in danger. Let us save the King.

North. See to it, gentlemen. I await the issue in my Swing-chair. Let the Barbarians but look on me and their weapons will drop.

Buller. All's right. A false alarm.

North. There was no alarm.

Buller. 'Twas but a SALUTE. THE BOYS have come back from Kilchurn. They are standing in front beside the spoil.

North. Widen the Portal. Artistically disposed! The whole like one huge Star-fish. Salmo ferox, centre—Pike, radii—Yellow-fins, circumference—Weight I should say the tenth of a ton. Call the Manciple. Manciple, you are responsible for the preservation of that Star-fish.

Buller. Sir, you forget yourself. The People must be fed. We are Seven. Twelve are on the troop roll—Nine strangers have sent in their cards—the Gillies are growing upon us—the Camp-followers have doubled the population since morn, and the circumambient Natives are waxing strong. Hunger is in the Camp—but for this supply Famine; *Iliacos intra muros* PECCATUR *et extra;* Dods reports that the Boiler is wroth, the furnace at a red heat, Pots and Pans a-simmer—the Culinary Spirit impatient to be at work. In such circumstances, the tenth of a ton is no great matter; but it is better than nothing. The mind of the Manciple may lie at rest, for that Star-fish will never see to-morrow's Sun; and motionless as he looks, he is hastening to the Shades.

North. Sir, you forget yourself. There is other animal matter in the world besides Fish. No penury of it in camp. I have here the Manciple's report. "One dozen plucked

Earochs—one ditto ditto Ducklings—d. d. d. March Chick—one Bubblyjock—one Side of Mutton—four Necks—six Sheep-heads, and their complement of Trotters—two Sheep, just slaughtered and yet in wholes—four Lambs ditto—the late Cladich-Calf—one small Stot—two lb. 40 Rounds in pickle—four Miscellaneous Pies of the First Order—six Hams—four dozen of Rein-deer Tongues—one dozen of Bears' Paws—two Barrels of——"

Buller. Stop. Let that suffice for the meanwhile.

North. The short shadow-hand on the face of Dial-Cruachan, to my instructed sense, stands at six. You young Oxonians, I know, always adorn for dinner, even when roughing it on service; and so, V. and W. do you. These two elderly gentlemen here are seen to most advantage in white neckcloths, and the OLD ONE is never so like himself as in a suit of black velvet. To your tents and toilets. In an hour we meet in the—DEESIDE.

DIES BOREALES.

No. II.

ENCAMPMENT AT CLADICH. TIME—*Eleven* A. M.

SCENE—*The Portal of the Pavilion.*

NORTH—BULLER—SEWARD.

Buller. I know there is nothing you dislike so much as personal observations——

North. On myself to myself—not at all on others.

Buller. Yet I cannot help telling you to your face, sir, that you are one of the finest looking old men——

North. Elderly gentlemen, if you please, sir.

Buller. In Britain, in Europe, in the World. I am perfectly serious, sir. You are.

North. You needed not to say you were perfectly serious; for I suffer no man to be ironical on Me, Mr. Buller. I am.

Buller. Such a change since we came to Cladich! Seward was equally shocked, with myself, at your looks on board the Steamer. So lean—so bent—so sallow—so haggard—in a word—so aged!

North. Were you shocked, Seward?

Seward. Buller has such a blunt way with him that he

often makes me blush. I was not shocked, my dear sir, but I was affected.

Buller. Turning to me, he said in a whisper, "What a wreck!"

North. I saw little alteration on you, Mr. Seward; but as to Buller, it was with the utmost difficulty I could be brought, by his reiterated asseverations, into a sort of quasi-belief in his personal identity; and even now, it is far from amounting to anything like a settled conviction. Why, his face is twice the breadth it used to be—and so red! It used to be narrow and pale. Then, what a bushy head—now, cocker it as he will, bald. In figure was he not slim? Now, stout's the word. Stout—stout—yes, Buller, you have grown stout, and will grow stouter—your doom is to be fat—I prophesy punch——

Buller. Spare me—spare me, sir. Seward should not have interrupted me—'twas but the first impression—and soon wore off—those Edinboro' people have much to answer for—unmercifully wearing you out at their ceaseless *soirées*—but since you came to Cladich, sir, CHRISTOPHER'S HIMSELF AGAIN—pardon my familiarity—nor can I now, after the minutest inspection, and severest scrutiny, detect one single additional wrinkle on face or forehead—nay, not a wrinkle at all—not one—so fresh of color, too, sir, that the irradiation is at times ruddy—and without losing an atom of expression, the countenance absolutely—plump. Yes, sir, plump's the word—plump, plump, plump.

North. Now you speak sensibly, and like yourself, my dear Buller. I wear well.

Buller. Your enemies circulated a report—

North. I did not think I had an enemy in the world.

Buller. Your friends, sir, had heard a rumor—that you had mounted a wig.

North. And was there, among them all, one so weak-minded as to believe it? But to be sure, there are no bounds to the credulity of mankind.

Buller. That you had lost your hair—and that, like Samson—

North. And by what Delilah had my locks been shorn?

Seward. It all originated, I verily believe, sir, in the moved imagination of the Pensive Public:

"Res est soliciti plena timoris Amor."

North. Buller, I see little, if any—no change whatever—on you, since the days of Deeside—nor on you, Seward. Yes, I do. Not now, when by yourselves; but when your boys are in Tent, ah! then I do indeed—a pleasant, a happy, a blessed change! Bright boys they are—delightful lads—noble youths—and so are my Two—emphasis on *my*—

Seward and Buller. Yes, all emphasis, and may the Four be friends for life.

North. In presence of us old folks, composed and respectful—in manly modesty attentive to every word we say—at times no doubt wearisome enough! Yet each ready, at a look or pause, to join in when we are at our gravest—and the solemn may be getting dull—enlivening the sleepy flow of our conversation as with rivulets issuing from pure sources in the hills of the morning—

Seward. Ay—ay; heaven bless them all!

North. Why, there is more than sense—more than talent—there is *genius* among them—in their eyes and on their tongues—though they have no suspicion of it—and that is the charm. Then how they rally one another! Witty fellows all Four. And the right sort of raillery. Gentlemen by birth and breeding, to whom in their wildest sallies vulgarity is impossible—to whom, on the giddy brink—the perilous edge—still adheres a native decorum superior to that of all the Schools.

Seward. They have their faults, sir—

North. So have we. And 'tis well for us. Without faults we should be unlovable.

Seward. In affection I spake.

North. I know you did. There is no such hateful sight on earth as a perfect character. He is one mass of corruption —for he is a hypocrite—*intus et in cute*—by the necessity of nature. The moment a perfect character enters a room—I leave it.

Seward. What if you happened to live in the neighborhood of the nuisance?

North. Emigrate. Or remain here—encamped for life—with imperfect characters—till the orders should issue—Strike Tent.

Buller. My Boy has a temper of his own.

North. Original—or acquired?

Buller. Naturally sweet-blooded—assuredly by the mother's side—but in her goodness she did all she could to spoil him. Some excuse—We have but Marmy.

North. And his father, naturally not quite so sweet-blooded, does all he can to preserve him? Between the two, a pretty Pickle he is. Has thine a temper of his own, too, Seward?

Seward. Hot.

North. Hereditary.

Seward. No—North. A milder, meeker, Christian Lady than his mother is not in England.

North. I confess I was at the moment not thinking of his mother. But somewhat too much of this. I hereby authorize the Boys of this Empire to have what tempers they choose—with one sole exception—THE SULKY.

Buller. The Edict is promulged.

North. Once, and once only, during one of the longest and best-spent lives on record, was I in the mood proscribed—and it endured most part of a whole day. The Anniversary of that day I observe, in severest solitude, with a salutary horror. And it is my Birthday. Ask me not, my friends, to reveal the Cause. Aloof from confession before man—we must keep to ourselves—as John Foster says—a corner of our own souls. A black corner it is—and enter it with or without a light—you see, here and there, something dismal—hideous—shapeless—nameless—each lying in its own place on the floor. There lies the CAUSE. It was the morning of my Ninth Year. As I kept sitting high upstairs by myself—one familiar face after another kept ever and anon looking in upon me—all with one expression! And one familiar voice after another—all with one tone—kept muttering at me—"*He's still in the Sulks!*" How I hated them with an intenser hatred—and chief them I before had loved best—at each opening and each shutting of that door! How I hated myself, as my blubbered face felt hotter and hotter—and I knew how ugly I must be, with my fixed fiery eyes. It was painful to sit on such a chair for hours in one posture, and to have so chained a child would have been great cruelty—but I was resolved to die, rather than change it; and had I been told by any one under an angel to get up and go to play, I would have spat in his face. It was a lonesome attic, and I had the fear of ghosts. But not then—my superstitious fancy was quelled by my troubled heart. Had I not deserved to be allowed to go? Did they not all know that all my happiness in this life depended on my being allowed to go? Could any one of them give a reason for not allowing me to go? What right had they to say that if I did go, I should never be able to find my way, by myself, back? What right had they to say that Roundy was a blackguard, and that he would lead me to the gallows? Never before, in all the world, had a good boy been used so on his birthday. They pretend to be sorry when I am sick—and when I say my prayers, they say theirs too; but I am sicker now—and they are not sorry, but angry—there's no use in prayers—and I won't read one verse in the Bible this night, should my aunt go down on her knees. And in the midst of such unworded soliloquies did the young blasphemer fall asleep.

Buller. Young Christopher North! Incredible.

North. I know not how long I slept; but on awaking, I saw an angel with a most beautiful face and most beautiful hair—a little young angel—about the same size as myself—sitting on a stool by my feet. "Are you quite well now, Christopher? Let us go to the meadows and gather flowers." Shame, sorrow, remorse, contrition, came to me with those innocent words—we wept together, and I was comforted. "I have been sinful"—"but you are forgiven." Down all the stairs hand in hand we glided; and there was no longer anger in any eyes—the whole house was happy. All voices were kinder—if that were possible—than they had been when I rose in the morning—a Boy in his Ninth Year. Parental hands smoothed my hair—parental lips kissed it—and parental greetings, only a little more cheerful than prayers, restored me to the Love I had never lost, and which I felt now had animated that brief and just displeasure. I had never heard then of Elysian fields; but I had often heard, and often had dreamt happy, happy dreams of fields of light in heaven. And such looked the fields to be, where fairest Mary Gordon and I gathered flowers, and spoke to the birds, and to one another, all day long—and again, when the day was gone, and the evening going, on till moontime, below and among the soft-burning stars.

Buller. And never has *Christopher been in the Sulks* since that day.

North. Under heaven I owe it all to that child's eyes. Still I sternly keep the Anniversary—for, beyond doubt, I was that day possessed with a Devil—and an angel it was, though human, that drove him out.

Seward. Your first Love?

North. In a week she was in heaven. My friends—in childhood—our whole future life would sometimes seem to be at the mercy of such small events as these. Small call them not—for they are great for good or for evil—because of the unfathomable mysteries that lie shrouded in the growth, on earth, of an immortal soul.

Seward. May I dare to ask you, sir—it is indeed a delicate—a more than delicate question—if the Anniversary—has been brought round with the revolving year since we encamped?

North. It has.

Seward. Ah! Buller! we know now the reason of his absence that day from the Pavilion and Deeside—of his utter seclusion—he was doing penance in the Swiss Giantess—a severe sojourn.

North. A Good Temper, friends—not a good Conscience—is the Blessing of Life.

Buller. Shocked to hear you say so, sir. Unsay it, my dear sir—unsay it—pernicious doctrine. It may get abroad.

North. THE SULKS!—the CELESTIALS. The Sulks are hell, sirs—the Celestials, by the very name, heaven. I take temper in its all-embracing sense of Physical, Mental, and Moral Atmosphere. Pure and serene—then we respire God's gifts, and are happier than we desire! Is not that divine? Foul and disturbed—then we are stifled by God's gifts—and are wickeder than we fear! Is not that devilish? A good Conscience and a bad Temper! Talk not to me, Young Men, of pernicious doctrine—it is a soul-saving doctrine—"millions of spiritual creatures walk unseen" teaching it—men's Thoughts, communing with heaven, have been teaching it—surely not all in vain—since Cain slew Abel.

Seward. The Sage!

Buller. Socrates.

North. Morose! Think for five minutes on what that word means—and on what that word contains—and you see the Man must be an Atheist. Sitting in the House of God *morosely!* Bright, bold, beautiful boys of ours, ye are not morose—heaven's air has free access through your open souls—a clear conscience carries the Friends in ther pastimes up the Mountains.

Seward. And their fathers before them.

North. And their great-grandfather—I mean their spiritual great-grandfather—myself—Christopher North. They are gathering up—even as we gathered up—images that will never die. Evanescent! Clouds—lights—shadows—glooms, the falling sound—the running murmur—and the swinging roar—as cataract, stream, and forest all alike seem wheeling by—these are not evanescent—for they will all keep coming and going—before their Imagination—all life-long at the bidding of the Will—or obedient to a Wish! Or by benign Law, whose might is a mystery, coming back from the far profound—remembered apparitions!

Seward. Dear sir.

North. Even my Image will sometimes reappear—and the Tents of Cladich—the Camp on Lochawe-side.

Buller. My dear sir—it will not be evanescent——

North. And withal such Devils! But I have given them *carte blanche.*

Seward. Nor will they abuse it.

North. I wonder when they sleep. Each has his own dormitory—the cluster forming the left wing of the Camp—but Deeside is not seldom broad awake till midnight; and though I am always up and out by six at the latest, never once have I caught a man of them napping, but either there they are each more blooming than the other, getting ready their gear for a start;—or, on sweeping the Loch with my glass, I see their heads, like wild-ducks—swimming—round Rabbit Island—as some wretch has baptized Inishail—or away to Inistrynish—or, for anything I know, to Port-Sonachan—swimming for a Medal given by the Club! Or there goes *Gutta Percha* by the Pass of Brandir or shooting away into the woods near Kilchurn. Twice have they been on the top of Cruachan—once for a clear hour, and once for a dark day—the very next morning, Marmaduke said, they would have "some more mountain," and the Four Cloud-compellers swept the whole range of Ben Bhuridh and Bein-Lurachan as far as the head of Glensrea. Though they said nothing about it, I heard of their having been over the hills behind us, t'other night, at Cairndow at a wedding. Why, only think, sirs, yesterday they were off by daylight to try their luck in Loch Dochart, and again I heard their merriment soon after we had retired. They must have footed it above forty miles. That Cornwall Clipper will be their death. And off again this morning—all on foot—to the Black Mount.

Buller. For what?

North. By permission of the Marquis, to shoot an Eagle. She is said to be again on egg—and to cliff-climbers her eyrie is within rifle-range. But let us forget the Boys—as they have forgot us.

Seward. The Loch is calmer to-day, sir, than we have yet seen it; but the calm is of a different character from yesterday's—that was serene, this is solemn—I had almost said austere. Yesterday there were few clouds; and such was the prevailing power of all those lovely woods on the islands, and along the mainland shores—that the whole reflection seemed sylvan. When gazing on such a sight, does not our feeling of the unrealities—the shadows—attach to the realities—the substances? So that the living trees—earth-rooted, and growing upwards—become almost as visionary as their inverted semblances in that commingling clime? Or is it that the life of the trees gives life to the images, and imagination believes that the whole, in its beauty, must belong by the same law, to the same world?

North. Let us understand, without seeking to destroy, our delusions—for has not this life of ours been wisely called the dream of a shadow!

Seward. To-day there are many clouds, and aloft they are beautiful; nor is the light of the sun not most gracious; but the repose of all that downward world affects me—I know not why—with sadness—it is beginning to look almost gloomy—and I seem to see the hush not of sleep, but of death. There is not the unboundaried expanse of yesterday—the loch looks narrower—and Cruachan closer to us, with all his heights.

Buller. I felt a drop of rain on the back of my hand.

Seward. It must have been, then, from your nose. There will be no rain this week. But a breath of air there is somewhere—for the mirror is dimmed, and the vision gone.

North. The drop was not from his nose, Seward, for here are three—and clear, pure drops too—on my Milton. I should not be at all surprised if we were to have a little rain.

Seward. Odd enough. I cannot conjecture where it comes from. It must be dew.

Buller. Who ever heard of dew dropping in large fat globules at meridan on a summer's day? It is getting very close and sultry. The interior must be, as Wordsworth says, "Like a Lion's den." Did you whisper, sir?

North. No. But something did. Look at the silver, Buller.

Buller. Thermometer 85. Barometer I can say nothing

about—but that it is very low indeed. A long way below Stormy.

North. What color would you call that glare about the the Crown of Cruachan? Yellow?

Seward. You may just as well call it yellow as not. I never saw such a color before—and don't care though I never see such again—for it is horrid. That *is* a—Glare.

North. Cowper says grandly,

> "A terrible sagacity informs
> The Poet's heart: he looks to distant storms;
> He hears the thunder ere the tempest lowers."

He is speaking of tempests in the moral world. You know the passage—it is a fine one—so indeed is the whole Epistle—Table-Talk. I am a bit of a Poet myself in smelling thunder. Early this morning I set it down for mid-day—and it is mid-day now.

Buller. Liker Evening.

North. Dimmish and darkish, certainly—but unlike Evening. I pray you look at the Sun.

Buller. What about him?

North. Though unclouded—he seems shrouded in his own solemn light—expecting thunder.

Buller. There is not much motion among the clouds.

North. Not yet. Merely what in Scotland we call a carry—yet that great central mass is double the size it was ten minutes ago—the City Churches are crowding round the Cathedral—and the whole assemblage lies under the shadow of the Citadel—with battlements and colonnades at once Fort and Temple.

Buller. Still some blue sky. Not very much. But some.

North. Cruachan! you are changing color.

Buller. Grim—very.

North. The Loch's like ink. I could dip my pen in it.

Seward. We are about to have thunder.

North. Weather-wise wizard—we are. That mutter was thunder. In five seconds you will hear some more. One—two—three—four—there; that was a growl. I call that good growling—sulky-sullen, savage growling, that makes the heart of Silence quake.

Seward. And mine.

North. What? Dying away! Some incomprehensible cause is turning the thunderous masses round towards Appin.

Seward. And I wish them a safe journey.

North. All right. They are coming this way—all at once—the whole Thunder-storm. Flash—roar.

> "Be thou as lightning in the eyes of France;
> For ere thou canst report I will be there,
> The thunder of my cannon shall be heard."

Who but Willy could have said *that!*

Seward. Who said what?

North. How ghastly all the trees!

Seward. I see no trees—nor anything else.

North. How can you, with that Flying Dutchman over your eyes?

Buller. I gave him my handkerchief—for at this moment I know his head is like to rend. I wish I had kept it to myself; but no use—the lightning is seen through lids and hands, and would be through stone walls.

North. Each flash has, of course, a thunder-clap of its own—if we knew where to look for it; but, to our senses, all connection between cause and effect is lost—such incessant flashings—and such multitudinous outbreaks—and such a continuous roll of outrageous echoes!

Buller. Coruscation—explosion—are but feeble words.

North. The Cathedral's on Fire.

Buller. I don't mind so much those wide flarings among the piled clouds, as these gleams——oh!

North. Where art thou, Cruachan? Ay—methinks I see thee—methinks I do not—thy Three Peaks may not pierce the masses that now oppress thee—but behind the broken midway clouds, those black purple breadths of solid earth are thine—thine those unmistakeable Cliffs—thine the assured beauty of that fearless Forest—and may the lightning scathe not one single tree!

Buller. Nor man.

North. This is your true total Eclipse of the Sun. Day, not night, is the time for thunder and lightning. Night can be dark of itself—nay, cannot help it; but when Day grows black, then is the blackness of darkness in the Bright One terrible;—and terror—Burke said well—is at the heart of the sublime. The Light, such as it is, sets off the power of the lightning—it pales to that flashing—and is forgotten in Fire. It smells of hell.

Seward. It is constitutional in the Sewards. North, I am sick.

North. Give way to gasping—and lie down—nothing can be done for you. The danger is not—

Seward. I am not afraid—I am faint.

North. You must speak louder, if you expect to be heard by ears of clay. Peals is not the word. "Peals on peals redoubled" is worse. There never was—and never will be a word in any language—for *all that.*

Buller. Unreasonable to expect it. Try twenty—in twenty languages.

North. Buller, you may count ten individual deluges—besides the descent of three at hand—conspicuous in the general Rain, which without them would be Rain sufficient for a Flood. Now the Camp has it—and let us enter the Pavilion. I don't think there is much wind here—yet far down the black Loch is silently whitening with waves like breakers; for here the Rain alone rules, and its rushing deadens the retiring thunder. The ebbing thunder! Still louder than any sea on any shore—but a diminishing loudness, though really vast, seems quelled; and, losing its power over the present, imagination follows it not into the distant region where it may be raging as bad as ever. Buller?

Buller. What?

North. How's Seward?

Seward. Much better. It is very, very kind of you, my dear sir, to carry me in your arms, and place me in your own Swing-chair. The change of atmosphere has revived me—but the Boys?

North. The Boys—why, they went to the Black Mount to shoot an eagle, and see a thunder-storm, and long before this they have had their hearts' desire. There are caves, Seward, in Buachail-Mor; and one recess I know—not a cave—but grander far than any cave—near the Fall of Eas-a-Bhrogich—far down below the bottom of the Fall, which in its long descent whitens the sable cliffs. Thither leads a winding access no storm can shake. In that recess you sit rock-surrounded—but with elbow-room for five hundred men—and all the light you have—and you would not wish for more—comes down upon you from a cupola far nearer heaven than that hung by Michael Angelo.

Seward. The Boys are safe.

North. Or the lone House of Dalness has received them—hospitable now as of yore—or the Huntsman's hut—or Shepherd's shieling—that word I love, and shall use it now—though shieling it is not, but a comfortable cottage—and the dwellers there fear not the thunder and the lightning—for they know they are in His hands—and talk cheerfully in the storm.

Seward. Over and gone. How breathable the atmosphere!

North. In the Forest of the Marquis and of Monzie, the horns of the Red-deer are again in motion. In my mind's eye—Harry—I see one—an enormous fellow—bigger than the big stag of Benmore himself—and not to be so easily brought to perform, by particular desire, the part of Moriens—giving himself a shake of his whole huge bulk, and a *caive* of his whole wide antlery—and then leading down from the Corrie, with Platonic affection, a herd of Hinds to the greensward islanded among brackens and heather—a spot equally adapted for feed, play, rumination, and sleep. And the Roes are glinting through the glades—and the Fleece are nibbling on the mountains' glittering breast—and the Cattle are grazing, and galloping, and lowing on the hills—and the furred folk, who are always dry, come out from crevices for a mouthful of the fresh air; and the whole four-footed creation are jocund—are happy!

Buller. What a picture!

North. And the Fowls of the Air—think ye not the Eagle, storm-driven not unalarmed along that league-long face of cliff, is now glad at heart, pruning the wing that shall carry him again, like a meteor, into the subsided skies?

Buller. What it is to have an imagination! Worth all my Estate.

North. Let us exchange.

Buller. Not possible. Strictly entailed.

North. Dock.

Buller. Mno.

North. And the little wren flits out from the back-door of her nest—too happy she to sing—and in a minute is back again, with a worm in her mouth, to her half-score gaping babies—the sole family in all the dell. And the sea-mews, sore against their will driven seawards, are returning by ones and twos, and thirties, and thousands, up Loch-Etive, and, dallying with what wind is still alive above the green transparency, drop down in successive parties of pleasure on the silver sands of Ardmatty, or lured onwards into the still leas of Glenliver, or the profounder quietude of the low mounds of Dalness.

Seward. My fancy is contented to feed on what is before my eyes.

Buller. Doff, then, the Flying Dutchman.

North. And thousands of Rills, on the first day of their apparent existence, are all happy too, and make me happy to look on them leaping and dancing down the rocks—and the River Etive, rejoicing in his strength, from far Kingshouse all along to the end of his journey, is happiest of them all; for the storm that has swollen has not discolored him, and with a pomp of clouds on his breast, he is flowing in his expanded beauty into his own desired Loch.

Seward. Gaze with me, my dear sir, on what lies before our eyes.

North. The Rainbow!

Buller. Four miles wide, and half a mile broad.

North. Thy own Rainbow, Cruachan—from end to end.

Seward. Is it fading—or is it brightening?—no, it is not fading—and to brighten is impossible. It is the beautiful at perfection—it is dissolving—it is gone.

Buller. I asked you, sir, have the Poets well handled Thunder?

North. I was waiting for the Rainbow. Many eyes besides ours are now regarding it—many hearts gladdened—but have you not often felt, Seward, as if such Apparitions came at a silent call in our souls—that we might behold them—and that the hour—or the moment—was given to us alone! So have I felt when walking alone among the great solitudes of Nature.

Seward. Lochawe is the name now for a dozen little lovely lakes! For, lo! as the vapors are rising, they disclose, here a bay that does not seem to be a bay, but complete in its own encircled stillness—there a bare grass island—yes it is Inishail—with a shore of mists—and there, with its Pines and Castle, Freoch, as if it were Loch Freoch, and not itself an Isle. Beautiful bewilderment! but of our own creating!—for thus Fancy is fain to dally with what we love—and would seek to estrange the familiar—as if Lochawe in its own simple grandeur were not all-sufficient for our gaze.

Buller. Let me try my hand. No—no—no—I can see and feel, have an eye and a heart for Scenery, as it is called, but am no hand at a description. My dear, sweet, soft-breasted, fair-fronted, bright-haired, delightful Cruachan — thy very name, how liquid with open vowels—not a consonant among them all—no Man-Mountain Thou—Thou art the LADY OF THE LAKE. I am in love with Thee—Thou must not think of retiring from the earth—Thou must not take the veil—off with it—off with it from those glorious shoulders—and come, in all Thy loveliness, to my long—my longing arms!

Seward. Is that the singing of larks?

North. No larks live here. The laverock is a Lowland bird, and loves our brairded fields and our pastoral braes; but the Highland mountains are not for him—he knows by instinct that they are haunted—though he never saw the shadow nor heard the sugh of the eagle's wing.

Seward. The singing from the woods seems to reach the sky. They have utterly forgotten their fear; or think you, sir, that birds know that what frightened them is gone, and that they sing with intenser joy because of the fear that kept them mute?

North. The lambs are frisking—and the sheep staring placidly at the Tents. I hear the hum of bees—returned—and returning from their straw-built Citadels. In the primal hour of his winged life, that wavering butterfly goes by in search of the sunshine that meets him; and happy for this generation of ephemerals that they first took wing on the afternoon of the day of the Great Storm.

Buller. How have the Poets, sir, handled thunder and lightning?

North. "Sæpe ego, cum flavis messorem induceret arvis
Agricola, et fragili jam stringeret hordea culmo,
Omnia ventorum concurrere prœlia vidi,
Quæ gravidam latè segetem ab radicibus imis
Sublimè expulsam eruerent: ita turbine nigro
Ferret hyems culmumque levem, stipulasque volantes.
Sæpe etiam immensum cœlo venit agmen aquarum,
Et fœdam glomerant tempestatem imbribus atris
Collectæ ex alto nubes: ruit arduus æther,
Et pluviâ ingenti sata læta, boumque labores
Diluit: implentur fossæ, et cava flumina crescunt
Cum sonitu, fervetque fretis spirantibus æquor.
Ipse Pater, mediâ nimborum in nocte, corusca
Fulmina molitur dextrâ: quo maxima motu
Terra tremit: fugêre feræ, et mortalia corda
Per gentes humilis stravit pavor: ille flagranti
Aut Atho, aut Rhodopen, aut alta Ceraunia telo
Dejicit: ingeminant Austri, et densissimus imber:
Nunc nemora ingenti vento, nunc littora plangunt."

Buller. You recite well, sir, and Latin better than English—not so sing-songy—and as sonorous: then Virgil, to be sure, is fitter for recitation than any Laker of you all——

North. I am not a Laker—I am a Locher.

Buller. Tweedledum—tweedledee.

North. That means the Tweed and the Dee? Content. One might have thought, Buller, that our Scottish Critics would have been puzzled to find a fault in that strain——

Buller. It is faultless; but not a Scotch critic worth a curse but yourself——

North. I cannot accept a compliment at the expense of all the rest of my countrymen. I cannot indeed.

Buller. Yes, you can.

North. There was Lord Kames—a man of great talents—a most ingenious man—and with an insight——

Buller. I never heard of him—was he a Scotch Peer?

North. One of the Fifteen. "A strained elevation"—says his Lordship—I am sure of the words, though I have not seen his Elements of Criticism for fifty years——

Buller. You are a creature of a wonderful memory.

North. "A strained elevation is attended with another inconvenience, that the author is apt to fall suddenly, as well as the reader; because it is not a little difficult to descend sweetly and easily from such elevation to the ordinary tone of the subject. The following is a good illustration of that observation" —and then his Lordship quotes the passage I recited—stopping with the words "*densissimus imber,*" which are thus made to conclude the description!

Buller. Oh! oh! oh! That's murder.

North. In the description of a storm—continues his Lordship—"to figure Jupiter throwing down huge mountains with his thunderbolts, is hyperbolically sublime, if I may use the expression; the tone of mind produced by that image is so distinct from the tone produced by a thick shower of rain, that the sudden transition *must be very unpleasant.*"

Buller. Suggestive of a great-coat. That's the way to deal with a great Poet. Clap your hand on the Poet's mouth in its fervor—shut up the words in mid-volley—and then tell him that he does not know how to descend sweetly and easily from strained elevation!

North. Nor do I agree with his Lordship that "to figure Jupiter throwing down huge mountains with his thunderbolts is hyperbolically sublime." As a part for a whole is a figure of speech, so is a whole for a part. Virgil says, "dejicit;" but he did not mean to say that Jupiter "tumbled down" Athos or Rhodope or the Acroceraunian range. He knew—for he saw them—that there they were in all their altitude after the storm—little if at all the worse. But Jupiter had struck—smitten—splintered—rent—trees and rocks—midway or on the summits—and the sight was terrific—and "dejicit" brings it before our imagination, which not for a moment pictures the whole mountain tumbling down. But great Poets know the power of words, and on great occasions how to use them—in this case—one—and small critics will not suffer their own senses to instruct them in Poetry—and hence the Elements of Criticism are not the Elements of Nature, and assist us not in comprehending the grandeur of reported storms.

Buller. Lay it into them, sir.

North. Good Dr. Hugh Blair again, who in his day had a high character for taste and judgment, agreed with Henry Home that "the transition is made too hastily—I am afraid—from the preceding sublime images, to a thick shower and the blowing of the south wind, and shows how difficult it frequently is to descend with grace, without seeming to fall." Nay, even Mr. Alison himself—one of the finest spirits that ever breathed on earth, says—"I acknowledge, indeed, that the 'pluviâ ingenti sata læta, boumque labores diluit,' is defensible from the connection of the imagery with the subject of the poem; but the 'implentur fossæ' is both an unnecessary and a degrading circumstance when compared with the magnificent effects that are described in the rest of the passage." In this quotation, too, the final grand line is inadvertently omitted—

> "Nunc nemora ingenti vento, nunc littora plangunt."

Buller. I never read Hugh Blair—but I have read—often, and always with increased delight—Mr. Alison's exquisite Essays on the nature and Principles of Taste, and Lord Jeffrey's admirable exposition of the Theory—in statement so clear, and in illustration so rich—worth all the Æsthetics of the Germans—Schiller excepted—in one Volume of Mist.

North. Mr. Alison had an original as well as a fine mind; and here he seems to have been momentarily beguiled into mistake by unconscious deference to the judgment of men—in his province far inferior to himself—whom in his modesty he admired. Mark. Virgil's main purpose is to describe the dangers—the losses to which the agriculturist is at all seasons exposed from wind and weather. And he sets them before us in plain and perspicuous language, not rising above the proper level of the didactic. Yet being a Poet he puts poetry into his description from the first and throughout. To say that the line "Et pluviâ," &c., is "*defensible* from the connection of the imagery with the subject of the Poem" is not enough. It is *necessitated.* Strike it out and you abolish the subject. And just so with "implentur fossæ." The "fossæ" we know in that country were numerous and wide, and, when swollen, dangerous—and the "cava flumina" well follow instantly—for the "fossæ" were their feeders—and we hear as well as see the rivers rushing to the sea—and we hear, too, as well as see, the sea itself. *There the description ends.* Virgil has done his work. But his imagination is moved, and there arises a new strain altogether. He is done with the agriculturists. And now he deals with man at large—with the whole human race.

He is now a Boanerges—a son of thunder—and he begins with Jove. The sublimity comes in a moment. "Ipse Pater, mediâ nimborum in nocte"—and is sustained to the close—the last line being great as the first—and all between accordant, and all true to nature. Without rain and wind, what would be a thunder-storm? The "densissimus imber!" obeys the laws—and so do the ingeminanting Austri—and the shaken woods and the stricken shores.

Buller Well done, Virgil—well done, North.

North. I cannot rest, Buller—I can have no peace of mind but in a successful defence of these Ditches. Why is a Ditch to be despised? Because it is dug? So is a grave. Is the Ditch—wet or dry—that must be passed by the Volunteers of the Fighting Division before the Fort can be stormed, too low a word for a Poet to use? Alas! on such an occasion well might he say, as he looked after the assault and saw the floating tartans—*implentur fossæ*—the Ditch is filled!

Buller. Ay, Mr. North, in that case the word Ditch—and the thing—would be dignified by danger, daring, and death. But here——

North. The case is the same—with a difference, for there is all the Danger—all the Daring—all the Death—that the incident or event admits of—and they are not small. Think for a moment. The Rain falls over the whole broad heart of the tilled earth—from the face of the fields it runs into the Ditches—the first unavoidable receptacles—these pour into the rivers—the rivers into the river mouths—and then you are in the Sea.

Buller. Go on sir, go on.

North. I am amazed—I am indignant, Buller. *Ruit arduus æther.* The steep or high ether rushes down! as we saw it rush down a few minutes ago. What happens?

"Et pluviâ ingenti sata læta boumque labores
Diluit!"

Alas! for the hopeful—hopeless husbandman now. What a multiplied and magnified expression have we here for the arable lands. All the glad seed-time vain—vain all industry of man and oxen—there you have the true agricultural pathos—washed away—set in a swim—deluged! Well has the Poet—in one great line—spoke the greatness of a great matter. Sudden affliction—visible desolation—imagined dearth.

Buller. Don't stop, sir, you speak to the President of our Agricultural Society—go on, sir, go on.

North. Now drop in—in its veriest place, and in two words, the *necessitated Implentur fossæ.* No pretence—no display—no phraseology—the nakedest, but quite effectual statement of the fact—which the farmer—I love that word farmer—has witnessed as often as he has ever seen the Coming—the Ditches that were dry ran full to the brim. The homely rustic fact, strong and impressive to the husbandman, cannot be dealt with by poetry otherwise than by setting it down in its bald simplicity. Seek to raise—to dress—to disguise—and you make it ridiculous. The Mantuan knew better—he says what must be said—and goes on—

Buller. He goes on—so do you, sir you both get on.

North. And now again begins Magnification,

"Et cava flumina crescunt
cum sonitu."

The "hollow-bedded rivers" grow, swell, visibly wax mighty and turbulent. You imagine that you stand on the bank and see the river that had shrunk into a thread getting broad enough to fill the capacity of its whole hollow bed. The rushing of arduous ether would not of itself have proved sufficient. Therefore glory to the Italian Ditches and glory to the Dumfriesshire Drains, which I have seen, in an hour, change the white murmuring Esk into a red rolling river, with as sweeping sway as ever attended the Arno on its way to inundate Florence.

Buller. Glory to the Ditches of the Vale of Arno—glory to the Drains of Dumfriesshire. Draw breath, sir. Now, go on, sir.

North. "Cum sonitu." Not as Father Thames rises—*silently*—till the flow lapse over lateral meadow-grounds for a mile on either side. But "cum sonitu," with a voice—with a roar—a mischievous roar—a roar of—ten thousand Ditches.

Buller. And then the "flumina"—"cava" no more—will be as clear as mud.

North. You have hit it. They will be—for the Arno in flood is like liquid mud—by no means enamoring, perhaps not even sublime—but showing you that it comes off the fields and along the Ditches—that you see swillings of the "sata læta boumque labores."

Buller. Agricultural Produce!

North. For a moment—a single moment—leave out the Ditches, and say merely, "The rain falls over the fields—the rivers swell roaring." No picture at all. You must have the fall over the surface—the gathering in the narrower artificial—the delivery into the wider natural channels—the fight of spate and surge at river mouth—

"Fervetque fretis spirantibus æquor."

The Ditches are indispensable in nature and in Virgil.

Buller. Put this glass of water to your lips, sir—not that I would recommend water to a man in a fit of eloquence—but I know you are abstinent—infatuated in your abjuration of wine. Go on—half-minute time.

North. I swear to defend—at the pen's point—against all Comers—the position—that the line

"Diluit: implentur fossæ, cava flumina crescunt
Cum sonitu—"

is, where it stands—and looking before and after—a perfect line; and that to strike out "implentur fossæ" would be an outrage on it—just equal, Buller, to my knocking out, without hesitation, your brains—for your brains do not contribute more to the flow of our conversation—than do the Ditches to that other spate.

Buller. That will do—you may stop.

North. I ask no man's permission—I obey no man's mandate—to stop. Now Virgil takes wing—now he blazes and soars. Now comes the power and spirit of the Storm gathered in the Person of the Sire—of him who wields the thunderbolt into which the Cyclops have forged storms of all sorts—wind and rain together—"*Tres Imbri torti radios!*" &c. You remember the magnificent mixture. And there we have VIRGILIUS *versus* HOMERUM.

Buller. You may sit down, sir.

North. I did not know I had stood up. Beg pardon.

Buller. I am putting Swing to rights for you, sir.

North. Methinks Jupiter is *twice* apparent—the first time, as the President of the Storm, which is agreeable to the dictates of reason and necessity;—the second—to my fancy—as delighting himself in the conscious exertion of power. What is he splintering Athos, or Rhodope, or the Acroceraunians for? The divine use of the Fulmen is to quell Titans, and to kill that mad fellow who was running up the ladder at Thebes, Capaneus. Let the Great Gods find *out their enemies now*—find out and finish them—and enemies they must have not a few among those prostrate crowds—"per gentes humilis stravit pavor." But shattering and shivering the mountain tops—which, as I take it, is here the prominent affair—and, as I said, the true meaning of "dejicit"—is mere pastime—as if Jupiter Tonans were disporting himself on a holiday.

Buller. Oh! sir, you have exhausted the subject—if not yourself—and us;—I beseech you sit down;—see, Swing solicits you—and oh! sir, you—we—all of us will find in a few minutes' silence a great relief after all that thunder.

North. You remember Lucretius?

Buller. No, I don't. To you I am not ashamed to confess that I read him with some difficulty. With ease, sir, do you?

North. I never knew a man who did but Bobus Smith; and so thoroughly was he imbued with the spirit of the great Epicurean, that Landor—himself the best Latinist living—equals him with Lucretius. The famous Thunder passage is very fine, but I cannot recollect every word; and the man who, in recitation, haggles and boggles at a great strain of a great poet deserves death without benefit of clergy. I do remember, however, that he does not descend from his elevation with such ease and grace as would have satisfied Henry Home and Hugh Blair—for he has so little notion of true dignity as to mention rain, as Virgil afterwards did, in immediate connection with thunder.

> "Quo de concussu sequitur *gravis imber* et uber,
> Omnis utei videatur in imbrem vortier æther,
> Atque ita præcipitans ad diluviem revocare."

Buller. What think you of the thunder in Thomson's Seasons?

North. What all the world thinks—that it is our very best British Thunder. He gives the Gathering, the General engagement, and the Retreat. In the Gathering there are touches and strokes that make all mankind shudder—the foreboding—the ominous! And the terror, when it comes, aggrandizes the premonitory symptoms. "Follows the loosened aggravated roar" is a line of power to bring the voice of thunder upon your soul on the most peaceable day. He, too—prevailing poet—feels the grandeur of the Rain. For instant on the words, "convulsing heaven and earth," ensue,

> "Down comes a deluge of sonorous hail,
> Or prone-descending rain."

Thomson had been in the heart of thunder-storms many a time before he left Scotland; and what always impresses me is the want of method—the confusion, I might almost say—in his description. Nothing contradictory in the proceedings of the storm; they all go on obediently to what we know of Nature's laws. But the effects of their agency on man and nature are given—not according to any scheme—but as they happen to come before the Poet's imagination, as they happened in reality. The pine is struck first—then the cattle and the sheep below—and then the castled cliff—and then the

> "Gloomy woods
> Start at the flash, and from their deep recess
> Wide-flaming out, their trembling inmates shake."

No regular ascending—or descending scale here; but wherever the lightning chooses to go, there it goes—the blind agent of indiscriminating destruction.

Buller. Capricious Zigzag.

North. Jemmy was overmuch given to mouthing in the *Seasons;* and in this description—matchless though it be—he sometimes out-mouths the big-mouthed thunder at his own bombast. Perhaps that is inevitable—you must, in confabulating with that Meteor, either imitate him, to keep him and yourself in countenance, or be, if not mute as a mouse, as thin-piped as a fly. In youth I used to go sounding to myself among the mountains the concluding lines of the Retreat.

"Amid Carnarvon's mountains rages loud
The repercussive roar; with mighty crush,
Into the flashing deep, from the rude rocks
Of Penmanmaur heaped hideous to the sky,
Tumble the smitten cliffs, and Snowdon's peak
Dissolving, instant yields his wint'ry load:
Far seen, the heights of heathy Cheviot blaze,
And Thule bellows through her utmost isles.

Are they good—or are they bad? I fear—not good. But I am dubious. The previous picture has been of one locality—a wide one—but within the visible horizon—enlarged somewhat by the imagination, which, as the schoolmen said, inflows into every act of the senses—and powerfully, no doubt, into the senses engaged in witnessing a thunder-storm. Many of the effects so faithfully, and some of them so tenderly painted, interest us by their picturesque particularity.

"Here the soft flocks, with that same harmless look
They wore alive, and ruminating still
In fancy's eye; and there the frowning bull,
And ox half-raised."

We are here in a confined world—close to us and near; and our sympathies with its inhabitants—human or brute—comprehend the very attitudes or postures in which the lightning found and left them; but the final verses waft us away from all that terror and pity—the geographical takes place of the pathetic—a visionary panorama of material objects supersedes the heart-throbbing region of the spiritual—for a mournful song instinct with the humanities, an ambitious bravura displaying the power and pride of the musician, now thinking not at all of us, and following the thunder only as affording him an opportunity for the display of his own art.

Buller. Are they good—or are they bad? I am dubious.

North. Thunder-storms travel fast and far—but here they

seem simultaneous; Thule is more vociferous than the whole of Wales together—yet perhaps the sound itself of the verses is the loudest of all—and we cease to hear the thunder in the din that describes it.

Buller. Severe—but just.

North. Ha! Thou comest in such a questionable shape—

Entrant. That I will speak to thee. How do you do, my dear sir? God bless you, how do you do?

North. Art thou a spirit of health, or goblin damned?

Entrant. A spirit of health.

North. It is—it is the voice of TALBOYS. Don't move an inch. Stand still for ten seconds—on the very same site, that I may have one steady look at you, to make assurance doubly sure—and then let us meet each other half-way in a Cornish hug.

Talboys. Are we going to wrestle already, Mr. North?

North. Stand still ten seconds more. He *is* He—You *are* you—gentlemen—H. G. Talboys—Seward, my crutch—Buller, your arm—

Talboys. Wonderful feat of agility! Feet up to the ceiling—

North. Don't say ceiling—

Talboys. Why not? ceiling—cœlum. Feet up to heaven.

North. An involuntary feat—the fault of Swing—sole fault—but I always forget it when agitated—

Buller. Some time or other, sir, you will fly backwards and fracture your skull.

North. There, we have recovered our equilibrium—now we are in grips, don't fear a fall—I hope you are not displeased with your reception.

Talboys. I wrote last night, sir, to say I was coming—but there being no speedier conveyance—I put the letter in my pocket, and there it is—

North. (*On reading "Dies Boreales.*—No. 1.")

A friend returned! spring bursting forth again!
The song of other years! which, when we roam,
Brings up all sweet and common things of home,
And sinks into the thirsty heart like rain!
Such the strong influence of the thrilling strain
By human love made sad and musical,
Yet full of high philosophy withal,
Poured from thy wizard harp o'er land and main!
A thousand hearts will waken at its call,
And breathe the prayer they breathed in earlier youth,—
May o'er thy brow no envious shadow fall!
Blaze in thine eye the eloquence of truth!
Thy righteous wrath the soul of guilt appal,
As lion's streaming hair or dragon's fiery tooth!

Talboys. I blush to think I have given you the wrong paper.

North. It is the right one. But may I ask what you have on your head?

Talboys. A hat. At least it was so an hour ago.

North. It never will be a hat again.

Talboys. A patent hat—a water proof hat—it was swimming, when I purchased it yesterday, in a pail—warranted against Lammas floods—

North. And in an hour it has come to this! Why, it has no more shape than a coal-heaver's.

Talboys. Oh! then it can be little the worse. For that is its natural artificial shape. It is constructed on that principle—and the patentee prides himself on its affording equal protection to head, shoulders, and back—helmet at once and shield.

North. But you must immediately put on dry clothes—

Talboys. The clothes I have on are as dry as if they had

been taking horse-exercise all morning before a laundry-fire. I am water proof all over—and I had need to be so—for between Inverary and Cladich there was much moisture in the atmosphere.

North. Do—do—go and put on dry clothes. Why the spot you stand on is absolutely swimming—

Talboys. My Sporting-jacket, sir, is a new invention—an invention of my own—to the sight silk—to the feel feathers—and of feathers is the texture—but that is a secret, don't blab it—and to rain I am impervious as a plover.

North. Do—do—go and put on dry clothes.

Talboys. Intended to have been here last night—left Glasgow yesterday morning—and had a most delightful forenoon of it in the Steamer to Tarbert. Loch Lomond fairly outshone herself—never before had I felt the full force of the words —"Fortunate Isles." The Bens were magnificent. At Tarbert—just as I was disembarking—who should be embarking but our friends Outram, M'Culloch, Macnee——

North. And why are they not here?

Talboys. And I was induced—I could not resist them—to take a trip on to Inverarnan. We returned to Tarbert and had a glorious afternoon till two this morning—thought I might lie down for an hour or two—but, after undressing, it occurred to me that it was advisable to redress—and be off instanter—so, wheeling round the head of Loch Long—never beheld the day so lovely—I glided up the gentle slope of Glencroe and sat down on "Rest and be thankful"—to hold a minute's colloquy with a hawk—or some sort of eagle or another, who seemed to think nobody at that hour had a right to be there but himself—covered him to a nicety with my rod—and had it been a gun, he was a dead bird. Down the other—that is, this side of the glen, which, so far from being precipitous, is known to be a descent but by the pretty little cataractettes playing at leap-frog—from your description I knew that must be Loch Fine—and that St. Catherine's. Shall I drop down and signalize the Inverary Steamer? I have not time—so through the woods of Ardkinglass—surely the most beautiful in this world—to Cairndow. Looked at my watch—had forgot to wind her up—set her by the sun—and on nearing the inn door an unaccountable impulse landed me in the parlor to the right. Breakfast on the table for somebody up stairs—whom nobody—so the girl said—could awaken—ate it—and the ten miles were but one to that celebrated Circuit Town. Saluted Dun-nuquech for your sake—and the Castle for the Duke's—and could have lingered all June among those gorgeous groves.

North. Do—do—go and put on dry clothes.

Talboys. Hitherto it had been cool—shady—breezy—the very day for such a saunter—when all at once it was an oven. I had occasion to note that fine line of the Poet's—"Where not a lime-leaf moves," as I passed under a tree of that species, with an umbrage some hundred feet in circumference, and a presentiment of what was coming whispered "Stop here"—but the Fates tempted me on—and if I am rather wet, sir, there is some excuse for it—for there was thunder and lightning, and a great tempest.

North. Not to-day? Here all has been hush.

Talboys. It came at once from all points of the compass—and they all met—all the storms—every mother's son of them—at a central point—where I happened to be. Of course, no house. Look for a house on an emergency, and if once in a million times you see one—the door is locked, and the people gone to Australia.

North. I insist on you putting on dry clothes. Don't try my temper.

Talboys. By-and-by I began to have my suspicions that I had been distracted from the road—and was in the Channel of the Airey. But on looking down I saw the Airey in his own channel—almost as drumly as the mire-burn—vulgarly called road—I was plashing up. Altogether the scene was most animating—and in a moment of intense exhilaration—not to weather-fend, but in defiance—I unfurled my Umbrella.

North. What, a Plover with a Parapluie?

Talboys. I use it, sir, but as a Parasol. Never but on this one occasion had it affronted rain.

North. The same we sat under, that dog-day, at Dunoon?

Talboys. The same. Whew! Up into the sky like the incarnation of a whirlwind! No turning outside in—too strong-ribbed for inversion—before the wind he flew—like a creature of the element—and gracefully accomplished the descent on an eminence about a mile off.

North. Near Orain-imali-chauan-mala-chuilish?

Talboys. I eyed him where he lay—not without anger. It had manifestly been a wilful act—he had torn himself from my grasp—and now he kept looking at me—at safe distance as he thought—like a wild animal suddenly undomesticated—and escaped into his native liberty. If he had sailed before the wind—why might not I? No need to *stalk* him—so I went at him right in front—but such another flounder! Then, sir, I first knew fatigue.

North.

> "So eagerly THE FIEND
> O'er bog, or steep, through strait, rough, dense, or rare,
> With head, hands, wings, or feet pursues his way,
> And swims, or sinks, or wades, or creeps, or flies."

Talboys. Finally I reached him—closed on him—when Eolus, or Eurus, or Notus, or Favonius—for all the heathen wind-gods were abroad—inflated him, and away he flew—rustling like a dragon-fly—and zig-zagging all fiery green in the gloom—sat down—as composedly as you would yourself, sir—on a knoll, in another region—engirdled with young birch-groves—as beautiful a resting-place, I must acknowledge, as, after a lyrical flight, could have been selected for repose by Mr. Wordsworth.

North. I know it—Arash-alaba-chalin-ora-begota-la-chona-hurie. Archy will go for it in the evening—all safe. But do go and put on dry clothes. What now, Billy?

Billy Balmer. Here are Mr. Talboy trunk, sir.

North. Who brought it?

Billy. Nea, Maister—I dan't kna'—I 'spose Carrier. I ken't reet weell—ance at Windermere-watter.

North. Swiss Giantess—Billy.

Billy. Ay—ay—sir.

North. You will find the Swiss Giantess as complete a dormitory as man can desire, Talboys. I reserve it for myself in event of rheumatism. Though lined with velvet, it is always cool—ventilated on a new principle—of which I took merely a hint from the Punka. My cot hangs in what used to be the Exhibition-room—and her Retreat is now a commodious Dressing-room. Billy, show Mr. Talboys to the Swiss Giantess.

Billy. Ay—ay, sir. This way, Mr. Talboy—this way, sir.

Talboys. What is your dinner-hour, Mr. North?

North. Sharp seven—seven sharp.

Talboys. And now 'tis but half-past two. Four hours for work. The Cladich—or whatever you call him—is rumbling disorderly in the wood; and I noted, as I crossed the bridge, that he was proud as a piper of being in Spate—but he looks more rational down in yonder meadows—and——HEAVEN HAVE MERCY ON ME! THERE'S LOCH AWE!!

North. I thought it queer that you never looked at it.

Talboys. Looked at it? How could I look at it? I don't

believe it was there. If it was—from the hill-top I had eyes but for the Camp—the Tents and the Trees—and "Thee the spirit of them all!" Let me have another eye-full—another soul-full of the Loch. But 'twill never do to be losing time in this way. Where's my creel—where's my creel?

North. On your shoulders—

Talboys. And my Book? Lost—lost—lost! Not in any one of all my pockets. I shall go mad.

North. Not far to go. Why your Book's in your hand.

Talboys. At eight?

North. Seven. Archy, follow him. In that state of excitement he will be walking with his spectacles on over some precipice. Keep your eye on him, Archy.

Archy. I can pretend to be carrying the landing-net, sir.

North. There's a specimen of a Scottish Lawyer, gentlemen. What do you think of him?

Buller. That he is without exception the most agreeable fellow, at first sight, I ever met in my life.

North. And so you would continue to think him, were you to see him twice a-week for twenty years. But he is far more than that—though, as the world goes, that is much: his mind is steel to the back-bone—his heart is sound as his lungs—his talents great—in literature, had he liked it, he might have excelled; but he has wisely chosen a better Profession—and his character now stands high as a Lawyer and a Judge. Yonder he goes! As fresh as a kitten after a score and three quarter miles at the least.

Buller. Seward—let's after him. Billy—the minnows.

Billy. Here's the Can, sirs.

Scene closes.

SCENE II.—*Interior of Deeside.*

TIME—*Seven* P. M.

NORTH—TALBOYS—BULLER—SEWARD.

North. Seward, face Buller. Talboys, face North. Fall to, gentlemen; to-day we dispense with regular service. Each man has his own distinct dinner before him, or in the immediate vicinity—soup, fish, flesh, fowl—and with all necessary accompaniments and sequences. How do you like the arrangement of the table, Talboys?

Talboys. The principle shows a profound knowledge of human nature, sir. In theory, self-love and social are the same—but in practice, self-love looks to your own plate—social to your neighbors'. By this felicitous multiplication of dinners—this One in Four—this Four in One—the harmony of the moral system is preserved—and all works together for the general good. Looked at artistically, we have here what the Germans and others say is essential to the beautiful and the sublime—Unity.

North. I believe the Four Dinners—if weighed separately—would be found not to differ by a pound. This man's fish might prove in the scale a few ounces heavier than that man's—but in such case, his fowl would be found just so many ounces lighter. And so on. The Puddings are cast in the same mould—and the things equal to the same thing, are equal to one another.

Talboys. The weight of each repast?

North. Calculated at twenty-five pounds.

Talboys. Grand total, one hundred. The golden mean.

North. From these general views, to descend to particulars. Soup (turtle) two pounds—Hotch, ditto—Fish (Trout) two pounds—Flesh (Jigot—black face five year old) six pounds—Fowl (Howtowdie boiled) five pounds—Duck (wild) three pounds—Tart (gooseberry) one pound—Pud (Variorum Edition) two pounds.

Buller. That is but twenty-three, sir! I have taken down the gentleman's words.

North. Polite—and grateful. But you have omitted sauces and creams, breads and cheeses. Did you ever know me incorrect in my figures, in any affirmation or denial, private or public?

Buller. Never. Beg pardon.

North. Now that the soups and fishes seem disposed of, I boldly ask you, one and all, gentlemen, if you ever beheld Four more tempting Jigots?

Talboys. I am still at my Fish. No fish so sweet as of one's own catching—so I have the advantage of you all. This one here—the one I am eating at this blessed moment—I killed in what the man with the Landing-net called the Birk Pool. I know him by his peculiar physiognomy—an odd cast in his eye—which has not left him on the gridiron. That Trout of my killing on your plate, Mr. Seward, made the fatal plunge at the tail of the stream so overhung with Alders that you can take it successfully only by the tail—and I know him by his color, almost as silvery as a whitling. Yours, Mr. Buller, was the third I killed—just where the river—for a river he is to-day, whatever he may be to-morrow—goes whirling into the Loch—and I can swear to him from his leopard spots. Illustrious sir, of him whom you have now disposed of—the finest of the Four—I remember saying inwardly, as with difficulty I encreeled him—for his shoulders were like a hog's—this for the King.

North. Your perfect Pounder, Talboys, is the beau-ideal of a Scottish Trout. How he cuts up! If much heavier—you are frustrated in your attempts to eat him thoroughly—have to search—probably in vain—for what in a perfect Pounder lies patent to the day—he is to back-bone comeatable—from gill to fork. Seward, you are an artist. Good creel?

Seward. I gave Mr. Talboys the first of the water, and followed him—a mere caprice—with the Archimedean Minnow. I had a run—but just as the monster opened his jaws to absorb—he suddenly eschewed the scentless phenomenon, and with a sullen plunge, sunk into the deep.

Buller. I tried the natural minnow after Seward—but I wished Archimedes at Syracuse—for the Screw had spread a panic—and in a panic the scaly people lose all power of discrimination, and fear to touch a minnow, lest it turn up a bit of tin or some other precious metal.

North. I have often been lost in conjecturing how you always manage to fill your creel, Talboys; for the truth is—and it must be spoken—you are no angler.

Talboys. I can afford to smile! I was no angler, sir, ten years ago—now I am. But how did I become one? By attending you, sir—for seven seasons—along the Tweed and the Yarrow, the Clyde and the Daer, the Tay and the Tummel, the Don and the Dee—and treasuring up lessons from the Great Master of the Art.

North. You surprise me! Why, you never put a single question to me about the art—always declined taking rod in hand—seemed reading some book or other, held close to your eyes—or lying on banks a-dose or poetizing—or facetious with the Old Man—or with the Old Man serious—and sometimes more than serious, as, sauntering along our winding way, we conversed of man, of nature, and of human life.

Talboys. I never lost a single word you said, sir, during

those days, breathing in every sense "vernal delight and joy," yet all the while I was taking lessons in the art. The flexure of your shoulder—the sweep of your arm—the twist of your wrist—your Delivery, and your Recovery—that union of grace and power—the utmost delicacy, with the most perfect precision—All these qualities of a heaven-born Angler, by which you might be known from all other men on the banks of the Whittadder on a Fast-day——

North. I never angled on a Fast-day.

Talboys. A *lapsus linguæ*—From a hundred anglers on the Daer, on the Queen's Birth-day——

North. My dear Friend, you ex——

Talboys. All those qualities of a heaven-born Angler I learned first to admire—then to understand—and then to imitate. For three years I practiced on the carpet—for three I essayed on a pond—for three I strove by the running waters—and still the Image of Christopher North was before me—till, emboldened by conscious acquisition and constant success, I came forth and took my place among the anglers of my country.

Buller. To-day I saw you fast in a tree.

Talboys. You mean my Fly.

Buller. First your Fly, and then, I think, yourself.

Talboys. I have seen *Il Maestro* himself in Timber, and in brushwood too. From him I learned to disentangle knots, intricate and perplexed far beyond the Gordian—"with frizzled hair implicit"—round twig, branch, or bole. Not more than half-a-dozen times of the forty that I may have been fast aloft—I speak mainly of my noviciate—have I had to effect liberation by sacrifice.

Seward. Pardon me, Mr. Talboys, for hinting that you smacked off your tail-fly to-day—I knew it by the sound.

Talboys. The sound! No trusting to an uncertain sound, Mr. Seward. Oh! I did so once—but intentionally—the hook had lost the barb—not a fish would it hold—so I whipped it off, and on with a Professor.

Buller. You lost one good fish in rather an awkward manner, Mr. Talboys.

Talboys. I did—that metal minnow of yours came with a splash within an inch of his nose—and no wonder he broke me—nay, I believe it was the minnow that broke me—and yet you can speak of *my* losing a good fish in rather an awkward manner!

North. It is melancholy to think that I have taught Young Scotland to excel myself in all the Arts that adorn and dignify life. Till I rose, Scotland was a barbarous country—

Talboys. Do say, my dear sir, semi-civilized.

North. Now it heads the Nations—and I may set.

Talboys. And why should that be a melancholy thought, sir?

North. Oh, Talboys—National Ingratitude! They are fast forgetting the man who made them what they are—in a few fleeting centuries the name of Christopher North will be in oblivion! Would you believe it possible, gentlemen, that even now, there are Scotsmen who never heard of the Fly that bears the name of me, its inventor—Killing Kit!

Buller. In Cornwall it is a household word.

Seward. And in all the Devons.

Buller. Men in Scotland who never heard the name of North!

North. Christopher North—who is he? Who do you mean by the Man of the Crutch?—The Knight of the Knout? Better never to have been born than thus to be virtually dead.

Seward. Sir, be comforted—you are under a delusion—Britain is ringing with your name.

North. Not that I care for noisy fame—but I do dearly love thee still.

Talboys. And you have it, sir—enjoy it and be thankful.

North. But it may be too still.

Talboys. My dear sir, what would you have?

North. I taught you, Talboys, to play Chess—and now you trumpet Staunton.

Talboys. Chess—where's the board? Let us have a game.

North. Drafts—and you quote Anderson and the Shepherd Laddie.

Talboys. Mr. North, why so querulous?

North. Where was the Art of Criticism? Where Prose? Young Scotland owes all her Composition to me—buries me in the earth—and then claims inspiration from heaven. "How sharper than a Serpent's tooth it is to have a thankless Child!" Peter—Peterkin—Pym—Stretch—where are your lazinesses—clear decks.

> "Away with Melancholy—
> Nor doleful changes ring
> On Life and human Folly,
> But merrily, merrily sing—fal la!"

Buller. What a sweet pipe! A single snatch of an old song from you, sir—

North. Why are you glowering at me, Talboys?

Talboys. It has come into my head, I know not how, to ask you a question.

North. Let it be an easy one—for I am languid..

Talboys. Pray, sir, what is the precise signification of the word "Classical?"

North. My dear Talboys, you seem to think that I have the power of answering, off-hand, any and every question a first-rate fellow chooses to ask me. Classical—classical! Why, I should say, in the first place—One and one other Mighty People—Those, the Kings of Thought—These, the Kings of the Earth.

Talboys. The Greeks—and Romans.

North. In the second place—

Talboys. Attend—do attend, gentlemen. And I hope I am not too much presuming on our not ancient friendship—for I feel that a few hours on Lochawe-side give the privilege of years—in suggesting that you will have the goodness to use the metal nut-crackers; they are more euphonious than ivory with walnuts.

North. In the second place—let me consider—Mr. Talboys—I should say—in the second place—yes, I have it—a Character of Art expressing itself by words: a mode—a mode of Poetry and Eloquence—FITNESS AND BEAUTY.

Talboys. Thank you, sir. Fitness and Beauty. Anything more?

North. Much more. We think of the Greeks and Romans, sir, as those in whom the Human Mind reached Superhuman Power.

Talboys. Superhuman?

North. We think so—comparing ourselves with them, we cannot help it. In the Hellenic Wit, we suppose Genius and Taste met at their height—the Inspiration Omnipotent—the Instinct unerring! The creations of Greek Poetry!—Ποιησις—a Making! There the soul seems to be free from its chains—happily self-lawed. "The Earth we pace" is there peopled with divine forms. Sculpture was the human Form glorified—deified. And as in marble, so in Song. Something common—terrestrial—adheres to *our* being, and weighs *us* down. They—the Hellenes—appear to us to have *really* walked—as we walk in our visions of exaltation—as if the Graces and the Muses held sway over daily and hourly existence, and not alone over work of Art and solemn occasion. No moral stain or imperfection can hinder them from appearing to us as the Light of human kind. Singular, that in Greece we reconcile ourselves to Heathenism.

Talboys. It may be that we are all Heathens at heart.

North. The enthusiast adores Greece—not knowing that Greece monarchizes over him, only because it is a miraculous mirror that resplendently and more beautifully reflects—himself—

> "Divisque videbit
> Permixtos Heroas, et IPSE videbitur illis."

Seward. Very fine.

North. O life of old, and long, long ago! In the meek, solemn, soul-stilling hush of Academic Bowers!

Seward. The Isis!

North. My youth returns. Come, spirits of the world that has been! Throw open the valvules of these your shrines, in which you stand around me, niched side by side, in visible presence, in this cathedral-like library! I read Historian, Poet, Orator, Voyager—a life that slid silently away in shades, or that bounded like a bark over the billows. I lift up the curtain of all ages—I stand under all skies—on the Capitol—on the Acropolis. Like that magician whose spirit, with a magical word, could leave his own bosom to inhabit another, I take upon myself every mode of existence. I read Thucydides, and I would be a Historian—Demosthenes, and I would be an orator—Homer, and I dread to believe myself called to be, in some shape or other, a servant of the Muse. Heroes and Hermits of Thought—Seers of the Invisible—Prophets of the Ineffable—Hierophants of profitable mysteries—Oracles of the Nations—Luminaries of that spiritual Heaven! I bid ye hail!

Buller. The fit is on him—he has not the slightest idea that he is in Deeside.

North. Ay—from the beginning a part of the race have separated themselves from the dusty, and the dust-devoured, turmoil of Action to Contemplation. Have thought—known—worshipped! And such knowledge Books keep. Books now crumbling like Towers and Pyramids—now outlasting them! Books that from age to age, and all the sections of mankind helping, build up the pile of Knowledge—a trophied Citadel. He who can read books as they should be read, peruses the operation of the Creator in his conscious, and in his unconscious Works, which yet we call upon to join, as if conscious, in our worship. Yet why—oh! why all this pains to attain that, through the labor of ages, which in the dewy, sunny prime of morn, one thrill of transport gives to me and to the Lark alike, summoning, lifting both heavenwards? Ah! perchance because the dewy, sunny prime does not last through the day! Because light poured into the eyes, and sweet breath inhaled, are not the whole of man's life here below—and because there is an Hereafter!

Seward. I know where he is, Buller. He called it well a Cathedral-like Library.

North. The breath of departed years floats here for my respiration. The pure air of heaven flows round about, but enters not. The sunbeams glide in, bedimmed as if in some haunt half-separated from Life, yet on our side of Death. Recess, hardly accessible—profound—of which I, the sole inmate, held under an uncomprehended restraint, breathe, move, and follow my own way and wise, apart from human mortals! Ye! tall, thick Volumes, that are each a treasure-house of austere or blazing thoughts, which of you shall I touch with sensitive fingers, of which violate the calmy austere repose? I dread what I desire. You may disturb—you may destroy me! Knowledge *pulsates* in me, as I receive it, communing with myself on my unquiet or tearful pillow—or as it visits me, brought on the streaming moonlight, or from the fields afire with noon-splendor, or looking at me from human eyes, and stirring round and around me in the tumult of men—Your knowledge comes in a holy stillness and chillness, as if spelt off tombstones.

Seward. Magdalen College Library, I do believe. Mr. North—Mr. North—awake—awake—here we are all in Dee-side.

North. Ay—ay—you say well, Seward. "Look at the studies of the Great Scholar, and see from how many quarters of the mind impulses may mingle to compose the motives that bear him on with indefatigable strength in his laborious career."

Seward. These were not my very words, sir—

North. Ay, Seward, you say well. From how many indeed! First among the prime, that peculiar aptitude and faculty, which may be called—a Taste and Genius for—Words.

Buller. I rather failed there in the Schools.

North. Yet you were in the First Class. There is implied in it, Seward, a readiness of logical discrimination in the Understanding, which apprehends the propriety of Words.

Buller. I got up my Logic passably and a little more.

North. For, Seward, the Thoughts, the Notions themselves—must be distinctly dissevered in the mind, which shall exactly apply to each Thought—Notion—its appropriate signs, its own Word.

Buller. You might as well have said "Buller"—for I beat Seward in my Logic.

North. But even to this task, Seward, of rightly distinguishing the meaning of Words, more than a mere precision of thinking—more than a clearness and strictness of the intellectual action is requisite.

Buller. And in Classics we were equal.

North. You will be convinced of this, Buller, if you recollect what Words express. The mind itself. For all its affections and sensibilities, Talboys, furnish a whole host of meanings, which must have names in Language. For mankind do not rest from enriching and refining their languages, until they have made them capable of giving the representation of their whole Spirit.

Talboys. The pupil of language, therefore, sir—pardon my presumption—before he can recognize the appropriation of the Sign, must recognize the thing signified?

North. And if the thing signified, Talboys, by the Word, be some profound, solemn, and moral affection—or if it be some wild, fanciful impression—or if it be some delicate shade or tinge of a tender sensibility—can anything be more evident than that the Scholar must have experienced in himself the solemn, or the wild, or the tenderly delicate feeling, before he is in the condition of affixing the right and true sense to the Word that expresses it?

Talboys. I should think so, sir.

Seward. The Words of Man paint the spirit of Man. The Words of a People depicture the Spirit of a people.

North. Well said, Seward. And, therefore, the Understanding that is to possess the Words of a language, in the Spirit in which they were or are spoken and written, must, by self-experience and sympathy, be able to converse, and have conversed, with the Spirit of the People, now and of old.

Buller. And yet what coarse fellows hold up their dunderheads as Scholars, forsooth, in these our days!

North. Hence it is an impossibility that a low and hard moral nature should furnish a high and fine Scholar. The intellectual endowments must be supported and made available by the concurrence of the sensitive nature—of the moral and the imaginative sensibilities.

Buller. What moral and imaginative sensibilities have they—the blear-eyed—the purblind—the pompous and the pedantic! But we have some true scholars—for example——

North. No names, Buller. Yes, Seward, the knowledge of Words is the Gate of Scholarship. Therefore I lay down upon the threshold of the Scholar's Studies this first condition of his high and worthy success, that he will not pluck the loftiest palm by means of acute, quick, clear, penetrating, sagacious, intellectual faculties alone—let him not hope it: that he requires to the highest renown also a capacious, profound, and tender soul.

Seward. Ay, sir, and I say so in all humility, this at the gateway, and upon the threshold. How much more when he *reads!*

North. Ay, Seward, you laid the emphasis well there—*reads.*

Seward. When the written Volumes of Mind from different and distant ages of the world, from its different and distant climates, are successively unrolled before his insatiable sight and his insatiable soul!

Buller. Take all things in moderation.

North. No—not the sacred hunger and thirst of the soul.

Buller. Greed—give—give.

North. From what unknown recesses, from what unlocked fountains in the depth of his own being, shall he bring into the light of day the thoughts by means of which he shall understand Homer, Pindar, Æschylus, Demosthenes, Plato, Aristotle—DISCOURSING! Shall understand them, as the younger did the elder—the cotemporaries did the cotemporaries—as each sublime spirit understood—himself?

Buller. Did each sublime spirit always understand himself?

Talboys. Urge that, Mr. Buller.

North. So—and so only—to read, is to be a Scholar.

Buller. Then I am none.

North. I did not say you were.

Buller. Thank you. What do you think of that, Mr. Talboys? Address Seward, sir.

North. I address you all three. Is the student smitten with the sacred love of Song? Is he sensible to the profound allurement of philosophic truth? Does he yearn to acquaint himself with the fates and fortunes of his kind? All these several desires are so many several inducements of learned study.

Buller. I understand that.

Talboys. Ditto.

North. And another inducement to such study is—an ear sensible to the Beauty of the Music of Words—and the metaphysical faculty of unraveling the causal process which the human mind followed in imparting to a Word, originally the sign of one Thought only, the power to signify a cognate second Thought, which shall displace the first possessor and exponent, usurp the throne, and rule for ever over an extended empire in the minds, or the hearts, or the souls of men.

Buller. Let him have his swing, Mr. Talboys.

Talboys. He has it in that chair.

North. A Taste and a Genius for Words! An ear for the beautiful music of Words! A happy justness in the perception of their strict proprieties! A fine skill in apprehending the secret relations of Thought with Thought—relations along which the mind moves with creative power, to find out for its own use, and for the use of all minds to come, some hitherto uncreated expression of an idea—an image—a sentiment—a passion? These dispositions, and these faculties of the Scholar in another Mind falling in with other faculties of genius, produce a student of a different name—THE POET.

Buller. Oh! my dear, dear sir, of Poetry we surely had enough—I don't say more than enough—a few days ago, sir.

North. Who is the Poet?

Buller. I beseech you let the Poet alone for this evening.

North. Well—I will. I remember the time, Seward, when there was a great clamor for a Standard of Taste. A definite measure of the indefinite!

Talboys. Which is impossible.

North. And there is a great clamor for a Standard of Morals. A definite measure of the indefinite!

Talboys. Which is impossible.

North. Why, gentlemen, the Faculty of Beauty *lives;* and in finite beings, which we are, Life changes incessantly. The Faculty of Moral Perception *lives*—and thereby it too changes for better and for worse. This is the Divine Law—at once encouraging and fearful—that Obedience brightens the moral eyesight—Sin darkens. Let all men know this, and keep it in mind always—that a single narrowest, simplest Duty, steadily practiced day after day, does more to support, and may do more to enlighten the soul of the Doer, than a course of Moral Philosophy taught by a tongue which a soul compounded of Bacon, Spenser, Shakspeare, Homer, Demosthenes, and Burke—to say nothing of Socrates, and Plato, and Aristotle, should inspire.

Buller. You put it strongly, sir.

Talboys. Undeniable doctrine.

North. Gentlemen, you will often find this question—"Is there a Standard of Taste?" inextricably confused with the question "Is there a true and a false Taste?" He who denies the one seems to deny the other. In like manner, "Is there a Right and Wrong?" And "is there accessible to us an infallible measure of Right and Wrong" are two questions entirely distinct, but often confused—for Logic fled the earth with Astræa.

Talboys. She did.

North. Talboys, you understand well enough the sense and culture of the Beautiful?

Talboys. Something of it, perhaps I do.

North. To feel—to love—to be swallowed up in the spirit and works of the Beautiful—in verse and in the visible Universe! That is a life—an enthusiasm—a worship. You find those who would if they could, and who pretend they can, attain the same end at less cost. They have taken lessons, and they will have their formalities go valid against their intuitions of the dedicated soul.

Talboys. But the lessons perish—the dedicated soul is a Power in all emergencies and extremities.

North. There are Pharisees of Beauty—and Pharisees of Morality.

Seward. At this day spiritual Christians lament that nine-tenths of Christians Judaize.

North. Nor without good reason. The Gospel is the Standard of Christian Morality. That is unquestionable. It is an authority without appeal, and under which undoubtedly all matters, uncertain before, will fall. But pray mark this—it is not a *positive standard,* in the ordinary meaning of that word—it is not one of which our common human understanding has only to require and to obtain the indications—which it has only to apply and observe.

Seward. I see your meaning, sir. The Gospel refers all moral intelligence to the Light of Love within our hearts. Therefore, the very reading of the canons, of every prescriptive line in it, must be by this light.

North. That is my meaning—but not my whole meaning, dear Seward. For take it, as it unequivocally declares itself to be, a Revelation—not simply of instruction, committed now and for ever to men in written human words, and so left—but accompanied with a perpetual agency to enable Will and Understanding to receive it; and then it will follow, I believe, that it is at every moment intelligible and applicable in its full sense, only by a direct and present inspiration—is it too much to say—anew revealing itself? "They shall be taught of God."

Seward. So far, then, from the Christian Morality being one of which the Standard is applicable by every Understanding, with like result in given cases, it is one that is different to every Christian in proportion to his obedience?

North. Even so. I suppose that none have ever reached the full understanding of it. It is an ever-growing illumination—a light more and more unto the perfect day—which day I suppose cannot be of the same life, in which we see as through a glass darkly.

Talboys. May I offer an illustration? The land shall descend to the eldest son—you shall love your neighbor as yourself. In the two codes these are foundation-stones. But see how they differ? There is the land—here is the eldest son—the right is clear and fast—and the case done with. But—do to thy neighbor? Do what? and to whom?

North. All human actions, all human affections, all human thoughts are then contained in the one Law—as the *subject* of which it defines the disposal. All mankind, but distributed into communities, and individuals all differently related to me, are contained in it, as the *parties* in respect of whom it defines the disposal!

Seward. And what is the Form? Do as thou wouldst it be done to thee!

North. Ay—my dear friend—the form resolves into a feeling. Love thy neighbor. That is all. Is a measure given? As thyself.

Seward. And is there no limitation?

North. By the whole apposition, thy love to thyself and thy neighbor are both to be put together in subordination to, and limitation and regulation by, thy Love to God. Love Him utterly—infinitely—with all thy mind, all thy heart, all thy strength. This is the entire book or canon—THE STANDARD. How wholly indefinite and formless to the Understanding! How full of light and form to the believing and loving Heart!

Seward. The Moon is up—how calm the night after all that tempest—and how steady the Stars! Images of enduring peace in the heart of nature—and of man. They, too, are a Revelation.

North. They, too, are the legible Book of God. Try to conceive how different the World must be to its rational inhabitant—with or without a Maker! Think of it as a soulless—will-less World. In one sense, it abounds as much with good to enjoy. But there is no good-giver. The banquet spread, but the Lord of the Mansion away. The feast—and neither grace nor welcome. The heaped enjoyment, without the gratitude.

Seward. Yet there have been Philosophers who so misbelieved.

North. Alas! there have been—and alas! there are. And what low souls must be theirs! The tone and temper of our feelings are determined by the objects with which we habitually converse. If we see beautiful scenes, they impart serenity—if sublime scenes, they elevate us. Will no serenity, no elevation come from contemplating Him, of whose Thought the Beautiful and the Sublime are but shadows!

Seward. No sincere or elevating influence be lost out of a World out of which He is lost?

North. *Now* we look upon Planets and Suns, and see Intelligence ruling them—on Seasons that succeed each other, and we apprehend Design—on plant and animal fitted to its place in the world, and furnished with its due means of existence, and repeated for ever in its kind—and we admire Wisdom. Oh! Atheist or Skeptic!—what a difference to Us if the marvellous Laws are here without a Lawgiver—if Design be here without a Designer—all the Order that wisdom could mean and effect, and not the Wisdom—if Chance, or Necessity, or Fate reigns here, and not Mind—if this Universe is matter of Astonishment merely, and not of adoration!

Seward. We are made better, nobler, sir, by the society of the good and the noble. Perhaps of ourselves unable to think high thoughts, and without the bold warmth that dares generously, we catch by degrees something of the mounting spirit, and of the ardor proper to the stronger souls with whom we live familiarly, and become sharers and imitators of virtues to which we could not have given birth. The devoted courage of a leader turns his followers into heroes—the patient death of one martyr inflames in a thousand slumbering bosoms a zeal answering to his own. And shall Perfect Goodness contemplated move no goodness in us? Shall His Holiness and Purity raise in us no desire to be holy and pure?—His infinite Love towards His creatures kindle no spark of love in us towards our fellow-creatures?

North. God bless you, my dear Seward—but you speak well. Our fellow-creatures! The name, the binding title, dissolves in air, if He is not our common Creator. Take away that bond of relationship among men, and according to circumstances they confront one another as friends or foes—but Brothers no longer—if not children of one Celestial Father.

Talboys. And if they no longer have immortal souls!

North. Oh! my friends!—if this winged and swift life be all our life, what a mournful taste have we had of possible happiness? We have, as it were, from some dark and cold edge of a bright world, just looked in and been plucked away again? Have we come to experience pleasure by fits and glimpses; but intertwined with pain, burdensome labor, with weariness, and with indifference? Have we come to try the solace and joy of a warm, fearless, and confiding affection, to be then chilled or blighted by bitterness, by separation, by change of heart, or by the dread sunderer of loves—Death? Have we found the gladness and the strength of knowledge, when some rays of truth have flashed in upon our souls, in the midst of error and uncertainty, or amidst continuous, necessitated, uninstructive avocations of the Understanding—and is that all? Have we felt in fortunate hour the charm of the Beautiful, that invests, as with a mantle, this visible Creation, or have we found ourselves lifted above the earth by sudden apprehension of sublimity? Have we had the consciousness of such feelings, which have seemed to us as if they might themselves make up a life—almost an angel's life—and were they "instant come and instant gone?" Have we known the consolation of DOING RIGHT, in the midst of much that we have done wrong? and was that also a coruscation of a transient sunshine? Have we lifted up our thoughts to see Him who is Love, and Light, and Truth, and Bliss, to be in the next instant plunged into the darkness of annihilation? Have all these things been but flowers that we have pulled by the side of a hard and tedious way, and that, after gladdening us for a brief season with hue and odor, wither in our hands, and are like ourselves—nothing?

Buller. I love you, sir, better and better every day.

North. We step the earth—we look abroad over it, and it seems immense—so does the sea. What ages had men lived—and knew but a small portion. They circumnavigate it now with a speed under which its vast bulk shrinks. But let the astronomer lift up his glass and he learns to believe in a total mass of matter, compared with which this great globe itself becomes an imponderable grain of dust. And so to each of us walking along the road of life, a year, a day, or an hour shall seem long. As we grow older, the time shortens; but when we lift up our eyes to look beyond this earth, our seventy years, and the few thousands of years which have rolled over

10

the human race, vanish into a point; for then we are measuring Time against Eternity.

Talboys. And if we can find ground for believing that this quickly-measured span of Life is but the beginning—the dim daybreak of a Life immeasurable, never attaining to its night—what *weight* shall we any longer allow to the cares, fears, toils, troubles, afflictions—which here have sometimes bowed down our strength to the ground—a burden more than we could bear.

North. They then all acquire a new character. That they are then felt as transitory must do something towards lightening their load. But more is disclosed in them; for they then appear as having an unsuspected worth and use. If this life be but the beginning of another, then it may be believed that the accidents and passages thereof have some bearing upon the conditions of that other, and we learn to look on this as a state of Probation. Let us out, and look at the sky.

DIES BOREALES.

No. III.

Scene—*Gutta Percha.*

Time—*Early Evening.*

North—Buller—Seward—Talboys.

North. Trim—trim—trim—

Talboys. Gentlemen, are you all seated?

North. Why into such strange vagaries fall as you would dance, Longfellow? Seize his skirts, Seward. Buller, cling to his knees. Billy, the boat hook—he will be—he is—overboard.

Talboys. Not at all. Gutta Percha is somewhat crank—and I am steadying her, sir.

North. What is that round your waist?

Talboys. My Air-girdle.

North. I insist upon you dropping it, Longman. It makes you reckless. I did not think you were such a selfish character.

Talboys. Alas! in this world, how are our noblest intentions misunderstood! I put it on, sir, that, in case of a capsize, I might more buoyantly bear you ashore.

North. Forgive me, my friend. But—be seated. Our craft is but indifferently well adapted to the gallopade. Be seated, I beseech you! Or if you will stand, do plant both feet —do not—do not alternate so—and above all do not, I implore you—show off on one, as if you were composing and reciting verses—There, down you are—and if there be not a hole in her bottom, Gutta Percha is safe against all the hidden rocks in Loch Awe.

Talboys. Let me take the stroke oar.

North. For sake of the ancient houses of the Sewards and the Bullers, sit where you are. We are already in four fathom water.

Talboys. The Lines.

Billy. Nea, nea—Mister Talboy. Nane shall steer Perch when He's afloat, but t'auld commodore.

North. Shove off, lads.

Talboys. Are we on earth, or in heaven?

Billy. On t'water.

North. Billy—mum.

Talboys. The Heavens are high—and they are deep. Fear would rise up from that Profound, if fear there could be in the perfectly Beautiful!

Seward. Perhaps there is—though it wants a name.

North. We know there is no danger—and therefore we should feel no fear. But we cannot wholly disencumber ourselves of the emotions that ordinarily great depth inspires—and verily I hold with Seward, while thus we hang over the sky-abyss below with suspended oars.

Seward. The Ideal rests on the Real—Imagination on Memory—and the Visionary, at its utmost, still retains relations with Truth.

Buller. Pray you to look at our Encampment. Nothing visionary there—

Talboys. Which Encampment?

Buller. On the hill-side—up yonder—at Cladich.

Talboys. You should have said so at first. I thought you meant that other down—

Buller. When I speak to you, I mean the *bona fide* flesh and blood Talboys, sitting by the side of the *bona fide* flesh and blood Christopher North, in Gutta Percha, and not that somewhat absurd, and, I trust, ideal personage, standing on his head in the water, or it may be the air, some fathoms below her keel —like a pearl-diver.

Talboys. Put up your hands—so—my dear Mr. North, and frame the picture.

North. And Maculloch not here! Why the hills behind Cladich, that people call tame, make a background that no art might meliorate. Cultivation climbs the green slopes, and overlays the green hill-ridges, while higher up all is rough, brown, heathery, rocky—and behind that undulating line, for the first time in my life, I see the peaks of mountains. From afar they are looking at the Tents. And far off as they are, the power of that Sycamore Grove connects them with our Encampment.

Talboys. Are you sure, sir, they are not clouds?

North. If clouds, so much the better. If mountains, they deserve to be clouds; and if clouds, they deserve to be mountains.

Seward. The long broad shadow of the Grove tames the white of the Tents—tones it—reduces it into harmony with the surrounding color—into keeping with the brown huts of the villagers, clustering on bank and brae on both sides of the hollow river.

North. The cozey Inn itself from its position is picturesque.

Talboys. The Swiss Giantess looks imposing—

Buller. So does the Van. But Deeside is the Pandemonium—

Talboys. Well translated by Paterson in his Notes on Milton, "All-Devil's-Hall."

North. Hush. And how lovely the foreground! Sloping upland—with single trees standing one by one, at distances wide enough to allow to each its own little grassy domain—with its circle of bracken or broom—or its own golden gorse grove—divided by the sylvan course of the hidden river itself, visible only when it glimpses into the Lock—Here, friends, we seem to see the united occupations of pastoral, agricultural—and—

Buller. Pardon me, sir, I have a proposition to make.

North. You might have waited a moment till—

Buller. Not a moment. We all Four see the background—and the middle-ground and the foreground—and all the ground round and about—and all the islands and their shadows—and all the mountains and theirs—and, towering high above all, that Cruachan of yours, who I firmly believe, is behind us—though 'twould twist my neck now to get a vizzy of him. No use then in describing all that lies within the visible horizon—there it is—let us enjoy it and be thankful—and let us talk this evening of whatever may happen to come into our respective heads—and I beg leave to add, sir, with all reverence, let's have fair play—let no single man—young or old—take more than his own lawful share—

North. Sir?

Buller. And let the subject of angling be tabooed—and all its endless botheration about baskets and rods, and reels and tackle—salmon, sea-trout, yellow-fin, perch, pike, and the Ferox—and no drivel about Deer and Eagles—

North. Sir? What's the meaning of all this—Seward, say—tell Talboys.

Buller. And let each man on opening his mouth be *timed* —and let it be two-minute time—and let me be time-keeper—but, in consideration of your years and habits, and presidency, let time to you, sir, be extended to two minutes and thirty seconds—and let us all talk time about—and let no man seek to nullify the law by talking at railway rate—and let no man who waives his right of turn, however often, think to make up for the loss by claiming quarter of an hour afterwards—and that, too, perhaps at the smartest of the soirée—and let there be no contradiction, either, round, flat, or angular—and let no man speak about what he understands—that is, has long studied and made himself master of—for that would be giving him an unfair —I had almost said—would be taking a mean advantage—and let no man—

North. Why, the mutiny at the Nore was nothing to this.

Buller. Lord High Admiral though you be, sir, you must obey the laws of the service—

North. I see how it is.

Buller. How is it?

North. But it will soon wear off—that's the saving virtue of Champagne.

Buller. Champagne, indeed! Small Beer, smaller than the smallest size. You have not the heart, sir, to give Champagne.

North. We had better put about, gentlemen, and go ashore.

Buller. My ever honored, long revered sir! I have got intoxicated on our Teetotal debauchery. The fumes of the water have gone to my head—and I need but a few drops of brandy to set me all right. Billy—the flask. There—I am as sober as a Judge.

North. Ay, 'tis thus, Buller, you wise wag, that you would let the "old man garrulous" into the secret of his own tendencies—too often unconscious he of the powers that have set so many asleep. I accept the law—but let it—do let it be three-minute time.

Buller. Five—ten—twenty—"with thee conversing, I forget all time."

North. Strike medium—Ten.

Buller. My dear sir, for a moment let me have that Spy-glass.

North. I must lay it down—for a Bevy of Fair Women are on the Mount—and are brought so near that I hear them laughing—especially the Prima Donna, whose Glass is in dangerous proximity with my nose.

Buller. Fling her a kiss, sir.

North. There—and how prettily she returns it!

Buller. Happy old man! Go where you will—

Talboys. Ulysses and the Syrens. Had he my air-girdle, he would swim ashore.

North. "Oh, mihi præteritos referat si Jupiter annos!"

Talboys. The words are regretful—but there is no regret in the voice that syllables them—it is clear as a bell, and as gladsome.

North. Talking of kissing, I hear one of the most melodious songs that ever flowed from lady's lip—

> "The current that with gentle motion glides,
> Thou knowest, being stopped, impatiently doth rage;
> But when his fair course is not hindered,
> He makes sweet music with the enameled stones,
> *Giving a gentle kiss to every sedge*
> *He overtaketh in his pilgrimage;*
> And so by many winding nooks he strays
> With willing sport to the wild ocean."

Is it not perfect?

Seward. It is. Music—Painting, and Poetry.

Buller. Sculpture and Architecture.

North. Buller, you're a blockhead. Dear Mr. Alison, in his charming *Essays on Taste*, finds a little fault in what seems to me a great beauty in this one of the sweetest passages in Shakspeare.

Buller. Sweetest. That's a miss-mollyish word.

North. Ass. One of the sweetest passages in Shakspeare. He finds fault with the Current kissing the Sedges. "The pleasing personification which we attribute to a brook is founded upon the faint belief of voluntary motion, and is immediately checked when the Poet *descends* to any minute or particular resemblance."

Seward. Descends!

North. The word, to my ear, does sound strangely; and though his expression, "faint belief," is a true and a fine one, yet here the doctrine does not apply. Nay, here we have a true notion inconsiderately misapplied. Without doubt Poets of more wit than sensibility do follow on a similitude beyond the suggestion of the contemplated subject. But the rippling of water against a sedge suggests a kiss—is, I believe, a kiss—liquid, soft, loving, *lipped.*

Buller. Beautiful.

North. Buller, you are a fellow of fine taste. Compare the whole catalogue of metaphorical kisses—admitted and claimable—and you will find this one of the most natural of them all. Pilgrimage, in Shakspeare's day, had dropt, in the speech of our Poets, from its early religious propriety, of seeking a holy place under a vow, into a roving of the region. See his "Passionate Pilgrim." If Shakspeare found the word so far generalized, then "wanderer through the woods," or plains, or through anything else, is the suggestion of the beholding. The river is more, indeed; being, like the pilgrim, on his way to a term, and an obliged way—"the wild ocean."

Seward. The "faint belief of voluntary motion"—Mr.

Alison's fine phrase—is one, and possibly the grounding incentive to impersonating the "current" here; but other elements enter in; liquidity—transparency—which suggests a spiritual nature, and Beauty which moves Love.

North. Ay, and the Poets of that age, in the fresher alacrity of their fancy, had a justification of comparisons, which do not occur as promptly to us, nor, when presented to us, delight so much as they would, were our fancy as alive as theirs. You might suspect, *à priori*, Ovid, Cowley, and Dryden, as likely to be led by indulgence of their ingenuity into passionless similitudes—and you may misdoubt even that Shakspeare was in danger of being so run away with. But let us have clear and unequivocal instances. This one assuredly is not of the number. It is exquisite.

Talboys. Mr. Alison, I presume to think, sir, should either have quoted the whole speech, or kept the whole in view, when animadverting on those two lines about the kissing Pilgrim. Julia, a Lady of Verona, beloved by Proteus, is only half-done—and now she comes—to herself.

> "Then let me go, and hinder not my course;
> I'll be as patient as a gentle stream,
> And make a pastime of each weary step,
> Till the last step have brought me to my love;
> And there I'll rest, as, after much turmoil,
> A blessed soul doth in Elysium."

The language of Shakspeare's Ladies is not the language we hear in real life. I wish it were. Real life would then be delightful indeed. Julia is privileged to be poetical far beyond the usage of the very best circles—far beyond that of any mortal creatures. For the God Shakspeare has made her and all her kin poetical—and if you object to any of the lines, you must object to them all. Eminently beautiful, sir, they are; and their beauty lies in the passionate, imaginative spirit that pervades the whole, and sustains the Similitude throughout, without a moment's flagging of the fancy, without a moment's departure from the truthfulness of the heart.

North. Talboys, I thank you—you are at the root.

Seward. A wonderful thing—altogether—is Impersonation.

North. It is indeed. If we would know the magnitude of the dominion which the disposition constraining us to impersonate has exercised over the human mind, we should have to go back unto those ages of the world when it exerted itself, uncontrolled by philosophy, and in obedience to religious impulses —when Impersonations of Natural Objects and Powers, of Moral Powers and of Notions entertained by the Understanding, filled the Temples of the Nations with visible Deities, and were worshiped with altars and incense, hymns and sacrifices.

Buller. Was ever before such disquisition begotten by—an imaginary kiss among the Sedges!

North. Hold your tongue, Buller. But if you would see how hard this dominion is to eradicate, look to the most civilized and enlightened times, when severe Truth has to the utmost cleansed the Understanding of illusions—and observe how tenaciously these imaginary Beings, endowed with imaginary life, hold their place in our Sculpture, Painting, and Poetry, and Eloquence—nay, in our common and quiet speech.

Seward. It is all full of them. The most prosaic of prosers uses poetical language without knowing it—and Poets without knowing to what extent and degree.

North. Ay, Seward, and were we to expatiate in the walks of the profounder emotions, we should sometimes be startled by the sudden apparitions of boldly impersonated Thoughts, upon occasions that did not seem to promise them—where you might have thought that interests of overwhelming moment would have effectually banished the play of imagination.

Talboys. Shakspeare is justified, then—and the Lady Julia spoke like a Lady in Love with all nature—and with Proteus.

Buller. A most beautiful day is this indeed—but it is a Puzzler.

> "The Swan on still St. Mary's Lake
> Floats double, Swan and Shadow;"

But here all the islands float double—and all the castles and abbeys—and all the hills and mountains—and all the clouds and boats and men—double, did I say—triple—quadruple—we are here, and there, and everywhere, and nowhere, all at the same moment. Inishail, I have you—no—Gutta Percha slides over you, and you have no material existence. Very well.

Seward. Is there no house on Inishail?

North. Not one—but the house appointed for all living. A Burial-place. I see it—but not one of you—for it is little noticeable, and seldom used—on an average, one funeral in the year. Forty years ago I stepped into a small snuff-shop in the Saltmarket, Glasgow, to replenish my shell—and found my friend was from Lochawe-side. I asked him if he often revisited his native shore, and he answered—seldom, and had not for a long time—but that though his lot did not allow him to live there, he hoped to be buried in Inishail. We struck up a friendship—his snuff was good, and so was his whisky, for it was unexcised. A few years ago, trolling for Feroces, I met a boat with a coffin, and in it the body of the old tobacconist.

Seward. "The Churchyard among the Mountains," in Wordsworth's *Excursion*, is alone sufficient for his immortality on earth.

North.—It is. So for Gray's is his Elegy. But some hundred and forty lines in all—no more—yet how comprehensive—how complete! "In a Country Churchyard!" Every generation there buries the whole hamlet—which is much the same as burying the whole world—or a whole world.

Seward.

"The rude forefathers of the hamlet sleep!"

All Peasants—diers and mourners! Utmost simplicity of all belonging to life—utmost simplicity of all belonging to death. Therefore, universally affecting.

North. Then the—Grayishness.

Buller. The what, sir?

North. The Grayishness. The exquisite scholarship, and the high artifice of the words and music—yet all in perfect adaptation to the scene and its essential character. Is there not in that union and communion of the solemn-profound, and the delicate-exquisite, something Cathedral-like? Which has the awe and infinitude of Deity and Eternity, and the prostrations and aspirations of adoration for its basis—expressed in the general structure and forms; and all this meeting and blent into the minute and fine elaboration of the ornaments? Like the odors that steal and creep on the soft, moist, evening air, whilst the dim hush of the Universal Temple dilates and elates. The least and the greatest in one. Why not? Is not that spiritual—angelical—divine! The least is not too exiguous for apprehension—the amplest exceeds not comprehension—and their united power is felt when not understood. I speak, Seward, of that which might be suggested for a primary fault in the Elegy—the contrast of the most artful, scholarly style, and the simple, rude, lowly, homely matter. But you shall see that every fancy seizes, and every memory holds especially those verses and wordings which bring out this contrast—that richest line—

"The breezy call of incense-breathing morn!"

is felt to be soon followed well by that simplest—

"No more shall rouse them from their lowly bed"—

where—I take "lowly" to imply low in earth—humbly turfed or flowered—and of the lowly.

Seward. And so, sir, the pomp of a Cathedral is described, though a village Church alone is in presence. So Milton, Cromwell, and other great powers are set in array—that which these were not, against that which those were.

North. Yet hear Dr. Thomas Brown—an acute metaphysician—but an obtuse critic—and no Poet at all. "The two images in this stanza ('Full many a gem,' &c.) certainly produce very different degrees of poetical delight. That which is borrowed from the rose blooming in solitude pleases in a very high degree, both as it contains a just and beautiful similitude, and still more as the similitude, is one of the most likely to have arisen in such a situation. But the simile in the first two lines of the stanza, though it may perhaps philosophically be as just, has no other charm, and strikes us immediately as not the natural suggestion of such a moment and such a scene. To a person moralizing amid a simple Churchyard, there is perhaps no object that would not sooner have occurred than this piece of minute jewelry—'a gem of purest ray serene, in the unfathomed caves of ocean.'"

Seward. A person moralizing! He forgot that person was Thomas Gray. And he never knew what you have told us now.

North. Why, my dear Seward, the Gem is the recognized most intense expression, from the natural world, of worth—inestimable priceless price—dependent on rarity and beauty. The Flower is a like intense expression, from the same world, of the power to call forth love. The first image is *felt* by every reader to be high, and *exalting* its object; the second to be tender, and openly *pathetic*. Of course it moves more, and of course it comes last. The Poet has just before spoken of Milton and Cromwell—of bards and kings—and history with all her wealth. Is the transition violent from these objects to Gems? He is moved by, but he is not bound to, the scene and time. His own thoughts emancipate. Brown seems utterly to have forgotten that the Poet himself is the Dramatic person of the Monologue. Shall he be restricted from using the richness and splendor of his own thoughts? That one stanza sums up the two or three preceding—and is perfectly attuned to the reigning mood, temper, or pathos.

Buller. Thank you, gentlemen. The Doctor is done brown.

North.

"The paths of glory lead but to the grave!"

Methinks I could read you a homily on that Text.

Buller. To-morrow, sir, if you please. To-morrow is Sunday—and you may read it to us as we glide to Divine Service at Dalmally—two of us to the Established and two of us to the Free Kirk.

North. Be it so. But you will not be displeased with me for quoting now, from heart-memory, a single sentence on the great line, from Beattie, and from Adam Fergusson. "It presents to the imagination a wide plain, where several roads appear, crowded with glittering multitudes, and issuing from different quarters, but drawing nearer and nearer as they advance, till they terminate in a dark and narrow house, where all their glories enter in succession, and disappear for ever."

Seward. Thank you, sir. That is Beattie?

North. It is. Fergusson's memorable words are—"If from this we are disposed to collect any inference adverse to the pursuits of glory, it may be asked whither do the paths of ignominy lead? If to the grave, also, then our choice of a life remains to be made on the grounds of its intrinsic value, without regard to an end which is common to every station of life we can lead, whether illustrious or obscure."

Seward. Very fine. Who says it? Fergusson—who was he?

North. The best of you Englishers are intolerably ignorant about Scotland. Do you know the Rev. John Mitford?

Seward. I do—and have for him the greatest respect.

North. So have I. He is one of our best editors—as Pickering is one of our best Publishers of the Poets. But I am somewhat doubtful of the truthfulness of his remarks on the opening of the Elegy, in the Appendix to his excellent Life of Gray. "The Curfew 'toll' is not the appropriate word—it was not a slow bell tolling for the dead."

Seward. True enough, not for the dead—but Gray then felt as if it were for the dying—and chose to say so—the parting day. Was it quick and "merry as a marriage-bell?" I can't think it—nor did Milton, "swinging *slow* with sullen roar." Gray was Il Penseroso. Prospero calls it the "solemn curfew." Toll is right.

North. But, says my friend Mitford, "there is another error, a confusion of time. The curfew tolls, and the ploughman returns from work. Now the ploughman returns two or three hours before the curfew rings; and 'the glimmering landscape' has 'long ceased to fade' before the curfew. The 'parting day' is also incorrect; the day had long finished. But if the word Curfew is taken simply for 'the Evening Bell,' then also is the time incorrect—and a *knell* is not tolled for the parting, but for the parted—'and leaves the world to darkness and to me.' 'Now fades the glimmering landscape on the sight.' Here the incidents, instead of being progressive, fall back, and make the picture confused and inharmonious; especially as it appears soon after that it was *not* dark. For 'the moping owl does to the moon complain.'"

Seward. Pardon me, sir, I cannot venture to answer all that

—but if Mitford be right, Gray must be very wrong indeed. Let me see—give us it over again—sentence by sentence—

Buller. No—no—no. Once is enough—and enough is as good as a feast.

North. Talboys?

Talboys. Since you have a great respect for Mr. Mitford, sir, so have I. But hitherto I have been a stranger to his merits.

Seward. The best of you Scottishers are intolerably ignorant about England.

Talboys. In the first place, Mr. North, when does the Curfew toll, or ring?—for hang me if I remember—or rather ever knew. And in the second place, when does the Evening Bell give tongue?—for hang me if I am much better informed as to his motions. Yet I should know something of the family of the Bells. Say—*eight* o'clock. Well. It is summer-time, I suppose; for you cannot believe that so dainty a person in health and habits, as the Poet Gray, would write an Elegy in a Country Churchyard in winter, and well on towards night. True, that is a way of speaking; he did not write it with his crow-quill, in his neat hand, on his neat vellum, on the only horizontal tomb-stone. But in the Churchyard he assumes to sit—probably under a Plane-tree, for sake of the congenial Gloom. Season of the year ascertained—Summer—time of Curfew—eight—then I can find no fault with the Ploughman. He comes in well—either as an image or a man. He must have been an honest, hard-working fellow, and worth the highest wages going between the years 1745 and 1750. At what hour do ploughmen leave the stilts in Cambridgeshire? We must not say at six. Different hours in different counties, Buller.

Buller. Go on—all's right, Talboys.

Talboys. It is not too much to believe that Hodge did not

grudge, occasionally, a half hour over, to a good master. Then he had to stable his horses—Star and Smiler—rub them down—bed them—fill rack and manger—water them—make sure their noses were in the oats—lock the stable before the nags were stolen—and then, and not till then,

"The Ploughman homeward plods his weary way."

For he does not sleep on the Farm—he has a wife and small family—that is, a large family of smallish children—in a Hamlet, at least two miles off—and he does not walk for a wager of a flitch of bacon and barrel of beer—but for his accustomed rasher and a jug—and such endearments as will restore his weariness up to the proper pitch for a sound night's sleep. God bless him!

Buller. Shorn of your beams, Mr. North eclipsed.

Talboys. The ploughman, then, does not return "two or three hours before the curfew rings." Nor has "the glimmering landscape long ceased to fade before the curfew." Nor is "the parting day incorrect." Nor "has the day long finished." Nor, when it may have finished, or may finish, can any man in the hamlet, during all that gradual subsiding of light and sound, take upon him to give any opinion at all.

North. My boy, Talboys.

Talboys. "And leave the world to darkness and to me." Ay—into his hut goes the ploughman, and leaves the world and me to darkness—which is coming—but not yet come—the Poet knows it is coming—near at hand its coming glooms; and Darkness shows her divinity as she is preparing to mount her throne.

North. Nothing can be better.

Talboys. "'Now fades the glimmering landscape on the sight.' Here the incident, instead of being progressive, falls back, and makes the picture confused and inharmonious."

Confused and inharmonious? By no manner of means. Nothing of the sort. There is no retrogression—the day has been unwilling to die—cannot believe she is dying—and cannot think 'tis for her the curfew is tolling; but the Poet feels it is even so; the glimmering and the fading, beautiful as they are, are sure symptoms—she is dying into Evening, and Evening will soon be the dying into Night; but to the Poet's eye how beautiful the transmutations! Nor knows he that the Moon has arisen, till, at the voice of the night-bird, he looks up the ivied church-tower, and there she is, whether full, waning, or crescent, there are not data for the Astronomer to declare.

North. My friend Mr. Mitford says of the line, "No more shall rouse them from their lowly bed"—That "here the epithet *lowly,* as applied to *bed,* occasions an ambiguity, as to whether the Poet means the bed on which they sleep, or the grave in which they are laid;" and he adds, "there can be no greater fault in composition than a doubtful meaning."

Talboys. There cannot be a more touching beauty. Lowly applies to both. From their lowly bed in their lowly dwellings among the quick, those joyous sounds used to awaken them; from their lowly bed in their lowly dwellings among the dead, those joyous sounds will awaken them never more: but a sound will awaken them when He comes to judge both the quick and the dead; and for them there is Christian hope—from

> "Many a holy text around them strewed
> That teach the rustic moralist to die."

North.

> "Their furrow oft the stubborn glebe hath broke;
> How jocund did they drive their team afield!
> How bowed the woods beneath their sturdy stroke!"

This stanza—says Mr. Mitford—"is made up of various pieces inlaid'—'Stubborn glebe' is from Gay; 'drive afield' from

Milton; 'sturdy stroke' from Spenser. Such is too much the system of Gray's composition, and therefore such the cause of his imperfections. Purity of language, accuracy of thought, and even similarity of rhyme, all give way to the introduction of certain poetical expressions; in fact, the beautiful jewel, when brought, does not fit into the new setting, or socket. Such is the difference between the flower stuck into the ground and those that grow from it." Talboys?

Buller. Why not—Buller?

Talboys. I give way to the gentleman.

Buller. Nor for worlds would I take the word out of any man's mouth.

Talboys. Gray took "stubborn glebe" from Gay. Why from Gay? It has been familiar in men's mouths from the introduction of agriculture into this Island. May not a Saxon gentleman say "drive their teams a-field" without charge of theft from Milton, who said "drove a-field." Who first said "Gee-ho, Dobbin?" Was Spenser the first—the only man before Milton—who used "sturdy stroke?"—and has nobody used it since Gray?

Buller. You could give a "sturdy stroke" yourself, Talboys. What's your weight?

Talboys. Gray's style *is* sometimes too composite—you yourself, sir, would not deny it is so—but Mr. Mitford's instances here are absurd, and the charge founded on them false. Gray seldom, if ever—say never, "*sacrifices* purity of language, and accuracy of thought," for the sake of introducing certain poetical expressions. "All give way" is a gross exaggeration. The beautiful words of the brethren, with which his loving memory was stored, came up in the hour of imagination, and took their place among the words as beautiful of his own congenial inspirations; the flowers he transplanted from poetry "languished not, grew dim, nor died;" for he had taken them up gently by the roots, and with some of the old mould adhering to their tendrils, and, true florist as he was, had prepared for them a richest soil in his own garden, which he held from nature, and which the sun and the dew of nature nourished, and will nourish for ever.

Buller. That face is not pleasant, sir. Nothing so disfigures a face as envy. Old Poets at last grow ugly all—but you, sir, are a Philosopher—and on your benign countenance 'twas but a passing cloud. There—you are as beautiful as ever—how comely in critical old age! Any farther fault to find with our friend Mitford?

North.

> "On some fond breast the parting soul relies,
> Some pious drops the closing eye requires;
> Even from the tomb the voice of nature cries,
> Even in our ashes live their wonted fires."

"'Pious drops' is from Ovid—piæ lachrymæ; 'closing eye' is from Pope—'voice of nature' from the Anthologia, and the last line from Chaucer—'Yet on our ashes cold is fire yreken.' *From so many quarries are the stones brought to form this elaborate Mosaic pavement.*" I say, for "piæ lachrymæ" all honor to Ovid—for "pious drops" all honor to Gray. "Closing eye" is *not* from Pope's Elegy; "voice of nature" is *not* from the Anthologia, but from Nature herself; Chaucer's line may have suggested Gray's, but the reader of Chaucer knows that Gray's has a tender and profound meaning which is not in Chaucer's at all—and he knows, too, that Mr. Mitford is not a reader of Chaucer—for were he, he could not have written "ashes" for "ashen." There were *no* quarries—there is *no* Mosaic. Mosaic pavement! Worse, if possible—more ostentatiously pedantic—even than stuck in flowers, jewels, settings, and sockets.

Talboys. The stanza is sacred to sorrow.

North. "From this Stanza," quoth Mitford, "the style of the composition drops into *a lower key;* the language is plainer, and is not in harmony with the splendid and elaborate diction of the former part." This objection is disposed of by what I said some minutes ago——

Buller. Half an hour ago—on *Grayishness.*

North. And I have only this farther to say, gentlemen, that though the language is plainer—yet it is solemn; nor is it unpoetical—for the hoary-headed swain was moved as he spake; the style, if it drop into a lower key, is accordant with that higher key on which the music was pitched that has not yet left our hearing. An Elegy is not an Ode—the close should be mournful as the opening—with loftier strain between—and it is so; and whatever we might have to say of the Epitaph—its final lines are "awful"—as every man must have felt them to be—whether thought on in our own lonely night-room—in the Churchyard of Granchester, where it is said Gray mused the Elegy—or by that Burial-ground in Inishail—or here afloat in the joyous sunshine for an hour privileged to be happy in a world of grief.

Buller. Let's change the subject, sir. May I ask what author you have in your other hand?

North. Alison on Taste.

Buller. You don't say so! I thought you quoted from memory.

North. So I did; but I have dog-eared a page or two.

Buller. I see no books lying about in the Pavilion—only Newspapers—and Magazines—and Reviews—and trash of that kind——

North. Without which, you, my good fellow, could not live a week.

Buller. The Spirit of the Age! The Age should be ashamed of herself for living from hand to mouth on Periodical Literature. The old Lady should indeed, sir. If the Pensive Public conceits herself to be the Thinking World—

North. Let us help to make her so. I have a decent little Library of some three hundred select volumes in the Van—my Plate-chest—and a few dozens of choice wines for my friends—of Champagne, which you, Buller, call small beer——

Buller. I retracted and apologized. Is that the key of the Van at your watch-chain?

North. It is. So many hundred people about the Encampment—sometimes among them suspicious strangers in paletots in search of the picturesque, and perhaps the pecuniary—that it is well to intrust the key to my own body-guard. It does not weigh an ounce. And *that* lock is not to be picked by the ghost of Huffey White.

Seward. But of the book in hand, sir?

North. "In that fine passage in the Second Book of the Georgics," says Mr. Alison, "in which Virgil celebrates the praises of his native country, after these fine lines—

> 'Hic ver assiduum, atque alienis mensibus æstas;
> Bis gravidæ pecudes, bis pomis utilis arbos.
> At rabidæ tigres absunt, et sæva leonum
> Semina: nec miseros fallunt aconita legentes:
> Nec rapit immensos orbes per humum, neque tanto
> Squameus in spiram tractu se colligit anguis.'

There is no reader whose enthusiasm is not checked by the cold and prosaic line which follows,—

> 'Adde tot egregias urbes, operumque laborem.'

The tameness and vulgarity of the transition dissipates at once the emotion we had shared with the Poet, and reduces him, in our opinion, to the level of a mere describer."

Seward. Cold and prosaic line! Tameness and vulgarity! I am struck mute.

North. I have no doubt that Mr. Alison distressed himself with "*Adde.*" It is a word from a merchant's counting-house, reckoning up his gains. And so much the better. Virgil is making out the balance-sheet of Italy—he is inventorying her wealth. Mr. Alison would have every word away from reality. Not so *the* Poet. Every now and then, they—the Poets—amuse themselves with dipping their pencils into the real, the common, the everyday, the homely. By so doing they arrest belief, which above everything they desire to hold fast. I should not wonder if you might catch Spenser at it, even. Shakspeare is full of it. There is nothing else prosaic in the passage; and if Virgil had had the bad taste to say "Ecce," instead of "Adde," I suppose no fault would have been found.

Seward. But what can Mr. Alison mean by the charge of tameness and *vulgarity?*

North. I have told you, sir.

Seward. You have not, sir.

North. I have, sir.

Seward. Yes—yes—yes. "Adde" is vulgar! I cannot think so.

North. The Cities of Italy, and the "operum labor," always have been and are an admiration. The words "Egregias urbes" suggest the general stateliness and wealth—"operumque laborem," the particular buildings—Temples, Basilicas, Theatres, and Great Works of the lower Utility. A summary and most vivid expression of a land possessed by intelligent, civilized, active, spirited, vigorous, tasteful inhabitants—also an eminent adorning of the land.

Seward. Lucretius says, that in spring the Cities are in flower—or on flower—or a flower—with children. And Lucan, at the beginning of the *Pharsalia,* describes the Ancient or Greek Cities desolate. They were fond and proud of their "tot egregiæ urbes" as the Modern Italians are—and with good reason.

North. How judiciously the Critics stop short of the lines that would overthrow their criterion always! The present case is an extraordinary example. Had Mr. Alison looked to the lines immediately following, he would not have objected to that One. For

> "Tot congesta manu præruptis oppida saxis,
> Fluminaque antiquos subter labentia muros"

is very beautiful—brings the whole under the domain of Poetry, by singular Picturesqueness, and by gathering the whole past history of Italy up—fetching it in with a word—*antiquos.*

Seward. I can form no conjecture as to the meaning of Mr. Alison's objections. He quotes a few fine lines from the "Praise of Italy," and then one line which he calls prosaic, and would have us to hold up our hands in wonder at the lame and impotent conclusion—at the sudden transformation of Virgil the Poet into Virgil the most prosaic of Prosers. You have said enough already, sir, to prove that he is in error even on his own showing;—but how can this fragmentary—this piecemeal mode of quotation—so common among critics of the lower school, and so unworthy of those of the higher—have found favor with Mr. Alison, one of the most candid and most enlightened of men? Some accidental prejudice from mere carelessness—but, once formed, retained in spite of the fine and true Taste which, unfettered, would have felt the fallacy, and vindicated his admired Virgil.

North. The "Laudes"—to which the Poet is brought by the preceding bold, sweeping, winged, and poetical strain about the indigenous vines of Italy—have twofold root—TREES and the glory of LANDS. Virgil kindles on the double suggestion —the trees of Italy compared to the trees of other regions.

They are the trees of primary human service and gladness—Oil and Wine. For see at once the deep, sound natural ground in human wants—the bounty of Nature—of Mother Earth—"whatever Earth, all bearing Mother, yields"—to her human children. That is the gate of entrance; but not prosaically—but two gate-posts of a most poetical mythus-fed husbandman. For we have Jason's fire-mouthed Bulls *ploughing*, and Cadmus-sown teeth of the dragon springing up in armed men. Then comes, instead, mild, benign, Man-loving Italy—"gravidæ fruges"—the heavy-eared corn—or rather big-teeming—the juice of Bacchus—the Olives, and the "broad herds of Cattle." Note—ye Virgilians—the Corn of Book First—the Oil and Wine of Book Second—and the Cattle of Book Third—for the sustaining Thought—the organic life of his Work moves in his heart.

Buller. And the Fourth—Bees—honey—and honey-makers are like Milkers—in a way small Milch-cows.

North. They are. Once a-foot—or a-wing—he hurries and rushes along, all through the "Laudes." The majestic victim-Bull of the Clitumnus—the incipient Spring—the double Summer—*the absence* of all envenomed and deadly broods—tigers—lions—aconite—serpents. This is NATURE'S FAVOR. Then *Man's Works*—cities and forts—(rock-fortresses)—the great lakes of Northern Italy—showing Man again in their vast edifications. Then Nature in veins of metals precious or useful—then Nature in her production of Man—the Marsi—the Sabellian youth—the Ligurian inured to labor—and the Volscian darters—then single mighty shapes and powers of Man—ROMANS—the Decii, the Marii, the Camilli,

"Scipiadas duros bello, et te, maxime Cæsar,"

The King of Men—the Lord of the Earth—the pacificator of the distracted Empire—which, to a Roman, is as much as to say the World. Then—hail Saturnian Land! Mother of Corn! Saturnian, because golden Saturn had reigned there—Mother, I suppose the rather because in *his* time corn sprung unsown —*sine semine*—She gave it from out of her own loving and cherishing bosom. *To Thee*, Italy, sing I my Ascræan or Hesiodic song. The Works and Days—the Greek Georgics are his avowed prototype—rude prototype to magnificence—like the Arab of the Desert transplanted to rear his empire of dazzling and picturesque civilization in the Pyrenean Peninsula.

Buller. Take breath, sir. Virgil said well—

"Adde tot egregias urbes operumque laborem."

Seward. Allow me one other word. Virgil—in the vivid lines quoted with admiration by Mr. Alison—lauds his beloved Italy for *the absence* of wild beasts and serpents—and he magnifies the whole race of serpents by his picture of One—the Serpent King—yet with subjects all equal in size to himself in our imagination. The Serpent is *in* the Poetry, but he is *not in* Italy. Is this a false artifice of composition—a vain ornament? Oh, no! He describes the Saturnian Land—the mother of corn and of men—bounteous, benign, golden, maternal Italy. The negation has the plenitude of life, which the fabulous absence of noxious reptiles has for the sacred Island of Ierne.

Buller. Erin-go-bragh!

Seward. Suddenly he sees another vision—not of what is absent but present; and then comes the line arraigned and condemned—followed by lines as great—

"Adde tot egregias urbes, operumque laborem,
Tot congesta manu præruptis oppida saxis,
Fluminaque antiquos subter labentia muros."

The first line grasps in one handful all the mighty, fair, wealthy CITIES of Italy—the second all the rock-cresting *Forts* of Italy —from the Alpine head to the sea-washed foot of the Peninsula.

The collective One Thought of the Human Might and Glory of Italy—as it appears on the countenance of the Land—or visible in its utmost concentration in the girdled Towns and Cities of Men.

Buller. "Adde" then is right, Seward. On that North and you are at one.

North. Yes, it is right, and any other word would be wrong. ADDE! Note the sharpness, Buller, of the significance—the vivacity of the short open sound. Fling it out—ring it out—sing it out. Look at the very repetition of the powerful "TOT"—"*tot* egregias"—"*tot* congesta"—witnessing by one of the first and commonest rules in the grammar of rhetoric—whether Virgil speaks in prose or in fire.

Buller. In fire.

North. Mr. Alison then goes on to say, "that the effect of the following nervous and beautiful lines, in the conclusion of the same Book, is *nearly destroyed* by a similar defect. After these lines,

> "Hanc olim veteres vitam coluêre Sabini,
> Hanc Remus et Frater; sic fortis Etruria crevit,
> Scilicet et rerum facta est pulcherrima Roma;"

We little expect the following *spiritless* conclusion:—

> "*Septemque una sibi muro circumdedit arces.*"

Seward. Oh! why does Mr. Alison call that line *spiritless?*

North. He gives no reason—assured by his own dissatisfaction, that he has but to quote it, and leave it in its own naked impotence.

Seward. I hope you do not think it spiritless, sir.

North. I think it contains the concentrated essence of spirit and of power. Let any one think of Rome, piled up in greatness, and grandeur, and glory—and a Wall round about—and in a moment his imagination is filled. What sort of a Wall?

A garden wall to keep out orchard thieves—or a modern wall of a French or Italian town to keep out wine and meat, that they may come in at the gate and pay toll? I trow not. But a Wall against the World armed and assailing? Remember that Virgil saw Rome—and that his hearers did—and that in his eyes and theirs she was Empress of the inhabited Earth. She held and called herself such—it was written in her face and on her forehead. The visible, tangible splendor and magnificence meant this, or they meant nothing. The stone and lime said this—and Virgil's line says it, sedately and in plain, simple phrase, which yet is a Climax.

Seward. As the dreaded Semiramis was flesh and blood—corporeal—made of the four elements—yet her soul and her empire spoke out of her—so spake they from the Face of Rome.

North. Ay, Seward—put these two things together—the Aspect that speaks Domination of the World, and the Wall that girds her with strength impregnable—and what more could you possibly demand from her Great Poet?

Seward. Arx is a Citadel—we may say an Acropolis. Athens had one Arx—so had Corinth. One Arx is enough to one Queenly City. But this Queen, within her one Wall, has enclosed Seven Arces—as if she were Seven Queens.

North. Well said, Seward. The Seven Hills appeared—and to this day do—to characterize the Supremacy of Rome. The Seven-Hilled City! You seem to have said everything—the Seven Hills are as a seven-pillared Throne—and all that is in one line—given by Virgil. Delete it—no, not for a thousand gold crowns.

Buller. Not for the Pigot Diamond—not for the Sea of Light.

North. Imagine Romulus tracing the circuit on which the walls were to rise of his little Rome—the walls ominously lustrated with a brother's blood. War after war humbles neighboring town after town, till the seas that bathe, and the mountains that guard Italy, enclose the confederated Republic. It is a step—a beginning. East and West, North and South, flies the Eagle, dipping its beak in the blood of battle-fields. Where it swoops, there fanning away the pride, and fame, and freedom of nations, with the wafture of its wings. Kingdoms and Empires that were, are no more than Provinces; till the haughty Roman, stretching out the fact to the limits of his ambitious desires, can with some plausibility deceive himself, and call the edges of the Earth the boundaries of his unmeasured Dominion.

Seward. "O Italy! Italy! would Thou wert stronger or less beautiful!"—was the mournful apostrophe of an Italian Poet, who saw, in the latter ages, his refined but enervated countrymen trampled under the foot of a more martial people from far beyond the Alps.

North. Good Manners giving a vital energy and efficacy to good Laws—in these few words, gentlemen, may be comprised the needful constituents of National Happiness and Prosperity —the foremost conditions.

Talboys. Ay—ay—sir. For good Laws without good Manners are an empty breath—whilst good Manners ask the protecting and preserving succor of good Laws. But the good Manners are of the first necessity, for they naturally produce the good Laws.

North. What does history show, Talboys, but nations risen up to flourish in wealth, power, and greatness, that with corrupted and luxurious manners have again sunk from their pre-eminence; whilst another purer and simpler people has in turn grown mighty, and taken their room in the world's eye—some hardy, simple, frugal race, perhaps, whom the seeming disfavor of nature constrains to assiduous labour, and who maintain in the lap of their mountains their independence and their pure and happy homes.

Talboys. The Luxury—the invading Goth and Hun—the dismembering—and new States uprisen upon the ruins of the World's fallen Empire. There is one line in Collins' *Ode to Freedom*—Mr. North—which I doubt if I understand.

North. Which?

Talboys.

> "No, Freedom, no—I will not tell
> How Rome before thy weeping face
> Pushed by a wild and artless race
> From off its wide, ambitious base,
> With heaviest sound a giant-statue fell—
> What time the northern Sons of Spoil awoke,
> And all the blended work of strength and grace,
> With many a rude repeated stroke,
> And many a barbarous yell, to thousand fragments broke."

North. Which?

Talboys. "How Rome before thy *weeping face.*"

North. Freedom wept at Rome's overthrow—though she had long been Freedom's enemy—and though her destroyers were Freedom's children—and "Spoil's Sons"—for how could Freedom look unmoved at the wreck "of all that blended work of strength and grace"—though raised by slaves at the beck of Tyrants? It was not always so.

Buller. Let me, Apollo-like, my dear sir, pinch your ear, and admonish you to return to the point from which, in discursive gyrations, you and Seward have been——

North. Like an Eagle giving an Eaglet lessons how to fly——

Buller. You promised solemnly, sir, not to mention Eagles this evening.

North. I did not, sir.

Buller. But, then, Seward is no Eaglet—he is, and long has been, a full-fledged bird, and can fly as well's yourself, sir.

North. There you're right. But then, making a discursive gyration round a point is not leaving it—and there you're wrong. Silly folk—not you, Buller, for you are a strong-minded, strong-bodied man—say "keep to the point"—knowing that if you quit it one inch, you will from their range of vision disappear —and then they comfort themselves by charging you with having melted among the clouds.

Buller. I was afraid, my dear sir, that having got your Eaglet on your back—or your Eaglet having got old Aquila on his—you would sail away with him—or he with you—"to prey in distant isles."

North. You promised solemnly, sir, not to mention Eagles this evening.

Buller. I did not, sir. But don't let us quarrel.

Seward. What does Virgil mean, sir, by "Rerum," in the line in which Mr. Alison thinks should have concluded the strain—

"Scilicet et rerum facta est pulcherrima Roma."

North. "Rerum"—what does he mean by "Rerum?" Let me perpend. Why, Seward, the legitimate meaning of Res here is a State—a Commonwealth. "The fairest of Powers—then—of Polities—of States."

Seward. Is that all the word means here?

North. Why, methinks we must explain. Observe, then, Seward, that Rome is the Town, as England the Island. Thus "England has become the fairest among the kingdoms of the Earth." This is equivalent, good English; and the only satisfactory and literal translation of the Latin verse. But here, the Physical and the Political are identified,—that is, England. England is the name at once of the Island—of so much earth limited out on the surface of the terraqueous globe—and of what besides? Of the Inhabitants? Yes? but of the Inhabitants (as the King never dies) perpetuated from generation to generation. Moreover, of this immortal inhabitation, further made one by blood and speech, laws, manners, and everything that makes a people. In short, England, properly the name of the land, is intended to be, at the same time, the name of the Nation.

> "England, with all thy faults, I love Thee still."

There Cowper speaks to both at once—the faults are of the men only—moral—for he does not mean fogs, and March east winds, and fever and agues. I love thee—is to the green fields and the white cliffs, as well as to all that still survives of the English heart and thought and character. And this absorption, sir, and compenetration of the two ideas—land into people, people into land—the exposition of which might, in good hands, be made beautiful—is a fruitful germ of Patriotism—an infinite blending of the spiritual and the corporeal. To Virgil, Rome the city was also Rome the Romans; and, therefore, sir, those Houses and Palaces, and that Wall, were to him as those green fields, and hills, and streams, and towns, and those cliffs are to Us. The girdled-in compendium of the Heaven's Favor and the Earth's Glory and Power.

> "Scilicet et RERUM facta est pulcherrima ROMA,
> Septemque una sibi muro circumdedit arces."

Do you all comprehend and adopt my explanation, gentlemen?

Talboys. I do.

Buller. I———do

Seward. I ask myself whether Virgil's "Rerum Pulcherrima" may not mean "Fairest of Things"—of Creatures—of earthly existences? To a young English reader, probably that is the first impression. It was, I think, mine. But fairest of earthly States and Seats of State is so much more idiomatic and to the purpose, that I conceive it—indubitable.

North. You all remember what Horatio sayeth to the soldiers in Hamlet, on the coming and going of the Ghost.

> "In the most high and palmy state of Rome,
> A little ere the mightiest Julius fell,
> The graves stood tenantless, and the sheeted dead
> Did squeak and gibber in the Roman streets;
> Stars shone with trains of fire, dews of blood fell;
> Disasters veiled the sun, and the moist star
> Upon whose influence Neptune's empire stands,
> Was sick almost to Doomsday with eclipse."

What does Horatio mean by high and palmy state? That Rome was in a flourishing condition?

Buller. That, I believe, sir, is a common impression. Hitherto it has been mine.

North. Let it be erased henceforth and for ever.

Buller. It is erased—I erase it.

North. Read henceforth and for ever high and palmy State. Write henceforth and for ever State with a towering Capital. Res! "Most high and palmy State" is precisely and literally "*Rerum Pulcherrima.*"

Seward. At your bidding—you cannot err.

North. I err not unfrequently—but not now, nor I believe this evening. Horatio, the Scholar, speaks to the two Danish Soldiers. They have brought him to be of their watch because he is a Scholar—and they are none. This relation of distinction is indeed the ground and life of the Scene.

> "Therefore I have entreated him, along
> With us to watch the minutes of the night;
> That if again this apparition come,
> He may approve our eyes, and speak to it."

Talboys.

"Thou art a Scholar—speak to it, Horatio."

North. You know, Talboys, that Scholars were actual Conjurors, in the mediæval belief, which has tales enow about Scholars in that capacity. Horatio comes, then, possessed with an especial Power; he knows how to deal with Ghosts—he could lay one, if need were. He is not merely a man of superior and cultivated intellect, whom intellectual inferiors engage to assist them in an emergency above the grasp—but he is the *very* man for the work.

Talboys. Have not the Commentators said as much, sir?

North. Perhaps—probably—who? If they have in plenitude, I say it again—because I once did not know it—or think of it—and I suppose that a great many persons die believing that the Two resort in the way of general dependence merely on Horatio.

Talboys. I believed, but I shall not die believing so.

North. Therefore, the scholarship of Horatio, and the non-scholarship of Bernardo and Marcellus, strike into the life, soul, essence, ground, foundation, fabric, and organization of this First Ghost Scene—sustain and build the whole Play.

Talboys. Eh?

North. Eh? Yes. But to the Point in hand. The Ghost has come and gone; and the Scholar addresses his Mates the two Non-Scholars. And show me the living Scholar who could speak as Horatio spake. Touching the matter that is in all their minds oppressively, *he* will transport *their* minds a flight suddenly of a thousand years, and a thousand miles or leagues—their untutored minds into the Region of History. He will take them to Rome—"*a little ere*"—and, therefore, before naming Rome, he lifts and he directs their imagination—"In the most high and palmy STATE." There had been Four Great

Empires of the World—and he will by these few words evoke in their minds the Image of the last and greatest. And now observe with what decision, as well as with what majesty, the nomination ensues—OF ROME.

Talboys. I feel it, sir.

North. Try, Talboys, to render "State" by any other word, and you will be put to it. You may analogize. It is for the Republic and City, what Realm or Kingdom is to us—at once place and indwelling Power. "State"—properly Republic—here specifically and pointedly means Reigning City. The Ghosts walked in the City—not in the Republic.

Talboys. I think I have you, sir—am not sure.

North. You have me—you are sure. Now suppose that, instead of the solemn, ceremonious, and stately robes in which Horatio attires the Glorious Rome, he had said simply, "in Rome," or "at Rome," where then his ψυχαγωγια—his leading of their spirits? Where his own scholar-enthusiasm, and love, and joy, and wonder? All gone? And where, Talboys, are they who, by here understanding "state" for "condition"—which every man alive does—

Talboys. Every man alive?

North. Yes, you did—confess you did. Where are they, I ask, who thus oblige Horatio to introduce his nomination of Rome—thus nakedly—and prosaically? Every hackneyer of this phrase—*state*—as every man alive hackneys it—is a nine-fold Murderer. He murders the Phrase; he murders the Speech; he murders Horatio; he murders the Ghost; he murders the Scene; he murders the Play; he murders Rome; he murders Shakspeare—and he murders Me.

Talboys. I am innocent.

North. Why, suppose Horatio to mean—"in the most glorious and victorious *condition* of Rome, on the Eve of Cæsar's death, the graves stood tenantless"—You ask—WHERE? See where you have got. A story told with two determinations of Time, and none of Place! Is that the way that Shakspeare, the intelligent and intelligible, recites a fact? No! But my explanation shows the Congruity or Parallelism. "In the *most high and palmy* State"—that is, City of Rome—ceremonious determination of Place—"a little ere the *mightiest* Julius fell" —ceremonious determination of Time.

Talboys. But is not the use of State, sir, for City, bold and singular?

North. It is. For Verse has her own Speech—though Wordsworth denies it in his Preface—and proves it by his Poetry, like his brethren Shakspeare and Milton. The language of Verse is rapid—abrept and abrupt. Horatio wants the notion of Republic; because properly the Republic is high and palmy, and not the wood, stone, and marble. So he manages an expeditious word that shall include both, and strike you at once. The word of a Poet strikes like a flash of lightning—it penetrates—it does not stay to be scanned—"probed, vexed, and criticised,"—it illuminates and is gone. But you must have eyes—and suffer nobody to shut them. I ask, then —Can any lawful, well-behaved Citizen, having weighed all this, and reviewed all these things, again violate the Poesy of the Avonian Swan, and his own muse-enlightened intelligence, by lending hand or tongue to the convicted and condemned VULGARISM?

Talboys. Now, then, and not till now, we Three know the full power of the lines—

"Scilicet et Rerum facta est pulcherrima Roma,
Septemque una sibi muro circumdedit arces."

North. Another word anent Virgil. Mr. Alison says— "There is a still more surprising instance of this fault in one of the most pathetic passages of the whole Poem, in the description of the disease among the cattle, which concludes the Third Georgic. The passage is as follows:—

> 'Ecce autem duro fumans sub vomere Taurus
> Concidit, et mixtum spumis vomit ore cruorem
> Extremosque ciet gemitus; it tristis arator,
> Mœrentem abjungens fraternâ morte juvencum,
> Atque opere in medio defixa relinquit aratra.'

The unhappy image in the second line is less calculated to excite compassion than disgust, and is singularly ill suited to the tone of tenderness and delicacy which the Poet has everywhere else so successfully maintained, in describing the progress of the loathsome disease." The line here objected to is the life of the description—and instead of offence, it is the clenching of the pathos. First of all, it is that which the poets always will have and the critics won't—the *Necessitated*—the Thing itself—the Matter in hand. It shapes—features—characterizes that particular Murrain. Leave it out—"the one Ox drops dead in the furrow, and the Ploughman detaches the other." It's a great pity, and very surprising—but that is NO PLAGUE. Suddenly he falls, and blood and foam gush mixed with his expiring breath. *That is a plague.* It has terror—affright—sensible horror—life vitiated, poisoned in its fountains. *Vomit*—a settled word, and one of the foremost, of the reversed, unnatural vital function. Besides, it is the true and proper word. Besides, it is vivid and picturesque, being the word of the Mouth. *Effundit* (which they would prefer—I do not mean it would stand in the verse) is general—might be from the ears. *Vomit* in itself says mouth. The poor mouth! whose function is to breathe, and to eat grass, and to caress—the visible organ of life—of vivification—and now of mortification. Taken from the dominion of the holy powers, and given up to the dark and nameless destroyer. "*Vomit ore Cruorem!*" The verse moans and groans for him—it may have in it a death rattle. How much more helpless and hopeless the real picture makes Arator's distress! Now, "*it tristis*" comes with effect.

Seward. Yes, Virgil, as in duty bound to do, faced the Cattle Plague in all its horrors. Had he not, he would have been false to Pales, the Goddess of Shepherds—to Apollo, who fed the herds of Admetus. So did his Master, Lucretius—whom he emulated—equalled, but not surpassed, in execution of the dismal but inevitable work. The whole land groaned under the visitation—nor was it confined to Cattle—it seemed as if the brute creation were about to perish. But his tender heart, near the close, singled out from the thousands one yoke of Steers—in two lines and a half told the death of one—in two lines and a half told the sadness of its owner—and in as many lines more told, too, of the survivor sinking, because his brother "was not"—and in as many more a lament for the cruel sufferings of the harmless creature—lines which, Scaliger says, he would rather have written than have been honored by the Lydian or the Persian king.

Buller. Perhaps you have said enough, Seward. It might have been better, perhaps, to have recited the whole passage.

North. Here is a sentence or two about Homer.

Buller. Then you are off. Oh! Sir—why not for an hour imitate that Moon and those Stars? How silently they shine! but what care you for the heavenly luminaries? In the majestic beauty of the nocturnal heavens vain man will not hold his peace.

Seward. Is that the murmur of the far off sea?

North. It is—the tide, may be, is on its return—is at "Connal's raging Ferry"—from Loch Etive—yet this is not its hour—'tis but the mysterious voice of Night.

Buller. Hush!

North. By moonlight and starlight, and to the voice of

Night, I read these words from Mr. Alison—"In the speech of Agamemnon to Idomeneus, in the Fourth Book of the Iliad, a circumstance is introduced altogether inconsistent both with the *dignity of the speech, and the Majesty of Epic Poetry:*—

'Divine Idomeneus! what thanks we owe
To worth like thine, what praise shall we bestow!
To Thee the foremost honors are decreed,
First in the fight, and every graceful deed.
For this, in banquets, when the generous bowls
Restore our blood, and raise the warriors' souls,
Though all the rest with stated rules be bound,
Unmixed, unmeasured, are thy goblets crowned.' "

Seward. That is Pope. Do you remember Homer himself, sir?

North. I do.

Ἰδομενεῦ, πέρι μέν σε τίω Δαναῶν ταχυπώλων,
ἠμὲν ἐνὶ πτολέμῳ ἠδ' ἄλλο ῳ ἐπὶ ἔργῳ,
ἠδ' ἐν δα θ', ὅτε πέρ τε γερούσιον αἴθοπα οἶνον
Ἀργείων οἱ ἄριστοι ἐνὶ κρητῆρσι κέρωνται.
εἴπερ γάρ τ' ἄλλοι γε καρη ομοωντες Ἀχαιοὶ
δαιτρον πίνωσιν, σὸν δὲ πλεῖον δέπας αἰεὶ
ἕστηχ' ὥσπερ ἐμοὶ, πιέειν, ὅτε θυμὸς ἀνώγοι,
ἀλλ' ὄρσευ πολεμόνδ', οἷος πάρος ευχεο εἶναι.

I believe you will find that in general men praise more truly, that is justly, deservedly, than they condemn. They praise from an impulse of love—that is, from a capacity. Nature protects love more than hate. Their condemnation is often mere incapacity—want of insight. Mr. Alison had elegance of apprehension—truth of taste—a fine sense of the beautiful—a sense of the sublime. His instances for praise are always well—often newly chosen, from an attraction felt in his own genial and noble breast. The true chord struck then. But he was somewhat too dainty-schooled—school-nursed and school-born.

A Judge and critic of Poetry should have been caught wild, and tamed; he should carry about him to the last some relish of the wood and the wilderness, as if he were ever in some danger of breaking away, and relapsing to them. He should know Poetry as a great power of the Universe—a sun—of which the Song—whosesoever—only catches and fixes a few rays. How different in thought was Epos to him and to Homer! Homer paints Manners—archaic, simple manners. Everybody feels—everybody says this—Mr. Alison must have known it—and could have said it as well as the best—

Seward. But the best often forget it. They seem to hold to this knowledge better now, Mr. North; and they do not make Homer answerable as a Poet, for the facts of which he is the historian—Why not rather accept than criticize?

North. I am sorry, Seward, for the Achæan Chiefs who had to drink δαιτρον—that is all. I had hoped that they had helped themselves.

Seward. Perhaps, sir, the Stint was a custom of only the οινον γερουσιον—a ceremonious Bowl!—and if so, undoubtedly with religious institution. The Feast is not honorary—only the Bowl: for anything that appears, Agamemnon, feasting his Princess, might say, "Now, for the Bowl of Honor"—and Idomeneus alone drinks. Or let the whole Feast be honorific, and the Bowl the sealing, and crowning, and characterizing solemnity. Now the distinction of the Stint, and the Full Bowl, selected for a signal of different honoring, has to me no longer anything irksome. It is no longer a grudged and scanted cheer—but lawful Assignment of Place.

Talboys. The moment you take it for Ceremonial, sir, you don't know what profound meaning may, or may not be in it. The phrase is very remarkable.

North. When the "Best of the Argives" mix in the Bowl "the honorific dark-glowing wine," or the dark-glowing wine of honor—when, ὅτε—quite a specific and peculiar occasion, and confined to the wine—you would almost think that the Chiefs themselves are the wine-mixers, and not the usual ministrants—which would perhaps express the descent of an antique use from a time and manners of still greater simplicity than those which Homer describes. Or take it merely, that in great solemnities, high persons do the functions proper to Servants. This we do know, that usually a servant, the Ταμιευς, or the οινοχοος, does mix the Bowl. By the way, Talboys, I think you will be not a little amused with old Chapman's translation of the passage.

Talboys. A fiery old Chap was George.

North. It runs thus—

"O Idomen, I ever loved thyself past all the Greeks,
In war, or any work of peace, at table, everywhere;
For when the best of Greeks, besides, mix ever at our cheer
My good old ardent wine with small, and our inferior mates
Drink ever that mixt wine measured too, thou drink'st without those rates
Our old wine *neat;* and ever more thy bowl stands like to mine;
To drink still when and what thou wilt; then rouse that heart of thine;
And whatsoever heretofore thou hast assumed to be,
This day be greater."

Talboys. Well done, Old Buck! This fervor and particularity are admirable. But, methinks, if I caught the words rightly, that George mistakes the meaning of γερουσιον—honorary; he has γερων γεροντος, an *old man*, singing in his ears; but old for wine would be quite a different word.

North. And he makes Agamemnon commend Idomeneus for drinking generously and honestly, whilst the others are afraid of their cups—as Claudius, King of Denmark, might praise one of his strong-headed courtiers, and laugh at Polonius.

Agamemnon does not say that Idomeneus's goblet was *not* mixed—was *neat*—rather we use to think that wine was always mixed—but whether "with small," as old Chapman says, or with water, I don't know—but I fancied water! But perhaps, Seward, the investigation of a Grecian Feast in heroic time, and in Attic, becomes an exigency. Chapman is at least determined—and wisely—to show that he is not afraid of the matter—that he saw nothing in it "altogether inconsistent with the dignity of the speech and the majesty of Epic Poetry."

Seward. Dignity! Majesty! They stand, sir, in the whole together—in the Manners taken collectively by themselves throughout the entire Iliad—and then taken as a part of the total delineation. Apply our modern notions of dignity and majesty to the Homeric Poetry, and we shall get a shock in every other page.

North. The Homeric, heroic manners! Heyne has a Treatise or Excursus—as you know—on the ἀυταρκεια—I think he calls it—of the Homeric Heroes—their waiting on themselves, or their self-sufficiency—where I think that he collects the picture.

Seward. I am ashamed to say I do not know it.

North. No matter. You see how this connects with the scheme of the Poem—in which, prevalent or conspicuous by the amplitude of the space which it occupies, is the individual prowess of heroes in field—conspicuous, too, by its moment in action. This is another and loftier mode of the ἀυταρκεια. The human bosom is a seat or fountain of power. Power goes forth, emanates in all directions, high and low, right and left. The Man is a terrestrial God. He takes counsel with his own heart, and he acts. "He conversed with his own magnanimous spirit"—or as Milton says of Abdiel meeting Satan—"And thus his own undaunted heart explored."

Seward. Yes, Mr. North, the Man is as a terrestrial God;

but—with continual recognition by the Poet and his heroes—as under the celestial Gods. And I apprehend, sir, that this two-fold way of representing man, in himself and towards them, is that which first separates the Homeric from and above all other Poetry, is its proper element of grandeur, in which we never bathe without coming out aggrandized.

North. Seward, you instruct me by——

Seward. Oh, no, sir! You instruct me——

North. We instruct each other. For this the heroes are all Demigods—that is, the son of a God, or Goddess, or the Descendant at a few Generations. Sarpedon is the Son of Jupiter, and his death by Patroclus is perhaps the passage of the whole Iliad that most specially and energetically, and most profoundly and pathetically, makes the Gods intimate to the life and being of men—presents the conduct of divinity and humanity with condescension there, and for elevation here. I do not mean that there is not more pomp of glorification about Achilles, for whom Jupiter comes from Olympus to Ida, and Vulcan forges arms—whose Mother-Goddess is Messenger to and from Jupiter, and into whose lips, when he is faint with toil and want of nourishment—abstaining in his passion of sorrow and vengeance—Minerva, descending, instils Nectar. But I doubt if there be anything so touching—*under this relation*—and so intimately aggrandizing as that other whole place—the hesitation of Jupiter whether he shall VIOLATE FATE, in order to save his own flesh and blood from its decreed stroke—the consolatory device of Juno (in remonstrating and dissuading) that he shall send Apollo to call Death and Sleep—a God-Messenger to God-Ministers—to bear the dead body from the battle-field to his own land and kin for due obsequies. And, lastly, those *drops of blood* which fall from the sky to the earth, as if the heart-tears of the Sire of all the worlds and their inhabitants.

Buller. You are always great, sir, on Homer. But, pray, have you any intention of returning to the αυταρκεια?

North. Ha ! Buller—do you speak? I have not wandered from it. But since you seem to think I have, think of Patroclus lighting a fire under a tripod with his own hands, to boil meat for Achilles' guests—of Achilles himself helping to lay the ransomed body of Hector on the car that was to take it away. This last is honorific and pathetic. Ministrations of all degrees for themselves, in their own affairs, characterize them all. From the least of these to Achilles fighting the River-God—which is an excess—all holds together—is of one meaning—and here, as everywhere, the least, and the familiar, and most homely, attests, vouches, makes evident, probable, and facile to credence, the highest, most uncouth, remote, and difficult otherwise of acceptation. Pitching the speculation lower, plentitude of the most robust, ardent, vigorous life overflows the Iliad—up from the animal to the divine—from the beautiful tall poplar by the river-side, which the wheelwright or wainwright fells. Eating, drinking, sleeping, thrusting through with spears, and hacking the live flesh off the bone—all go together and help one another—and make the "Majesty and Dignity"—or what not—of the Homeric Epos. But I see, Buller, that you are *timeing me*—and I am ashamed to confess that I have exceeded the assigned limit. Gentlemen, I ask all your pardons.

Buller. Timeing you—my dear sir! Look—'tis only my snuff-box—your own gift—with your own haunted Head on the lid—inspired work of Laurence Macdonald.

North. Give it me—why there—there—by your own unhappy awkwardness—it has gone—gone—to the bottom of the deepest part of the Loch!

Buller. I don't care. It *was* my chronometer! The Box is safe.

North. And so is the Chronometer. Here it is—I was laughing at you in my sleeve.

Buller. Another Herman Boaz!—Bless my eyes, there is Kilchurn! It must be—there is no other such huge Castle, surely, at the head of the Loch—and no other such mountains—

North. You promised solemnly, sir, not to say a single word about Loch Awe or its appurtenance, this Evening—so did every mother's son of us at your order—and 'twas well—for we have seen them and felt them all—at times not the less profoundly—as the visionary pomp keeps all the while gliding slowly by—perpetual accompaniment of our discourse, not uninspired, perhaps, by the beauty or the grandeur, as our imagination was among the ideal creations of genius—with the far-off in place and in time—with generations and empires.

> "When dark oblivion swallows cities up,
> And mighty States, characterless, are grated
> To dusty nothing."

Seward. In the declining light I wonder your eyes can see to read print.

North. My eyes are at a loss with Small Pica—but veritable Pica I can master, yet, after sunset. Indeed, I am sharpest-sighted by twilight, like a cat or an owl.

Buller. Have you any more annotations on Alison?

North. Many. The flaws are few. I verily believe these are all. To elucidate his Truths—in Taste and in Morals—would require from us Four a far longer Dialogue. Alison's Essays should be reprinted in one Pocket Volume—Wisdom and Goodness are in that family hereditary—the editing would be a work of Love—and in Bohn's Standard Library they would confer benefit on thousands who now know but their name.

Seward. My dear sir, last time we voyaged the Loch, you

said a few words—perhaps you may remember it—about those philosophers—Alison—the "Man of Taste," as Thomas Campbell loved to call him—assuredly is not of the number—who have insisted on the natural Beauty of Virtue, and natural Deformity of Vice, and have appeared to place our capacity of distinguishing Right from Wrong chiefly, if not solely, on the sense of this Beauty and of this Deformity—

North. I remember saying, my dear Seward, that they have drawn their views too much from the consideration of the state of these feelings in men who had been long exercised in the pure speculative contemplation of moral Goodness and Truth, as well as in the calmness and purity of a tranquil, virtuous life. Was it so?

Seward. It was.

North. In such minds, when all the calm faculties of the soul are wedded in happy union to the image of Virtue, there is, I have no doubt, that habitual feeling for which the term Beauty furnishes a natural and just expression. But I apprehend that this is not the true expression of that serious and solemn feeling which accompanies the understanding of the qualities of Moral Action in the minds of the generality of men. They who in the midst of their own unhappy perversions, are visited with knowledge of those immutable distinctions, and they who in the ordinary struggles and trials incident to our condition, maintain their conduct in unison with their strongly grounded principles and better aspirations, would seldom, I apprehend, employ this language for the description of feelings which can hardly be separated from the ideas of an awful responsibility involving the happiness and misery of the accountable subjects of a moral order of Government.

Seward. You think, sir, that to assign this perception of Beauty and Deformity, as the groundwork of our Moral Nature, is to rest on too slight a foundatioa that part of man's constitution which is first in importance to his welfare?

North. Assuredly, my dear friend, I do. Nay, I do not fear to say that the Emotion, which may properly be termed a Feeling of Beauty in Virtue, takes place at those times when the deepest affection of our souls towards Good and Evil acts less strongly, and when the Emotion we feel is derived more from Imagination—and—

Seward. And may I venture to suggest, sir, that as Imagination, which is so strong a principle in our minds, will take its temper from any prevalent feelings, and even from any fixed and permanent habits of mind, so our Feeling of Beauty and Deformity shall be different to different men, either according to the predominant strength of natural principles, or according to their course of life?

North. Even so. And therefore this general disposition of Imagination to receive its character will apply, no doubt, where the prevailing feelings and habits are of a Moral cast; and hence in minds engaged in calm intellectual speculation, and maintaining their own moral nature rather in innocence and simplicity of life than in the midst of difficult and trying situations and in conflict with passions, there can be no doubt that the Imagination will give itself up to this general Moral Cast of Mind, and feel Beauty and Deformity vividly and uniformly in the contemplation of the moral quality of actions and moral states of character.

Seward. But your words imply—do they not, sir?—that such is the temper of their calmer minds, and not the emotion which is known when, from any great act of Virtue, or Crime, which comes suddenly upon them, their Moral Spirit rises up in its native strength, to declare its own Affection and its own Judgment?

North. Just so. Besides, my excellent friend, if you consider well the feeling which takes possession of us, on contemplating some splendid act of heroic and self-devoting Virtue, we shall find that the sort of enthusiastic transport which may kindle towards him who has performed it, is not perfectly a moral transport at all; but it is a burst of love and admiration. Take out, then, from any such emotion, what Imagination, and Love, and Sympathy have supplied, and leave only what the Moral Spirit recognizes of Moral Will in the act, and you will find that much of that dazzling and splendid Beauty which produced the transport of loving admiration is removed.

Seward. And if so, sir, then must it be very important that we should not deceive ourselves, and rely upon the warmth of emotion we may feel towards generous and heroic actions as evidence of the force of Moral Principle in our own breasts, which requires to be ascertained by a very different test—

North. Ay, Seward; and it is important, also, that we should learn to acknowledge and to respect, in those who, without the capacity of such vivid feelings, are yet conscientiously faithful to the known Moral Law, the merit and dignity of their Moral Obedience. We must allow to Virtue, my dearest Seward, all that is her due—her countenance beautiful in its sweet serenity—her voice gentle and mild—her demeanor graceful—and a simple majesty in the flowing folds of her stainless raiment. So may we picture her to our imagination, and to our hearts. But we must beware of making such abstractions fantastic and visionary, lest we come at last to think of emotions of Virtue and Taste as one and the same—a fatal error indeed—and that would rob human life of much of its melancholy grandeur. The beauty of Virtue is but the smile on her celestial countenance—and may be admired—loved—by those who hold but little communion with her inner heart—and it may be overlooked by those who pay to her the most devout worship.

Talboys. Methinks, sir, that the moral emotion, with which we regard actions greatly right or greatly wrong, is no transport; it is an earnest, solemn feeling of a mind knowing there is no peace for living souls, except in their Moral Obedience, and therefore receiving a deep and grateful assurance of the peace of one soul more, in witnessing its adherence to its virtue; and the pain which is suffered from crime is much more allied to sorrow, in contemplating the wilful departure of a spirit from its only possible Good, than to those feelings of repugnance and hate which characterize the temper of our common human emotion towards crimes offering violence and outrage to humanity.

North. I believe that, though darkness lies round and about us seeking to solve such questions, a feeling of deep satisfaction in witnessing the adherence to Moral Rectitude, and of deep pain in witnessing the departure from it, are the necessary results of a moral sensibility; but, taken in their elementary simplicity, they have, I think, a character distinct from those many other emotions which will necessarily blend with them, in the heart of one human being looking upon the actions of another —"because that we have all one human heart."

Talboys. Who can doubt that Religion infuses power and exaltation into the Arts? The bare History teaches this. In Greece, Poetry sang of Gods, and of Heroes, in whose transactions Gods moved. Sculpture moulded forms which were attempted expressions of Divine Attributes. Architecture constructed Temples. *De facto,* the Grecian Arts rose out of Religion. And were not the same Arts, of revived Italy, religious?

Buller. They all require for their foundation and support a great pervading sympathy—some Feeling that holds a whole national breast. This is needed to munificently defraying the Costlier Arts—no base consideration at bottom. For it is *a* life-bond of this life, that is freely dropped, when men freely and generously contribute their means to the honor of Religion. There is a sentiment in opening your purse.

Seward. Yes, Buller—without that sentiment no man can love noble Art. The true, deep, grand support of Genius is the confidence of universal sympathy. Homer sings because Greece listens. Phidias pours out his soul over marble, gold, and ivory, because he knows that at Olympia united Greece will wonder and will worship. Think how Poet is dumb and Sculptor lame, who foreknows that what he *would* sing, what he *would* carve, will neither be felt nor understood.

Buller. The Religion of a people furnishes the sympathy which both *pays and applauds.*

Talboys. And Religion affords to the Artist in Words or Forms the highest Norms of Thought—sublime, beautiful, solemn—withal the sense of Aspiration—possibly of Inspiration.

North. And it guards Philosophy—and preserves it, by spiritual influence, from degradation worse than death. The mind is first excited into activity through the impressions made by external objects on the senses. The French metaphysicians —pretending to follow Locke—proceeded to discover in the mind a mere compound of Sensations, and of Ideas drawn from Sensations. Sensations, and Ideas that were the Relics of Sensations—nothing more.

Talboys. And thus, sir, by degrees, the Mind appeared to them to be nothing else than a product of the body—say rather a state of the body.

North. A self-degradation, my friend, which to the utmost removes the mind from God. And this Creed was welcome to those to whom the belief in Him was irksome. That which we see and touch became to such Philosophers the whole of Reality. Deity—the Relation of the Creation to the Creator

—the hope of a Futurity beyond the grave—vanished from the Belief of Materialists living in, and by, and to—Sensation.

Seward. And with what a horrid sympathy was the creed welcomed!

North. Ay, Seward, I who lived nearer the time—perhaps better than you can—know the evil. Not in the schools alone, or in the solitude of philosophical thought, the doctrine of an arid speculation circulated, like a thin and unwholesome blood, through the veins of polite literature; not in the schools alone, but in the gorgeous and gay saloons, where the highly-born, the courtly, and the wealthy, winged the lazy hours with light or dissolute pleasures—there the Philosophy which fettered the soul in the pleasing bands of the Senses, which plucked it back from a feared immortality, which opened a gulf of infinite separation between it and its Maker, was cordially entertained—there it pointed the jest and the jibe. Skepticism a study—the zeal of Unbelief! Principles of false thought appeared suddenly and widely as principles of false passion and of false action. Doubts, difficulties, guesses, fine spinnings of the perverse brain, seized upon the temper of the times—became the springs of public and popular movements—engines of political change. The Venerations of Time were changed into Abominations. A Will strong to overthrow—hostile to Order—anarchical—"intended siege and defiance to Heaven." The irreligious Philosophy of the calmer time now bore its fruits. The Century had prepared the explosion that signalized its close—Impiety was the name of the Giant whom these throes of the convulsed earth had borne into the day, and down together went Throne and Altar. But where are we?

Buller. At the river mouth.

North. What! at home.

Buller. See the Tent-Lights—hear the Tent-Music.

North. Your arm, Talboys—till I disembark. Up to the Mount I shall then climb, unassisted but by the Crutch.

DIES BOREALES.

No. IV.

SCENE—*The Pavilion.*

TIME—*One* P. M.

BULLER—SEWARD—TALBOYS—NORTH.

Talboys. Here he is—here he is! I traced him by Crutch-print to the Van—like an old Stag of Ten to his lair by the Slot.

Seward. Thank Heaven! But was this right, my dear sir?

Buller. Your Majesty ought not thus to have secreted yourself from your subjects.

Seward. We feared you had absconded—abdicated—and retired into a Monastery.

Buller. We have all been miserable about you since an early hour in the morning—invisible to mortal eye since yester bed-going gong—regal couch manifestly unslept in—tent after tent scrutinized as narrowly as if for a mouse—Swiss Giantess searched as if by custom-house officers—no Christopher in the Encampment—what can I compare it to—but a Bee-hive that had lost its Queen. The very Drones were in a ferment—the

14*

workers demented—dismal the hum of grief and rage—of national lamentation and civil war.

North. Billy could have told you of my retreat.

Seward. Billy was in a state of distraction—rushed to the Van—and, finding it empty, fainted.

North. Billy saw me in the Van—and I told him to shut the spring smartly—and be mum.

Buller. Villain!

North. Obedience to orders is the sum-total of Duty. Most of the men seem tolerably sober—those whom despair had driven to drink have been sent to sleeping-quarters—the Camp has recovered from its alarm—and is fit for Inspection by the General Commanding the Forces.

Seward. But have you breakfasted, my dear sir?

North. Leave me alone for that. What have you all been about?

Talboys. We three started at Five for Luib, in high glee.

North. What! in face of my prediction? Did I not tell you that in that dull, dingy, dirty, ochre sunset—in that wan moon and those tallow-candle stars—I saw the morning's Deluge.

Buller. But did you not also quote Sir David Brewster? "In the atmosphere in which he lives and breathes, and the phenomena of which he daily sees, and feels, and describes, and measures, the philosopher stands in acknowledged ignorance of the laws which govern it. He has ascertained, indeed, its extent, its weight, and its composition; but though he has mastered the law of heat and moisture, and studied the electric agencies which influence its condition, he cannot predict, or even approximate to a prediction, whether on the morrow the sun shall shine, or the rain fall, or the wind blow, or the lightning descend."

North. And all that is perfectly true. Nevertheless, we

weather-wise and weather-foolish people—not Philosophers but Empirics—sailors and shepherds—with all our eyes on the lower and the higher heavens—gather up prognostications of the character of the coming time—an hour or a day—take in our canvass and set our storm-jib—or run for some bay where the prudent ship shall ride at anchor, as safe and almost as motionless as if she were in a dry-dock; or off to the far hill-side to look after the silly sheep—yet not so silly either—for there they are, instinctive of a change, lying secured by that black belt of Scotch-Firs against the tempest brewing over Lockerby or Lochmaben—far from the loun Bilholm Braes!—You Three started at Five o'clock for Luib?

Talboys. I rejoice we did. A close carriage is in all weathers detestable—your vehicle should be open to all skyey influences—with nothing about it that can be set up or let down—otherwise some one or other of the party—on some pretence or other—will be for shutting you all in. And then—Farewell, Thou green Earth—Thou fair Day—and ye Skies! It had apparently been raining for some little time—

North. For six hours, and more heavily, I do think, than I ever heard it rain before in this watery world. Having detected a few drops in the ceiling of my cubiculum, I had slipt away to the Van on the first blash of the business—and from that hour to this have been under the Waterfall—as snug as a Kelpie.

Talboys. In we got—well jammed together—a single gentleman, or even two, would have been blown out—and after some remonstrances with the old Greys, we were off to Luib. Long before we were nearly half-way up the brae behind the Camp, Seward complained that the water was running down his back—but ere we reached the top, that inconvenience and every other was merged. The carriage seemed to be in a sinking state, somewhere about Achlian; and rolling before the rain-storm—horses we saw none—it needed no great power of imagination to fear we were in the Loch. At this juncture we came all at once close upon—and into—an appalling crash, and squash, and splash—a plunging, rushing, groaning, and moaning, and roaring—which for half-a-minute baffled conjecture. The Bridge—you know it, sir—the old Bridge, that Seward was never tired of sketching—going—going—gone; down it went—men, horses, all, at the very parapet, and sent us with a *jaup* in among the Woods.

North. Do you mean to say you were on the Bridge as it sunk?

Talboys. I know nothing about it. How should I? We were in the heart of the Noise—we were in the heart of the Water—we were in the heart of the Wood—we, the vehicle, the horses—the same horses, I believe, that were standing behind the Camp when we mounted—though I had not seen them distinctly since, till I recognized them madly galloping in their traces up and down the foaming banks.

North. Were you all on this side of the river?

Talboys. Ultimately we were—else how could we have got here? You seem incredulous, sir. Mind me—I don't say we were on the Bridge—and went down with it. It is an open question—and in the absence of dispassionate witnesses must be settled by probabilities. Sorry that, though the Driver saved himself, the Vehicle in the mean time should be lost—with all the Rods.

North. They will be recovered on a change of weather. How and when got ye back?

Talboys. On horseback. Buller behind Seward—myself before a man who occasionally wore a look of the Driver. I hope it was he—if it was not—the *Driver* must have been drowned. We had now the wind—that is, the storm—that is, the hurricane, in our faces—and the animals every other minute wheeled about and stood rooted for many minutes to the road, with their tails towards Cladich. My body had fortunately lost all sensation hours before we regained the Camp.

North. Hours! How long did it take you to accomplish the two miles?

Talboys. I did not time it; but we entered the Great Gate of the Camp to the sound of the Breakfast Bagpipes.

Seward. As soon as we had changed ourselves—as you say in Scotland——

Talboys. Let's bother Mr. North no more about it. With exception of the Bridge, 'tis not worth talking of—and we ought to be thankful it was not Night. Then what a delightful feeling of security now, sir, from all intrusion of vagrant visitors from the Dalmally side! By this time communication must be cut off with Edinburgh and Glasgow—*via* Inverary—so the Camp is virtually insulated. In ordinary weather, there is no calling the Camp our own. So far back as yesterday only, 8 English—4 German—3 French—2 Italian—1 Irish, all Male, many mustached—and from those and other countries, nearly an equal number of Female—some mustached too—"but that not much."

North. Impossible indeed it is to enjoy one hour's consciousness of secure solitude, in this most unsedentary age of the world.—Look there. Who the deuce are you, sir? Do you belong to Cloud-land—and have you made an involuntary descent in the deluge? Or are you of the earth earthy? Off, sir,—off to the back premises. Enter the Pavilion at your peril, you Phenomenon. Turn him out, Talboys.

Talboys. Then I must turn out myself. I stepped forth for a moment to the Front——

North. And have in that moment been transmogrified into the Man of the Moon. A false alarm. But methinks you might have been satisfied with the Bridge.

Talboys. It is clearing up, sir—it is clearing up—pails and buckets, barrels and hogsheads, fountains and tanks, are no longer the order of the day. Jupiter Pluvius is descending on Juno with moderated impetuosity—is restricting himself to watering pans and garden engines—there is reason to suspect, from the look of the atmosphere, that the supplies are running short—that in a few hours the glass will be up to Stormy—and hurrah, then, for a week of fine, sunshiny, shadowy, breezy, balmy, angling Weather! Why, it is almost fair now. I do trust that we shall have no more of those dry, dusty, sandy, gravelly days, so unlike Lochawe-side, and natural only in Modern Athens or the Great Desert. Hark! it is clearing up. That is always the way with thorough-bred-rain—desperate spurt or rush at the end—a burst when blown—dead-beat——

Seward. Mr. North, matters are looking serious, sir.

North. I believe there is no real danger.

Seward. The Pole is cracking——

Talboys. Creacking. All the difference in the world between these two words. The insertion of the letter E converts danger into safety—trepidation into confidence—a tent into a Rock.

Buller. I have always forgot to ask if the Camp is insured?

North. An insurance was effected, on favorable terms, on the Swiss Giantess before she came into my possession—the Trustees are answerable for the Van—the texture of the Tents is tough to resist the Winds—and the stuff itself was re-steeped during winter in pyroligneous acid of my own invention, which has been found as successful with canvass as with timber. Deeside, the Pavilion and her fair Sisterhood are impervious alike to Wet and Dry Rot—Fire and Water.

Talboys. You can have no idea, sir, of the beautiful running of our drains. When were they dug?

North. Yestreen—at dusk. Not a field in Scotland the worse of being drained—my lease from Monzie allows it—a good landlord deserves a good tenant; and though it is rather late in the year for such operations, I ventured on the experiment—partly for sake of the field itself, and partly for sake of self-preservation. Not pioneers, and miners, and sappers alone—the whole Force were employed under the Knave of Spades—open drains meanwhile—to be all covered in—with tiles—ere we shift quarters.

Talboys. A continuance of this weather for a day or two will bring them up in shoals from the Lock—Undoubtedly we shall have Eels. I delight in drain-angling. Silver Eels! Gold fish! You shall be wheeled out, my dear sir, in Swing, and the hand of your own Talboys shall disengage the first "Fish without Fins" from the Wizard's Hook.

Seward. And he shall be sketched by his own Seward, in a moment of triumph, and lithographed by Schenck for the forthcoming Edition of Tom Stoddart.

Buller. And his own Buller shall make the chips fly like Michael Angelo—and from the marble block evolve a Christopher Piscator not unworthy a Steele—or a Macdonald.

North. Lay aside your tackle, Talboys, and let us talk.

Talboys. I am never so talkative as over my tackle.

Buller. Lay it aside, then, Talboys, at Mr. North's request.

Talboys. Would, my dear Sir, you had been with me on Thursday, to witness the exploits of this GRIESLY PALMER. Miles up Glensrae, you come—suddenly on the left—in a little glen of its own—on such a jewel of a Waterfall. Not ten feet fall—in the pleasure-grounds of a lowland mansion 'twould be called a Cascade. But soft as its voice is, there is something in it that speaks the Cataract. You discern the Gaelic gurgle—and feel that the Fountain is high up in some spot of greensward among heather-hills. Snow-white it is not—almost as translucent as the pool into which it glides. You see through it the green ledge it slides over with a gentle touch—and seeking its own way, for a few moments, among some mossy cones, it slips, without being wearied, into its place of rest, which it disturbs not beyond a dimple that beautifies the quivering reflection of the sky. A few birch-trees—one much taller than the rest—are all the trees that are there—but that sweetest of all scents assures you of the hawthorn—and old as the hills—stunted in size—but full-leaved and budded as if in their prime—a few hawthorns close by among the clefts. But why prattle thus to you, my dear sir?—no doubt you know it well—for what beautiful secret in the Highlands is unknown to Christopher North?

North. I do know it well; and your description—so much better than I could have drawn—has brought it from the dimmer regions of memory, "into the study of imagination."

Talboys. After a few circling sweeps to show myself my command of my gear, and to give the Naiad warning to take care of her nose, I let drop this GRIESLY PALMER, who alighted as if he had wings. A Grilse! I cried—a Grilse! No a Sea-trout—an amber Witch—a White Lady—a Daughter of Pearl—whom with gentle violence and quick dispatch I solicited to the yellow sands—and folding not my arms, as is usual in works of fiction, slightly round her waist—but both hands, with all their ten fingers, grasping her neck and shoulders to put the fair creature out of pain—in with her—in with her into my Creel—and again to business. It is on the First Victim of the Day, especially if, as in this case, a Bouncer, an angler fondly dwells in reminiscence—each successive captive—however engrossing the capture—loses its distinct individuality in the fast accumulating crowd; and when, at close of day, sitting down among the broom, to empty and to count, it is on the First Victim that the angler's eye reposes—in refilling, it is the first victim you lay aside to crown the treasure—in wending homewards it is on the First Victim's biography you muse; and at home—in the Pavilion—it is the First Victim you submit to the critical ken of Christopher——

Buller. Especially if, as in this case, she be a Bouncer.

North. You pride yourself on your recitation of poetry, Talboys. Charm us with the finest descriptive passage you can remember from the British Poets. Not too loud—not too loud—this is not Exeter Hall—nor are you about to address the Water-witch from the top of Ben-Lomond.

Talboys.

"But thou, Clitumnus! in thy sweetest wave
Of the most living crystal that was e'er
The haunt of river nymph, to gaze and lave
Her limbs where nothing hid them, thou dost rear
Thy grassy banks, whereon the milk-white steer
Grazes; the purest god of gentle waters!
And most serene of aspect, and most clear;
Surely that stream was unprofaned by slaughters—
A mirror and a bath for Beauty's youngest daughters!

"And on thy happy shore a Temple still,
Of small and delicate proportion, keeps,
Upon a mild declivity of hill,
Its memory of thee; beneath it sweeps
Thy current's calmness: oft from out it leaps
The finny darter with the glittering scales,
Who dwells and revels in thy glassy deeps;
While, chance, some scattered water-lily sails
Down where the shallower wave still tells its bubbling tales.

"Pass not unblest the genius of the place!
If through the air a zephyr more serene
Win to the brow, 'tis his; and if ye trace
Along his margin a more eloquent green,
If on the heart the freshness of the scene

Sprinkle its coolness, and from the dry dust
Of weary life a moment lave it clean
With Nature's baptism—'tis to him ye must
Pay orisons for this suspension of disgust."

North. Admirably said and sung. Your low tones, Talboys, are earnest and impressive; and you recite, like all true lovers of song, in the spirit of soliloquy, as if you were yourself the sole listener. How I hate Spouting. Your elocutionist makes his mouth a *jet d'eau*—and by his gestures calls on all the auditors to behold the performance. From the lips of the man who has music in his soul, the words of inspiration flow as from a natural fountain, for his soul has made them its own—and delights to feel in their beauty an adequate expression of its own emotions.

Talboys. I spoke them to myself—but I was still aware of *your* presence, my dear sir.

North. The Stanzas are fine—but are they the finest in Descriptive Poetry?

Talboys. I do not say so, sir. Any request of yours I interpret liberally, and accede to at once. Finer stanzas there may be—many; but I took them because they first came to heart. "Beautiful exceedingly" they are—they may not be faultless.

North. Sir Walter has said—"Perhaps there are no verses in our language of happier descriptive power than the two stanzas which characterize the Clitumnus."

Talboys. Then I am right.

North. Perhaps you are. Scott loved Byron—and it is ennobling to hear one great Poet praising another: yet the stanzas which so delighted our Minstrel may not be so felicitous as they seemed to be to his moved imagination.

Talboys. Possibly not.

North. In the First Stanza what do we find? An apostrophe—"Thou, Clitumnus," not yet quite an Impersonation—a few lines on, an Impersonation of the Stream—

> "——the purest God of gentlest waters!
> And most serene of aspect, and most clear."

What is gained by this Impersonation? Nothing. For the qualities here attributed to the River-God are the very same that had already been attributed to the water—purity—serenity—clearness. "Sweetest wave of the most living crystal"—affects us just as much—here I think more than the two lines about the God. And observe, that no sooner is the God introduced than he disappears. His coming and his going are alike unsatisfactory—for his coming gives us no new emotion, and his going is instantly followed by lines that have no relation to his Godship at all.

Talboys. Why—why—I really don't know.

North. I have mildly—and inoffensively to all the world—that is, to all us Four—shown one imperfection; and I think—I feel there is another—in this Stanza. "The sweetest wave of the most living crystal" is visioned to us in the opening lines as the haunt "of river nymph, to gaze and lave her limbs where nothing hid them,"—and we are pleased; it is visioned to us, in the concluding line, as "the mirror and the bath for Beauty's youngest daughters"—and we are not pleased; or if we are, but for a moment—for it is, as nearly as may be, the same vision over again—a mirror and a bath!

Talboys. But then, sir—

North. Well?

Talboys. Go on, sir.

North. I am not sure that I understand "Beauty's youngest daughters."

Talboys. Why, small maidens from ten to twelve years old,

who in their innocent beauty may bathe without danger, and in their innocent self-admiration may gaze without fear.

North. Then is the expression at once commonplace and obscure.

Talboys. Don't say so, sir.

North. Think you Byron means the Graces?

Talboys. He does—he does—the Graces sure enough—the Graces.

North. Whatever it means—it means no more than we had before. A descriptive Stanza should ever be progressive, and at the close complete. To my feeling, "slaughters" had better been kept far away from the imagination as from the eyes. I know Byron alludes here to the Sanguinetto of the preceding Stanza. But he ought not to have alluded to it—the contrast was complete without such reference—between the river we are delighting in and the blood-named torrent that has passed away. Why, then, force such an image back upon us—when of ourselves we should never have thought of it, and it is the last image we should desire to see?

Talboys. Allow me a few minutes to consider—

North. A day. Will you be so good, Talboys, as tell me in ten words the meaning of—in the next Stanza—"keeps its memory of Thee?"

Talboys. I will immediately.

North. To my mind—angler as I am—

Talboys. The Prince of Anglers.

North. To my mind, two lines and a half about Fishes are here too much—"finny darter" seems conceited—and "dwells and *revels*" needlessly strong—and the *frequent rising* of "finny darters with the glittering scales" to me seems hardly consistent with the solemn serenity inspired by the Temple "of small and delicate proportion" "keeping its memory of Thee,"—whatever that may mean;—nor do I think that a poetical mind like

Byron's, if fully possessed in ideal contemplation with the beauty of the whole, would have thought so much of such an occurrence, or dwelt upon it with so many words.

Talboys. I wish that finny darters with the glittering scales had oft leaped from out thy current's calmness, Thou Glenorchy, yesterday—but not a fin could I stir with finest tackle and Double-Nothings.

North. That is no answer, either one way or another, to my gentle demur to the perfection of the stanzas. The "scattered water-lily" may be well enough—so let it pass—with this ob, that the flower of the water-lily is not easily separated from its stalk—and is not, in that state, eligible as an image of peace.

Talboys. It is of beauty.

North. Be it so. But is "scattered" the right word? No. A water-lily to be *scattered* must be *torn*—for you scatter many, not one—a fleet, not a ship—a flock of sheep, not one lamb. A solitary water-lily—broken off and drifting by, has, as you said, its own beauty—and Byron doubtlessly intended that—but he has not said it—he has said the reverse—for a "scattered" water-lily is a dishevelled water-lily—a water-lily no more—a dispersed or dispersing multitude of leaves—of what had been a moment before—a Flower.

Talboys. The image pleases every body—take it as you find it, and be content.

North. I take it as I find it, and am not content; I take it as I don't find it, and am. Then I gently demur to "still tells its bubbling tales." In Gray's line—

"And pore upon the brook that babbles by,"

the word "babbles" is the right one—a mitigated "brawling" —a continuous murmur without meaning, till you give it one or many—like that of some ceaseless female human being, pleasantly accompanying your reveries that have no relation to what you hear. Her blameless babble has that effect—and were it to stop, you would awake. But Byron's "shallower wave still tells its *bubbling tales*"—a tale is still about something—however small—and pray what is that something? Nothing. "Tales," then, is not the *very* word here—nor will "bubbling" make it so—at best it is a prettyism rather than Poetry. The Poet is becoming a Poetaster.

Talboys. I shall never recite another finest descriptive passage from the whole range of our British Poets—during the course of my life—in this Pavilion.

North. Let us look at the Temple.

Talboys. Be done, I beseech you, sir.

North. Talboys, you have as logical—as legal a head as any man I know.

Talboys. What has a logical or legal head to do with Byron's description of the Clitumnus?

North. As much as with any other "Process." And you know it. But you are in a most contradictory—I had almost said captious mood, this forenoon—and will not imbibe genially—

Talboys. Imbibe genially—acids—after having imbibed in the body immeasurable rain.

North. Let us look at the Temple. "A Temple still" might mean a still temple.

Talboys. But it doesn't.

North. A Poet's meaning should never, through awkwardness, be ambiguous. But no more of that. "Keeps its Memory of Thee" suggests to my mind that the Temple, dedicated of old to the River-God, retains, under the new religion of the land, evidence of the old Deification and Worship. The Temple survives to express to us of another day and faith, a Deification and worship of Thee—Clitumnus—dictated by the same apprehension of thy characteristic Beauty in the hearts of those old worshippers that now possesses ours looking on Thee. Thou art unchanged—the sensitive and imaginative intelligence of Thee in man is unchanged—although times have changed—states, nations—and, to the eyes of man, the heavens themselves! If all this be meant—all this is not said—in the words you admire.

Talboys. I cannot say, as an honest man, that I distinctly understand you, my dear sir.

North. You understand me better than you understand Byron.

Talboys. I understand neither of you.

North. The poetical thought seems to be here—that the Temple rises up spontaneously on the bank—under the power of the Beautiful in the river—a permanent self-sprung reflection of *that* Beautiful—as indeed, to imagination, all things appear to create themselves!

Talboys. You speak like yourself now, sir.

North. But look here, my good Talboys. The statue of Achilles may "keep its memory"—granting the locution to be good, which it is not—of Achilles—for Achilles is no more. Sink—in a rapture of thought—the hand of the artist—think that the statues of Achilles *came of themselves*—as unsown flowers come—for poets to express to all ages the departed Achilles. They keep—as long as they remain unperished—"their memory of Achilles"—they were from the beginning voluntary and intentional conservators of the Memory of the Hero. But *Clitumnus is here*—alive to this hour, and with every prospect of outliving his own Temple. What do you say to that?

Talboys. To what?

North. Finally—if that reminiscence of the Heathen Deification, which I first proposed, was in Byron's mind—and he means by "still keeps its memory of Thee" memory of the

River-God—and of the Worship of the River-God—then all he says about the mere natural river—its leaping fishes, and so forth, is wide of his own purpose—and what is worse—implies an absurdity—a reminiscence—not of the past—but of the present.

Talboys. If all that were submitted to me for the Pursuer, in Printed Papers—I should appoint answers to be given in by the Defender—within seven days—and within seven days after that—give judgment.

North. Keep your temper, Mr. Testy. As I have no wish to sour you for the rest of the day, I shall say little about the Third Stanza. "Pass not unblest the Genius of the Place," would to me be a more impressive prayer, if there were more *spirituality* in the preceding stanzas—and in the lines which follow it; for the Genius of the Place has been acting, and continues to act, almost solely on the Senses. And who is the Genius of the Place! The River-God—he to whom the Gentile worship built that Temple. But Byron says, most unpoetically, "along his margin"—along the margin of the Genius of the Place! Then, how flat—how poor—after "the Genius of the Place"—"*the freshness of the Scene*"—for the freshness of *the Scene* bless the genius of *the Place!* Is that language flowing from the emotion of a Poet's heart? And the last line spoils all; for he whom we are to bless—the River-God—or the Genius of the Place—has given the heart but a "moment's" cleanness from dry dust—but a moment's, and no more! And never did hard, coarse Misanthropy so mar a Poet's purpose as by the shocking prose that is left grating on our souls—"*suspension of disgust!*" So, after all this beauty—and all this enjoyment of beauty—well or ill painted by the Poet—you *must pay orisons* to the River-God or the Genius—whom you had been called on to *bless*—for a mere momentary suspension of disgust to all our fellow-creatures—a disgust that would return as strong—or stronger than ever—as soon as you got to Rome.

Talboys. I confess I don't like it.

North. "MUST!" There are NEEDS of all sorts, shapes, and sizes. There is terrible necessity—there is bitter necessity—there is grinding necessity—there is fine—delicate—loving—playful necessity.

Talboys. Sir?

North. There are MUSTS that fly upon the wings of devils—Musts that fly upon the wings of angels—Musts that walk upon the feet of men—Musts that flutter upon the wings of Fairies—But I am dreaming!—Say on.

Talboys. I think the day's clearing—let us launch Gutta Percha, Buller, and troll for a Ferox.

North. Then fling that Tarpaulin over your Feather-Jacket, on which you plume yourself, and don't forget your Gig-Parasol, Longfellow—for the rain-gauge is running over, so are the water-butts, and I hear the Loch surging its way up to the Camp. The Cladich Cataract is a stunner. Sit down, my dear Talboys. Recite away.

Talboys. No.

North. Gentlemen, I call on Mister Buller.

Buller.

"The roar of waters!—from the headlong height
Velino cleaves the way-worn precipice;
The fall of waters! rapid as the light
The flashing mass foams shaking the abyss;
The hell of waters! where they howl and hiss,
And boil in endless torture; while the sweat
Of their great agony, wrung out from this
Their Phlegethon, curls round the rocks of jet
That gird the gulf around, in pitiless horror set,

"And mounts in spray the skies, and thence again
Returns in an unceasing shower, which round,

With its unemptied cloud of gentle rain
Is an eternal April to the ground,
Making it all one emerald! how profound
The gulf! and how the giant element
From rock to rock leaps with delirious bound
Crushing the cliffs, which, downward worn and rent
With his fierce footsteps, yield in chasms a fearful vent

"To the broad column which rolls on, and shows
More like the fountain of an infant sea
Torn from the womb of mountains by the throes
Of a new world, than only thus to be
Parent of rivers, which flow gushingly
With many windings, through the vale;—Look back;
Lo! where it comes like an eternity,
As if to sweep down all things in its track,
Charming the eye with dread—a matchless cataract,

"Horribly beautiful! but on the verge,
From side to side, beneath the glittering morn,
An Iris sits, amidst the infernal surge,
Like Hope upon a death-bed, and unworn
Its steady dyes, while all around is torn
By the distracted waters, hears serene
Its brilliant hues with all their beams unshorn;
Resembling, 'mid the torture of the scene,
Love watching Madness with unalterable mien."

North. In the First Stanza there is a very peculiar and a very striking form—or construction—The Roar of Waters—The Fall of Waters—The Hell of Waters.

Buller. You admire it.

North. I do.

Talboys. Don't believe him, Buller. Let's be off—there is no rain worth mentioning—see—there's a Fly. Oh! 'tis but a Red Professor dangling from my bonnet—a Red Professor with tinsy and a tail. Come, Seward, here's the Chess-Board. Let us make out the Main.

North. The four lines about the Roar and the Fall are good——

Talboys. Indeed, sir.

North. Mind your game, sir. Seward, you may give him a Pawn. The next four—about Hell—are bad.

Talboys. Indeed, sir.

North. Seward, you may likewise give him a Knight. As bad as can be. For there is an incredible confusion of tormented and tormentor. They howl, and hiss, and boil in endless torture—they are suffering the Pains of Hell—they are in Hell. "But the sweat of their great agony is wrung out from this their Phlegethon." Where is this their Phlegethon? Why, this their Phlegethon is—themselves! Look down—there is no other river—but the Velino.

Buller. Hear Virgil—

> "Mœnia lata videt, triplici circumdata muro,
> Quæ rapidus flammis ambit torrentibus amnis
> Tartareus Phlegethon, torquetque sonantia saxa."

No Phlegethon with torrents of fire surrounding and shaking Byron's Hell. I do not understand it—an unaccountable blunder.

North. In next stanza, what is gained by

> "How profound
> The gulf! and how the giant element
> From rock to rock leaps with delirious bound!"

Nothing. In the First Stanza, we had the "abyss," "the gulf," and the agony—all and more than we have here.

Seward. Check-mate.

Talboys. Confound the board!—no, not the board—but Hurwitz himself could not play in such an infernal clatter.

North. Buller has not got to the word "infernal" yet, Phillidor—but he will by-and-by. "Crushing the Cliffs"—

crushing is not the right word—it is the wrong one—for not such is the process—visible or invisible. "*Downward* worn" is silly. "Fierce footsteps," to my imagination, is tame and out of place—though it may not be to yours;—and I thunder in the ears of the Chess-players that the first half of the next stanza—the third—is as bad writing as is to be found in Byron.

Talboys. Or in North.

North. Seward—you may give him likewise a Bishop—

> "Look back:
> Lo! where it comes like an Eternity."

I do not say that is not sublime. If it is an image of Eternity—sublime it must be—but the Poet has chosen his time badly for inspiring us with that thought—for we look back on what he had pictured to us as falling into hell—and then flowing diffused "only thus to be parents of rivers that flow gushingly with many windings through the vale"—images of Time.

> "As if to sweep down all things in its track,"

is well enough for an ordinary cataract, but not for a cataract that comes "like an Eternity."

Talboys.

> "Charming the eye with dread—a matchless cataract,
> Horribly beautiful."

Seward. One game each.

Talboys. Let us go to the Swiss Giantess to play out the Main.

North. In Stanza Fourth—"But *on the verge,*" is very like nonsense—

Talboys. Not at all.

North. The Swiss Giantess is expecting you—good-by,

my dear Talboys. Now, Buller, I wish you, seriously and calmly, to think on this image—

> "An Iris sits, amidst the infernal surge,
> Like Hope upon a death-bed."

Did Hope—could Hope ever sit by *such* a death-bed! The infernal surge—the hell of waters—the howling—the hissing—the boiling in endless torture—the sweat of the great agony wrung out—and more of the same sort—*these image the death-bed.* Hope has sat beside many a sad—many a miserable death-bed—but not by such as this; and yet, here, such a death-bed is hinted at as not uncommon—in a few words—"like Hope upon a death-bed." The smile came not of itself—it was sought for—and had far better have been away. There is much bad writing here, too—"unworn"—"unshorn"—"torn"—"dyes"—"hues"—"beams"—"torture *of the scene*"—epithet heaped on epithet, without any clear perception or sincere emotion—the Iris changing from Hope upon a death-bed to Love watching Madness—both of which I pronounce, before that portion of mankind assembled in this Tent, to be on the FALSETTO—and wide from the thoughts that visit the suffering souls of the children of men remembering this life's greatest calamities.

Seward. Yet throughout, sir, there is Power.

North. Power! My dear Seward, who denies it? But great Power—true poetical Power—is self-collected—not turbulent though dealing with turbulence—in its own stately passion dominating physical nature in its utmost distraction—and in her blind forces seeing a grandeur—a sublimity that only becomes visible or audible to the senses, through the action of imagination creating its own consistent ideal world out of that turmoil—making the fury of falling waters appeal to our Moral Being, from whose depths and heights rise emotions echoing all the tones of the thundering cataract. In these stanzas of Byron, the main Power is in the Cataract—not in the Poetry—loud to the ear—to the eye flashing and foaming—full of noise and fury, signifying not much to the soul, as it stuns and confounds the senses—while its more spiritual significations are uncertain or unintelligible, accepted with doubt, or rejected without hesitation, because felt to be false and deceitful, and but brilliant mockeries of the Truth.

Talboys. Spare Byron, who is a Poet—and castigate some popular Versifier.

North. I will not spare Byron—and just because he is a Poet. For popular Versifiers, they may pipe at their pleasure, but aloof from our Tents—chirp anywhere but in this Encampment; and if there be a Gowdspink or Yellow-hammer among them, let us incline our ear kindly to his chattering or his yammering, "low doun in the broom," or high up on his apple-tree, in outfield or orchard, and pray that never naughty schoolboy may harry his nest.

Seward. Would Sir Walter's Poetry stand such critical examination?

North. All—or nearly so—directly dealing with War—Fighting in all its branches. Indeed, with any kind of Action he seldom fails—in Reflection, often—and, strange to say, almost as often in description of Nature, though there in his happier hours he excels.

Seward. I was always expecting, during that discussion about the Clitumnus, that you would have brought in Virgil.

North. Ay, Maro—in description—is superior to them all—in the Æneid as well as in the Georgics. But we have no time to speak of his Pictures now—only just let me ask you—Do you remember what Payne Knight says of Æneas?

Seward. No, for I never read it.

North. Payne Knight, in his *Analytical Inquiry into the*

Principles of Taste—a work of high authority in his own day, and containing many truths vigorously expounded, though characterized throughout by arrogance and presumption—speaks of that "selfish coldness with which the Æneas of Virgil treats the unfortunate princess, *whose affections he had seduced,*" and adds, that "Every modern reader of the Æneid finds that the Episode of Dido, though in itself the most exquisite piece of composition existing, weakens extremely the subsequent interest of the Poem, it being impossible to sympathize either cordially or kindly with the fortunes or exertions of a hero who sneaks away from his high-minded and much-injured benefactress in a manner so base and unmanly. When, too, we find him soon after imitating all the atrocities, and surpassing the utmost arrogance, of the furious and vindictive Achilles, without displaying any of his generosity, pride, or energy, he becomes at once mean and odious, and only excites scorn and indignation; especially when, at the conclusion, he presents to Lavinia a hand stained with the blood of her favored lover, whom he had stabbed while begging for quarter, and after being rendered incapable of resistance." Is not this, Seward, much too strong?

Seward. I think, sir, it is not only much too strong, but outrageous; and that we are bound, in justice to Virgil, to have clearly before our mind his own Idea of his Hero.

Talboys. To try that Æneas by the rules of poetry and of morality; and if we find his character such as neither our imagination nor our moral sense will suffer us to regard with favor—to admire either in Hero or Man—then to throw the Æneid aside.

Buller. And take up his Georgics.

Talboys. To love Virgil we need not forget Homer—but to sympathize with Æneas, our imaginations must not be filled with Achilles.

Seward. Troy is dust—the Son of Thetis dead. Let us go with the Fugitives and their Leader.

Talboys. Let us believe from the first that they seek a Destined Seat—under One Man, who knows his mission, and is worthy to fulfil it. Has Virgil so sustained the character of that Man—of that Hero? Or has he, from ineptitude, and unequal to so great a subject—let him sink below our nobler sympathies—nay, unconscious of failure of his purpose, as Payne Knight says, accommodated him to our contempt?

Seward. For seven years he has been that Man—that Hero. One Night's Tale has shown him—as he is—for I presume that Virgil—and not Payne Knight—was his Maker. If that speech was all a lie—and the Son of Anchises, not a gallant and pious Prince, but a hypocrite and a coward—shut the Book or burn it.

Talboys. Much gossip—of which any honest old woman, had she uttered the half of it, would have been ashamed before she had finished her tea—has been scribbled by divers male pens—stupid or spritely—on that magnificent Recital. Æneas, it has been said, by his own account, skulked during the Town Sack—and funked during the Sea Storm. And how, it has been asked, came he to lose Creusa? Pious indeed! A truly pious man, say they, does not speak of his piety—he takes care of his household gods without talking about Lares and Penates. Many critics—some not without name—have been such—unrepentant—old women. Come we to Dido.

North. Be cautious for I fear I have been in fault myself towards Æneas for his part in that transaction.

Talboys. I take the account of it from Virgil. Indeed, I do not know of any scandalous chronicle of Carthage or Tyre. A Trojan Prince and a Tyrian Queen—say at once a Man and a Woman—on sudden temptation and unforeseen opportunity—SIN—and they continue to sin. As pious men as Æneas—

and as kingly and heroic too, have so sinned far worse than that—yet have not been excommunicated from the fellowship of saints, kings, or heroes.

Seward. To say that Æneas "seduces Dido," in the sense that Payne Knight uses the word, is a calumnious vulgarism.

Talboys. And shows a sulky resolution to shut his eyes—and keep them shut.

Seward. Had he said that in the Schools at Oxford, he would have been plucked at his Little-go. But I forget—there was no plucking in those days—and indeed I rather think he was not an University Man.

North. Nevertheless he was a Scholar.

Seward. Not nevertheless, sir—notwithstanding, sir.

North. I sit corrected.

Seward. Neither did Infelix Elissa seduce him—desperately in love as she was—'twas not the storm of her own will that drove her into that fatal cave.

Talboys. Against Venus and Juno combined, alas! for poor Dido at last!

Seward. Æneas was in her eyes what Othello was in Desdemona's. No Desdemona she—no "gentle lady"—nor was Virgil a Shakspeare. Yet those remonstrances—and that raving—and that suicide!

Talboys. Ay, Dan Virgil feared not to put the condemnation of his Hero into those lips of fire—to let her winged curses pursue the Pious Perfidious as he puts to sea. But what is truth—passion—nature from the reproachful and raving—the tender and the truculent—the repentant and the revengeful—the true and the false Dido—for she had forgot and she remembers Sychæus—when cut up into bits of bad law, and framed into an Indictment through which the Junior Jehu at the Scottish Bar might drive a Coach and Six!

Seward. But he forsook her! He did—and in obedience

to the will of heaven. Throughout the whole of his Tale of Troy, at that fatal banquet, he tells her whither, and to what fated region, the fleet is bound—he is not sailing under sealed orders—Dido hears the Hero's destiny from the lips of Mœstissimus Hector, from the lips of Creusa's Shade. But Dido is deaf to all those solemn enunciations—none so deaf as those who will not hear; the Likeness of Ascanius lying by her on her Royal Couch fired her vital blood—and she already is so insane as to dream of lying ere long on that God-like breast. He had forgot—and he remembers his duty—yes—his duty; according to the Creed of his country—of the whole heathen world—in deserting Dido, he obeyed the Gods.

Talboys. He sneaked away! says Knight. Go he must—would it have been more heroic to set fire to the Town, and embark in the General Illumination?

Seward. Would Payne Knight have seriously advised Virgil to marry Æneas, in good earnest, to Dido, and make him King of Carthage?

Buller. Would they have been a happy couple?

Seward. Does not our sympathy go with Æneas to the Shades? Is he unworthy to look on the Campos Lugentes? On the Elysian Fields? To be shown by Anchises the Shades of the predestined Heroes of unexisting Rome?

Talboys. Do we—because of Dido—despise him when first he kens, on a calm bright morning, that great Grove on the Latian shore near the mouth of the Tiber.

> "Æneas, primique duces, et pulcher Iulus,
> Corpora sub ramis deponunt arboris altæ,
> Instituuntque dapes."

Seward. But he was a robber—a pirate—an invader—an usurper—so say the Payne Knights. Virgil sanctifies the Landing with the spirit of peace—and a hundred olive-crowned

Envoys are sent to Laurentum with such peace-offerings as had never been laid at the feet of an Ausonian King.

Talboys. Nothing can exceed in simple grandeur the advent of Æneas—the reception of the Envoys by old Latinus. The right of the Prince to the region he has reached is established by grant human and divine. Surely a father, who is a king, may dispose of his daughter in marriage—and here he must; he knew, from omen, and oracle, the Hour and the Man. Lavinia belonged to Æneas—not to Turnus—though we must not severely blame the fiery Rutulian because he would not give her up. Amata, in and out of her wits, was on his side; but their betrothment—if betrothed they were—was unhallowed—and might not blind in face of Fate.

Buller. Turnus was in the wrong from beginning to end. Virgil, however, has made him a hero—and idiots have said that he eclipses Æneas—the same idiots, who, at the same time, have told us that Virgil could not paint a hero at all.

Talboys. That his genius has no martial fervor. Had the blockheads read the Rising—the Gathering—in the Seventh Æneid?

North. Sir Walter himself had much of it by heart—and I have seen the "repeated air" kindle the aspect, and uplift the Lion-Port of the greatest War-Poet that ever blew the trumpet.

Seward. Æneas at the Court of Evander—that fine old Grecian! There he is a Hero to be loved—and Pallas loved him—and he loved Pallas—and all men with hearts love Virgil for their sakes.

Talboys. And is he not a Hero, when relanding from sea at the mouth of his own Tiber, with his Etrurian Allies—some thousands strong? And does he not then act the Hero? Virgil was no War-Poet! Second only to Homer, I hold—

Seward. An imitator of Homer! With fights of the

Homeric age--how could he help it? But he is, in much, original on the battle-field--and is there in all the Iliad a Lausus, or a Pallas?—

Buller. Or a Camilla?

Seward. Fighting is at the best a sad business—but Payne Knight is offensive on the cruelty—the ferocity of Æneas. I wish Virgil had not made him seize and sacrifice the Eight Young Men to appease the Manes of Pallas. Such sacrifice Virgil believed to be agreeable to the manners of the time—and, if usual to the most worthy, here assuredly due. In the final Great Battle,

> "Away to heaven, respective Lenity,
> And fire-eyed Fury be my conduct now."

Buller. Knight is a ninny on the Single Combat. In all the previous circumstances regarding it, Turnus behaved ill—now that he must fight, he fights well: 'tis as fair a fight as ever was fought in the field of old Epic Poetry; tutelary interposition alternates in favor of either Prince; the bare notion of either outliving defeat never entered any mind but Payne Knight's: nor did any other fingers ever fumble such a charge against the hero of an Epic as "Stabbing while begging for quarter"—but a momentary weakness in Turnus which was not without its effect on Æneas, till at sight of *that Belt,* he sheathed the steel.

Talboys. Payne works himself up, in the conclusion of the passage, into an absolute maniac.

North. Good manners, Talboys—no insult—remember Mr. Knight has been long dead.

Talboys. So has Æneas—so has Virgil.

North. True. Young gentlemen, I have listened with much pleasure to your animated and judicious dialogue. Shall I now give Judgment?

Buller. Lengthy?

North. Not more than an hour.

Buller. Then, if you please, my Lord, to-morrow.

North. You must all three be somewhat fatigued by the exercise of so much critical acumen. So do you, Talboys, and Seward, unbend the bow at another game of Chess; and you, Buller, reanimate the jaded Moral Sentiments by a sharp letter to Marmaduke, insinuating that if he don't return to the Tents within a week, or at least write to say that he and Hal, Volusene and Woodburn, are not going to return at all, but to join the Rajah of Sarawak, the Grand Lama, or Prester John—which I fear is but too probable from the general tone and tenor of their life and conversation for some days before their Secession from the Established Camp—there will be a general breaking of Mothers' hearts, and in his own particular case, a cutting off with a shilling, or disinheriting of the heir apparent of one of the finest Estates in Cornwall. But I forget—these Entails will be the ruin of England. What! Billy, is that you?

Billy. Measter, here's a Fish and a Ferocious.

Talboys. Ha! what Whappers!

Buller. More like Fish before the Flood than after it.

Seward. After it, indeed! During it. What is Billy saying, Mr. North? That Coomerlan' dialect's Hottentot to my Devonshire ears.

North. They have been spoiled by the Doric delicacies of the "Exmoor Courship." He tells me that Archy M'Callum, the Cornwall Clipper, and himself, each in a cow-hide, having ventured down to the River Mouth to look after and bale Gutta Percha, foregathered with an involuntary invasion of divers gigantic Fishes, who had made bad their landing on our shores, and that after a desperate resistance they succeeded in securing the Two Leaders—a Salmo Salar and a Salmo Ferox—see on snout and shoulder tokens of the Oar. Thirty—and

Twenty Pounders—Billy says; I should have thought they were respectively a third more. No mean Windfall. They will tell on the Spread. I retire to my Sanctum for my Siesta.

Talboys. Let me invest you, my dear Sir, with my Feathers.

Buller. Do—do take my Tarpaulin.

Seward. Billy, your Cow-hide.

North. I need none of your gimcracks—for I seek the Sanctum by a subterranean—beg your pardon—a Subter-Awning Passage.

Scene II.—*Deeside.*

Time—*Seven* P. C.

North—Buller—Seward—Talboys.

North. How little time or disposition for anything like serious Thinking, or Reading, out of people's own profession or trade, in this Railway World! The busy-bodies of these rattling times, even in their leisure hours, do not affect an interest in studies their fathers and their grandfathers, in the same rank of life, pursued, even systematically, on many an Evening sacred from the distraction that ceased with the day.

Talboys. Not all busy-bodies, my good sir—think of——

North. I have thought of them—and I know their worth—their liberality and their enlightenment. In all our cities and towns—and villages—and in all orders of the people—there is Mind—Intelligence, and Knowledge; and the more's the shame in that too general appetence for mere amusement in literature, perpetually craving for a change of diet—for something new in the light way—while anything of any substance is "with sputtering noise rejected" as tough to the teeth, and hard of digestion—however sweet and nutritious; would they but taste and try.

Seward. I hope you don't mean to allude to Charles Dickens?

North. Assuredly not. Charles Dickens is a man of original and genial genius—his popularity is a proof of the goodness of the heart of the people; and the love of him and his writings—though not so thoughtful as it might be—does honor to that strength in the English character which is indestructible by any influences, and survives in the midst of frivolity, and folly, and of mental depravations, worse than both.

Seward. Don't look so savage, sir.

North. I am not savage—I am serene. Set the Literature of the day aside altogether—and tell me if you think our conversation since dinner would not have been thought *dull* by many not altogether uneducated persons, who pride themselves not a little on their intellectuality and on their full participation in the Spirit of the Age?

Talboys. Our conversation since dinner DULL!! No—no—no. Many poor creatures, indeed, there are among them—even among those of them who work the Press—pigmies with pap feeding a Giant who sneezes them away when sick of them into small offices in the Customs or Excise;—but not one of our privileged brethren of the Guild—with a true ticket to show—but would have been delighted with such dialogue—but would be delighted with its continuation—and thankful to know that he, "a wiser and a better man, will rise to-morrow morn."

Seward. Do, my dear sir—resume your discoursing about those Greeks.

North. I was about to say, Seward, that those shrewd and just observers, and at the same time delicate thinkers, the ancient Greeks did, as you well know, snatch from amongst the ordinary processes which nature pursues, in respect of inferior animal life, a singularly beautiful Type or Emblem, expressively imaging to Fancy that bursting disclosure of Life from the bosom of Death, which is implied in the extrication of the soul from its corporeal prison, when this astonishing change is highly, ardently, and joyfully contemplated. Those old festal religionists—who carried into the solemnities of their worship the buoyant gladsomeness of their own sprightly and fervid secular life, and contrived to invest even the artful splendor and passionate human interest of their dramatic representations with the name and character of a sacred ceremony—found for that soaring and refulgent escape of a spirit from the dungeon and chains of the flesh, into its native celestial day, a fine and touching similitude in the liberation of a beautiful Insect, the gorgeously-winged aerial Butterfly, from the living tomb in which nature has, during a season, cased and urned its torpid and death-like repose.

Seward. Nor, my dear sir, was this life-conscious penetration or intuition of a keen and kindling intelligence into the dreadful, the desolate, the cloud-covered Future, the casual thought of adventuring Genius, transmitted in some happier verse only, or in some gracious and visible poesy of a fine chisel; but the Symbol and the Thing symbolized were so bound together in the understanding of the nation, that in the Greek language the name borne by the Insect and the name designating the Soul is one and the same—ΨΥΧΗ.

North. Insects! They have come out, by their original egg-birth, into an active life. They have crept and eaten—and slept and eaten—creeping and sleeping, and eating—still waxing in size, and travelling on from fitted pasture to pasture, they have in not many suns reached the utmost of the minute dimensions allotted them—the goal of their slow-footed wanderings, and the term, shall we say—*of their life.*

Seward. No! But of that *first period,* through which they have made some display of themselves as living agents. They have reached *this* term. And look at them—now.

North. Ay—look at them—now. Wonder on wonder! For now a miraculous instinct guides and compels the creature —who has, as it were, completed one life—who has accomplished one stage of his existence—to entomb himself. And he accordingly builds or spins himself a tomb—or he buries himself in his grave. Shall I say, that she herself, his guardian, his directress, Great Nature, *coffins* him? Enclosed in a firm shell—hidden from all eyes—torpid, in a death-like sleep—*not dead*—he waits the appointed hour, which the days and nights bring, and which having come—his renovation, his resuscitation is come. And now the sepulture no longer holds him! Now the prisoner of the tomb has right again to converse with embalmed air and with glittering sunbeams—now, the reptile that *was*—unrecognizably transformed from himself —a glad, bright, mounting creature, unfurls on either side the translucent or the richly-hued pinions that shall waft him at his liking from blossom, to blossom or lift him in a rapture of aimless joyancy to disport and rock himself on the soft-flowing undulating breeze.

Seward. My dearest sir, the Greek in his darkness, or uncertain twilight of belief, has culled and perpetuated his beautiful emblem. Will the Christian look unmoved upon the singular imaging, which, amidst the manifold strangely-charactered secrets of nature, he finds of his own sealed and sure faith?

North. No, Seward. The philosophical Theologian claims in this likeness more than an apt simile, pleasing to the stirred fancy. He sees here an ANALOGY—and this Analogy he proposes as one link in a chain of argumentation, by which he would show that Reason might dare to win from Nature, as a Hope, the truth which it holds from God as revealed knowledge.

Seward. I presume, sir, you allude to Butler's Analogy. I have studied it.

North. I do—to the First Chapter of that Great Work. This parallelism, or apprehended resemblance between an event continually occurring and seen in nature, and one unseen but continually conceived as occurring upon the uttermost brink and edge of nature—this correspondency, which took such fast hold of the Imagination of the Greeks, has, as you know, my dear friends, in these latter days been acknowledged by calm and profound Reason, looking around on every side for evidences or imitations of the Immortality of the Soul.

Buller. Will you be so good, sir, as let me have the volume to study of an evening in my own Tent?

North. Certainly. And for many other evenings—in your own Library at home.

Talboys. Please, sir, to state Butler's argument in your own words and way.

North. For Butler's style is hard and dry. A living being undergoes a vicissitude by which on a sudden he passes from a state in which he has long continued into a new state, and with it into a new scene of existence. The transition is from a narrow confinement into an ample liberty—and this change of circumstances is accompanied in the subject with a large and congruous increment of powers. They believe this who believe the Immortality of the Soul. But the fact is, that changes bearing this description do indeed happen in Nature, under our very eyes, at every moment; this method of progress being universal in her living kingdoms. Such a marvellous change is literally undergone by innumerable kinds, the human animal included, in the instant in which they pass out from the darkness and imprisonment of the womb into the light and open liberty of this breathing world. Birth has been the image of a death, which is itself nothing else than a birth from one straightened life into another ampler and freer. The ordering of Nature, then, is an ordering of Progression, whereby new and enlarged states are attained, and, simultaneously therewith, new and enlarged powers; and all this is not slowly, gradually, and insensibly, but suddenly and *per saltum*.

Talboys. This analogy, then, sir, or whatever there is that is in common to *birth* as we *know* it, and to *death* as we *conceive* it, is to be understood as an evidence set in the ordering of Nature, and justifying or tending to justify such our conception of Death?

North. Exactly so. And you say well, my good Talboys, "justifying or tending to justify." For we are all along fully sensible that a vast difference—a difference prodigious and utterly confounding to the imagination—holds betwixt the case *from* which we reason, *birth*—or that further expansion of life in some breathing kinds which might he held as a *second birth* —betwixt these cases, I say, and the case *to* which we reason, DEATH!

Talboys. Prodigious and utterly confounding to the imagination indeed! For in these physiological instances, either the same body, or a body changing by such slow and insensible degrees that it seems to us to be the same body, accompanies, encloses, and contains the same life—from the first moment in which that life comes under our observation to that in which it vanishes from our cognizance; whereas, sir, in the case to which we apply the Analogy—our own Death—the life is supposed to survive in complete separation from the body, in and by its union with which we have known it and seen it manifested.

North. Excellently well put, my friend. I see you have studied Butler.

Talboys. I have—but not for some years. The Analogy is not a Book to be forgotten.

North. This difference between the case from which we

reason, and the case to which we reason, there is no attempt whatever at concealing—quite the contrary—it stands written, you know, my friend, upon the very Front of the Argument. This difference itself is the very motive and occasion of the Whole Argument! Were there not *this difference* between the cases which furnish the Analogy, and the case to which the Analogy is applied—had we certainly known and seen a Life continued, although suddenly passing out from the body where it had hitherto resided—or were *Death* not the formidable disruption which it is of a hitherto subsisting union—the cases would be identical, and there would be nothing to reason about or to inquire. There *is* this startling difference—and accordingly the Analogy described has been proposed by Butler merely as a first step in the Argument.

Talboys. It remains to be seen, then, whether any further considerations can be proposed which will bring the cases nearer together, and diminish to our minds the difficulty presented by the sudden separation.

North. Just so. What ground, then, my dear young friends—for you seem and are young to me—what ground, my friends, is there for believing that the Death which we see, can affect the living agent which we do not see? Butler makes his approaches cautiously, and his attack manfully—and this is the course of his Argument. I begin with examining my present condition of existence, and find myself to be a being endowed with certain Powers and Capacities—for I act, I enjoy, I suffer.

Talboys. Of this much there can be no doubt; for of all this an unerring consciousness assures me. Therefore, at the outset, I hold this one secure position—that I exist, the possessor of certain powers and capacities.

North. But that I do now before Death exist, endued with certain powers and capacities, affords a presumptive or *primâ facie* probability that I shall after death continue to exist, possessing these powers and capacities—

Buller. How is that, sir?

North. You do well to put that question, my dear Buller —a *primâ facie* probability, unless there be some positive reason to think that death is the "destruction of Me, the living Being, and of these my living Faculties."

Buller. A presumptive or *primâ facie* probability, sir? Why does Butler say so?

North. "Because there is in every case a probability that *all* things will continue as we experience they are, in *all* respects, except those in which we have some reason to think they will be altered."

Buller. You will pardon me, sir, I am sure, for having asked the question.

North. It was not only a proper question, but a necessary one. Butler wisely says—"This is that kind of Presumption or Probability from Analogy, expressed in the very word CONTINUANCE, which seems our only natural reason for believing the course of the world will continue to-morrow, as it has done so far as our experience or knowledge of history can carry us back." I give you, here, the Bishop's very words—and I believe that in them is affirmed a truth that no skepticism can shake.

Talboys. If I mistake not, sir, the Bishop here frankly admits, that were we not fortified against a natural impression, with some better instruction than unreflecting Nature's, the spontaneous disposition of our Mind would undoubtedly be an expectation that in this great catastrophe of our mortal estate, We Ourselves must perish; but he contends—does he not, sir?—that it would be a blind fear, and without rational ground.

North. Yes—that it is an impression of the illusory faculty,

Imagination, and not an inference of Reason. There would arise, he says, "a general confused suspicion, that in the great shock and alteration which we shall undergo by death, We, *i. e.* our living Powers, might be wholly destroyed;"—but he adds solemnly, "there is no particular distinct ground or reason for this apprehension, so far as I can find."

Talboys. Such "general confused suspicion," then, is not justified?

North. Butler holds that any justifying ground of the apprehension that, in the shock of death, I, the living Being, or, which is the same thing, These my powers of acting, enjoying, and suffering, shall be extinguished and cease, must be found either in "the reason of the Thing," itself, or in "the Analogy of Nature." To say that a legitimate ground of attributing to the sensible mortal change a power of extinguishing the inward life is to be found in the Reason of the Thing, is as much as to say, that when considering the essential nature of this great and tremendous, or at least dreaded change, Death, and upon also considering *what* these powers of acting, of enjoying, of suffering, truly *are*, and *in what manner*, absolutely, they subsist in us—there does appear to lie therein demonstration, or evidence, or likelihood, that the change, Death, will swallow up such living Powers—and that We shall no longer *be.*

Talboys. In short, sir, that from considering *what* Death is, and *upon what* these Powers and their exercise depend, there is *reason* to think, that the Powers or their exercise will or *must* cease with Death.

North. The very point. And the Bishop's answer is bold, short, and decisive. We cannot *from* considering what Death is, draw this or any other conclusion, *for we do not know what Death is!* We know only certain effects of Death—the stopping of certain sensible actions—the dissolution of certain sensible parts. We can draw no conclusion, for we do not possess the premises.

Seward. From your Exposition, sir, I feel that the meaning of the First Chapter of the Analogy is dawning into clearer and clearer light.

North. Inconsiderately, my dear sir, we seem indeed to ourselves to know what Death is; but this is from confounding the Thing and its Effects. For we see effects: at first the stoppage of certain sensible actions—afterwards, the dissolution of certain sensible parts. But *what* it is that has happened—*wherefore* the blood no longer flows—the limbs no longer move—*that* we do not see. We do not see it with our eyes—we do not discern it by any inference of our understanding. It is a *fact* that seems to lie shrouded forever from our faculties in awful and impenetrable mystery. That fact—the produce of an instant—which has happened *within, and in the dark*—that fact come to pass in an indivisible point of time—that stern fact—ere the happening of which the Man was alive—an inhabitant of this breathing world—united to ourselves——our Father, Brother, Friend—at least our Fellow Creature—by the happening, *he* is gone—is forever irrecoverably sundered from this world, and from us its inhabitants—IS DEAD—and that which lies outstretched before our saddened eyes is only his mortal remains—a breathless corpse—an inanimate, insensible clod of clay:—Upon that interior *sudden* fact—*sudden*, at last, how slowly and gradually soever prepared—since the utmost attenuation of a thread is a thing totally distinct from its ending, from its becoming no thread at all, and since, up to that moment, there was a possibility that some extraordinary, perhaps physical application might for an hour or a few minutes have rallied life, or might have reawakened consciousness, and eye, and voice——upon that elusive *Essence* and *self* of Death no curious searching of ours has laid, or, it may be well assumed, will ever lay hold. When the organs of sense no longer minister to Perception, or the organs of motion to any change of posture—when the blood stopped in its flow thickens and grows cold—and the fair and stately form, the glory of the Almighty's Hand, the burning shrine of a Spirit that lately rejoiced in feeling, in thought, and in power, lies like a garment done with and thrown away—"a kneaded clod"—ready to lose feature and substance —and to yield back its atoms to the dominion of the blind elements from which they were gathered and compacted—— *What is Death?* And what grounds have we for inferring that an event manifested to us as a phenomenon of the Body, which alone we touch, and hear, and see, has or has not reached into the Mind, which is for us Now just as it always was, a Thing utterly removed and exempt from the cognizance and apprehension of our bodily senses? The Mind, or Spirit, the unknown Substance, in which Feeling, and Thought, and Will, and the Spring of Life were—was united to this corporeal frame; and, being united to it, animated it, poured through it sensibility and motion, glowing and creative life—crimsoned the lips and cheeks—flashed in the eye—and murmured music from the tongue; *now*, the two—Body and Soul—are *disunited* —and we behold one-half the consequence—the Thing of dust relapses to the dust:—we dare to divine the other half of the consequence—the quickening Spark, the sentient Intelligence, the Being gifted with Life, the Image of the Maker, in Man, has reascended, has returned thither whence it came, into the Hand of God.

Seward. If, sir, we were without light from the revealed Word of God, if we were left, by the help of reason, standing upon the brink of Time, dimly guessing, and inquiringly exploring, to find for ourselves the grounds of Hope and Fear, would your description, my dear Master, of that which has happened, seem to our Natural Faculties impossible? Surely not.

North. My dear Seward, we have the means of rendering some answer to that question. The nations of the world have been, more or less, in the condition supposed. Self-left, they have borne the burden of the dread secret, which for them only the grave could resolve; but they never were able to sit at rest in the darkness. Importunate and insuppressible desire, in their bosoms, knocked at the gate of the invisible world, and seemed to hear an answer from beyond. The belief in a long life of ages to follow this fleet dream—imaginary revelations of regions bright or dark—the mansions of bliss or of sorrow—an existence to come, and often of retribution to come—has been the religion of Mankind—here in the rudest elementary shape—here in elaborated systems.

Seward. Ay, sir; methinks the Hell of Virgil—and his Elysian Fields are examples of a high, solemn, and beautiful poetry. But they have a much deeper interest for a man studious, in earnest, of his fellow-men. Since they really express the notions under which men have with serious belief shadowed out for themselves the worlds to which the grave is a portal. The true moral spirit that breathes in his enumeration of the Crimes that are punished, of the Virtues that have earned and found their reward, and some scattered awful warnings—are impressive even to us Christians.

North. Yes, Seward, they are. Hearken to the attestation of the civilized and the barbarous. Universally there is a cry from the human heart, beseeching, as it were, of the Unknown Power which reigns in the Order and in the Mutations of Things, the prolongation of this vanishing breath—the renovation, in undiscovered spheres, of this too brief existence—an appeal from the tyranny of the tomb—a prayer against annihilation. Only at the top of Civilization, sometimes a cold and barren philosophy, degenerate from nature, and bastard to reason, has limited its sullen view to the horizon of this

Earth—has shut out and refused all ulterior, happy, or dreary anticipation.

Seward. You may now, assured of our profound attention—return to Butler—if indeed you have left him——

North. I have and I have not. A few minutes ago I was expounding—in my own words—and for the reason assigned, will continue to do so—his argument. If, not knowing what death is, we are not entitled to argue, from the nature of death, that this change must put an end to Ourselves, and those essential powers in our mind which we are conscious of exerting—just as little can we argue from the nature of these powers, and from their manner of subsisting in us, that they are liable to be affected and impaired, or destroyed by death. For what do we know of these powers, and of the conditions on which we hold them, and of the mind in which they dwell? Just as much as we do of the great change, Death itself—that is to say—NOTHING.

Talboys. We know the powers of our mind solely by their manifestations.

North. But people in general do not think so—and many metaphysicians have written as if they had forgot that it is only from the manifestation that we give name to the Power. We know the fact of Seeing, Hearing, Remembering, Reasoning—the feeling of Beauty—the actual pleasure of Moral Approbation, the pain of Moral Disapprobation—the state—pleasure or pain of loving—the state—pleasure or pain of hating—the fire of anger—the frost of fear—the curiosity to know—the thirst for distinction—the exultation of conscious Power—all these, and a thousand more, we know abundantly: our conscious Life is nothing else but such knowledge endlessly diversified. But the POWERS themselves, which are thus exerted—what *they* are—*how* they subsist in us ready for exertion—of this we know—NOTHING.

Talboys. We know something of the Conditions upon which the exercise of these Powers depends—or by which it is influenced. Thus we know, that for seeing, we must possess that wondrous piece of living mechanism, the eye, in its healthy condition. We know further, that a delicate and complicated system of nerves, which convey the visual impressions from the eye itself to the seeing power, must be healthy and unobstructed. We know that a sound and healthy state of the brain is necessary to these manifestations—that accidents befalling the Brain totally disorder the manifestations of these powers—turning the clear, self-possessed mind into a wild anarchy—a Chaos—that other accidents befalling the same organ suspend all manifestations. We know that sleep stops the use of many powers—and that deep sleep—at least as far as any intimations that reach our waking state go—stops them all. We know that a nerve tied or cut stops the sensation—stops the motory volition which usually travels along it. We know how bodily lassitude—how abstinence—how excess—affects the ability of the mind to exert its powers. In short, the most untutored experience of every one amongst us all shows bodily conditions, upon which the activity of the faculties which are seated in the mind, depends. And within the mind itself we know how one manifestation aids or counteracts another—how Hope invigorates—how Fear disables—how Intrepidity keeps the understanding clear—

North. You are well illustrating Butler, Talboys. Then again we know that *for Seeing,* we must have that wonderful piece of living mechanism perfectly constructed and in good order—that a certain delicate and complicated system of nerves extending from the eye inwards, is appointed to transmit the immediate impressions of light from this exterior organ of sight to the percipient Mind—that these nerves allotted to the function of seeing, must be free from any accidental pressure; knowledge admirable, curious, useful; but when all is done, all investigated, that our eyes, and fingers, and instruments, and thoughts, can reach—*What*, beyond all this marvellous Apparatus of seeing, is *That which sees*—what the percipient *Mind* is—that is a mystery into which no created Being ever had a glimpse. Or what is that immediate connection between the Mind itself, and those delicate corporeal adjustments—whereby certain *tremblings*, or other momentary changes of state in a set of nerves, upon the sudden, turn into Colors—into Sight—INTO THE VISION OF A UNIVERSE.

Seward. Does Butler say all that, sir?

North. In his own dry way perhaps he may. These, my friends, are Wonders into which Reason looks, astonished; or, more properly speaking, into which she looks not, nor, self-knowing, attempts to look. But, reverent and afraid, she repeats that attitude which the Great Poet has ascribed to "brightest cherubim" before the footstool of the Omnipotent Throne, who

"Approach not, but with both wings veil their eyes."

Talboys. For indeed at the next step beyond lies only the mystery of Omnipotence—that mystery which connects the world, open and known to us, to the world withheld and unknown.

North. The same with regard to Pleasure and Pain. *What* enjoys Pleasure or suffers Pain?—all that is, to our clearest, sharpest-sighted science, nothing else but darkness—but black unfathomable night. Therefore, since we know not what Death itself is—and since we know not what this Living Mind is, nor what any of its powers and capacities are—what conclusion, taken in the nature of these unknown subjects, can we possibly be warranted in drawing as to the influence which this unknown change, Death, will exert upon this unknown Being—Mind—and upon its unknown faculties and sensibilities?—None.

Seward. Shall unknown Death destroy this unknown Mind and its unknown capacities? It is just as likely, for anything that Reason can see, that it will set them free to a larger and more powerful existence. And if we have any reason upon other grounds to expect this—then by so much the more likely.

North. We know that this Eye and its apparatus of nerves no longer shall serve for *seeing*—we know that these muscles and their nerves shall no longer serve for *moving*—we know that this marvellous Brain itself no longer shall serve, as we are led to believe that it now serves, for *thinking*—we know that this bounding heart never again shall throb and quicken, with all its leaping pulses, with joy—that pain of this body shall never again *tire* the mind, and that pain of this mind shall never again *tire* this body, once pillowed and covered up in its bed of imperturbable slumber. And there ends our knowledge. But that this Mind, which, united to these muscles and their nerves, sent out vigorous and swift motions through them—which, united to this Brain, compelled this Brain to serve it as the minister of its thinkings upon this Earth and in this mode of its Being—which, united to this Frame, in it, and through it, and from it, felt for Happiness and for Misery—that this Mind, once *disunited* from all these, its instruments and servants, shall therefore perish, or shall therefore forego the endowment of its powers, which it manifested by these its instruments—of that we have no warranty—of that there is no probability.

Talboys. Much rather, sir, might a probability lie quite the other way. For if the structure of this corporeal frame places at the service of the Mind some five or six senses, enabling it, by so many avenues, to communicate with this external world, this very structure shuts up the Mind in those few senses, ties it down to the capacities of exactness and sensibility for which *they* are framed. But we have no reason at all to think that these few modes of sensibility, which we call our external senses, are *all* the modes of sensibility of which our spirits are capable. Much rather we must believe that, if it pleased, or shall ever please, the Creator to open in this Mind, in a new world, new modes of sensation, the susceptibility for these modes is already there for another set of senses. Now we are confined to an eye that sees distinctly at a few paces of distance. We have no reason for thinking that, united with a finer organ of sight, we should not see far more exquisitely; and thus, sir, our notices of the dependence in which the Mind now subsists upon the body do of themselves lead us to infer its own self-subsistency.

North. What we are called upon to do, my friends, is to set Reason against Imagination and against Habit. We have to lift ourselves up above the limited sphere of sensible experience. We have to *believe* that something more *is* than that which we see—than that which we know.

Talboys. Yet, sir, even the facts of Mind, revealed to us living in these bodies, are enough to show us that more is than these bodies—since we feel that WE ARE, and that it is impossible for us to regard these bodies otherwise than as *possessions of ours*—utterly impossible to regard them as Ourselves.

North. We distinguish between the acts of Mind, inwardly exerted—the acts, for instance, of Reason, of Memory, and of Affection—and acts of the Mind communicating through the senses with the external world. But Butler seems to me to go too far when he says, "I confess that in sensation the mind uses the body; but in reflection I have no reason to think that the mind uses the body." But, my dear friends, I, Christopher North, think, on the contrary, that the Mind uses the Brain for a thinking instrument; and that much thought fatigues the Brain, and causes an oppressive flow of the blood to the Brain, and otherwise disorders that organ. And altogether I should be exceedingly sorry to rest the Immortality of the Soul upon so doubtful an assumption as that the Brain is not, in any respect or sort, the Mind's Organ of Thinking. I see no need for so timid a sheltering of the argument. On the contrary, the simple doctrine, to my thought, is this—The Mind, as we know it, is implicated and mixed up with the Body—*throughout*—in all its ordinary actions. This corporeal frame is a system of organs, or Instruments, which the Mind employs in a thousand ways. They are its *instruments*—all of them are—and none of them is itself. What does it matter to me that there is one more organ—the Brain—for one more function—thinking? Unless the Mind were in itself a seeing thing—that is, a thing able to see—it could not use the Eye for seeing; and unless the Mind were a thinking thing, it could not use the Brain for thinking. The most intimate implication of itself with its instruments in the functions which constitute our consciousness, proves nothing in the world to me, against its essential distinctness from them, and against the possibility of its living and acting in separation from them, and when they are dissolved. So far from it, when I see that the body chills with fear, and glows with love, I am ready to call fear a cold, and love a warm passion, and to say that the Mind uses its bodily frame in fearing and in loving. All these things have to do with manifestations of my mind to itself, Now, whilst implicated in this body. Let me lift myself above imagination—or let my imagination soar and carry my reason on its wings—I leave the body to moulder, and I go sentient, volent, intelligent, whithersoever *I* am called.

Talboys. It seems a timidity unworthy of Butler to make the distinction. Such a distinction might be used to invalidate his whole doctrine.

North. It might—if granted—and legitimately. But the

course is plain, and the tenor steadfast. As a child, you think that your finger is a part of yourself, and that you feel with it. Afterwards, you find that it can be cut off without *diminishing you:* and physiologists tell you, and you believe, that it does not feel, but sends up antecedents of feeling to the brain. Am I to stop anywhere? Not in the body. As my finger is no part of Me, no more is my liver, or my stomach, or my heart—*or my brain.* When I have overworked myself, I feel a lassitude, distinctly local, in my brain—*inside of my head*—and therewithal an indolence, inertness, inability of thinking. If reflection—as Butler more than insinuates—hesitatingly says—is independent of my brain and body, whence the lassitude? And how did James Watt get unconquerable headaches with meditating Steam-engines?

Talboys. It is childish, sir, to stagger at degrees, when we have admitted the kind. The Bishop's whole argument is to show, that the thing in us which feels, wills, thinks, is distinct from our body; that I am one thing, and my body another.

North. HAVE WE SOULS? If we have—they can live after the body—cannot perish with it; if we have not—wo betide us all!

Seward. Will you, sir, be pleased to sum up the Argument of the First Chapter of the Analogy?

North. No. Do you. You have heard it—and you understand it.

Seward. I cannot venture on it.

North. Do you, my excellent Talboys—for you know the Book as well as I do myself.

Talboys. That the Order of Nature shows us great and wonderful changes, which the living being undergoes—and arising from beginnings inconceivably low, to higher and higher conditions of consciousness and action;—That hence an exaltation of our Powers by the change Death, would be congruous to the progress—which we have witnessed in other creatures, and have experienced in ourselves;—That the fact, that before Death we possess Powers of acting, and suffering, and enjoying, affords a *primâ facie* probability that, after death, we shall continue to possess them; because it is a constant presumption in Nature, and one upon which we constantly reason and rely, speculatively and practically, that all things will continue as they are, unless a cause appear sufficient for changing them;—But that in Death nothing appears which should suffice to *destroy* the Powers of Action, Enjoyment, and Suffering, in a Living Being;—For that in all we know of Death we know the destruction of parts *instrumental* to the uses of a Living Being;—But that of any destruction reaching, or that we have reason to suppose to reach the Living Being, we know nothing;—That the Unity of Consciousness persuades us that the Being in which Consciousness essentially resides is one and indivisible—by any accident, Death inclusive, indiscerptible;—That the progress of diseases, growing till they kill the mortal body, but leaving the Faculties of the Soul in full force to the last gasp of living breath, is a particular argument, establishing this independence of the Living Being—the Spirit—which is the Man himself—upon the accidents which may befall the perishable Frame.

North. Having seen, then, a Natural Probability that the principle within us, which is the seat and source of Thought and Feeling, and of such Life as can be imparted to the Body, will subsist undestroyed by the changes of the Body—and having recognized the undoubted Power of the Creator—if it pleases Him—indefinitely to prolong the life which He has given—how would you and I, my dear Friends, proceed—from the ground thus gained—and on which—with Butler—we take our stand—to speak farther of reasons for believing in the Immortality of the Soul?

Seward. I feel, sir, that I have already taken more than my own part in this conversation. We should have to inquire, sir, whether in His known attributes, and in the known modes of His government, we could ascertain any causes making it probable that He will thus prolong our existence—and we find many such grounds of confidence.

North. Go on, my dear Seward.

Seward. If you please, sir, be yours the closing words—for the Night.

North. The implanted longing in every human bosom for such permanent existence—the fixed anticipation of it—and the recoil from annihilation—seem to us intimation vouchsafed by the Creator of His designs towards us;—the horror with which Remorse awakened by sin looks beyond the Grave, partakes of the same prophetical inspiration. We see how precisely the lower animals are fitted to the places which they hold upon the earth, with instincts that exactly supply their needs, with no powers that are not here satisfied—while we, as if out of place, only through much difficult experience can adapt ourselves to the physical circumstances into which we are introduced—and thus, in one respect, furnished below our condition, are, on the other hand, by the aspirations of our higher faculties, raised infinitely above it—as if intimating that whilst those creatures *here* fulfil the purpose of their creation, *here* we do not—and, therefore, look onward;—That whilst our other Powers, of which the use is over, decline in the course of nature as Death approaches, our Moral and Intellectual Faculties often go on advancing to the last, as if showing that they were drawing nigh to their proper sphere of action;—That whilst the Laws regulating the Course of Human Affairs visibly proceed from a Ruler who favors Virtue, and who frowns upon Vice, yet that a just retribution does not seem uniformly carried out in the good success of well-doers, and the ill success of evil-doers—so that we are led on by the constitution of our souls to look forward to a world in which that which here looks like Moral Disorder, might be reduced into Order, and the Justice of the Ruler and the consistency of his Laws vindicated;—That in studying the arrangements of this world, we see that in many cases dispositions of Human affairs, which, upon their first aspect, appeared to us evil, being more clearly examined and better known, resulted in good—and thence draw a hope that the stroke which daunts our imagination, as though it were the worst of evils, will prove, when known, a dispensation of bounty—"Death the Gate of Life," opening into a world in which His beneficent hand, if not nearer to us than here, will be more steadily visible—no clouds interposing between the eyes of our soul and their Sun;—That the perplexity which oppresses our Understanding from the sight of this world, in which the Good and Evil seem intermixed and crossing each other, almost vanishes, when we lift up our thoughts to contemplate this mutable scene as a place of Probation and of Discipline, where sorrows and Sufferings are given to school us to Virtue—as the Arena where Virtue strives in the laborious and perilous contest, of which it shall hereafter receive the well-won and glorious crown;—That we draw confidence in the same conclusions, from observing how closely allied and agreeing to each other are the Two Great Truths of Natural Religion, the Belief in God and the Belief in our own Immortality; so that, when we have received the idea of God, as the Great Governor of the Universe, the belief in our own prolonged existence appears to us as a necessary part of that Government; or if, upon the physical arguments, we have admitted the independent conviction of our Immortality, this doctrine appears to us barren and comfortless, until we understand that this continuance of our Being is to bring us into the more untroubled fruition of that Light, which here shines upon us, often through mist and cloud;—That in all these high doctrines we are instructed to rest more securely, as we find the growing harmony of one solemn conviction with another—as we find that all our better and nobler Faculties co-operate with one another—and these predominating principles carry us to these convictions—so that our Understanding then first begins to possess itself in strength and light when the heart has accepted the Moral Law;—But that our Understanding is only fully at ease, and our Moral Nature itself, with all its affections, only fully supported and expanded, when both together have borne us on to the knowledge of Him who is the sole Source of Law—the highest Object of Thought—the Favorer of Virtue—towards whom Love may eternally grow, and still be infinitely less than His due—till we have reached this knowledge, and with it the steadfast hope that the last act of this Life joins us to Him—does not for ever shut us up in the night of Oblivion;—And we have strengthened ourselves in inferences forced upon us by remembering how humankind has consented in these Beliefs, as if they were a part of our Nature—and by remembering further, how, by the force of these Beliefs, human Societies have subsisted and been held together—how Laws have been sanctioned, and how Virtues, Wisdom, and all the good and great works of the Human Spirit, have, under these influences, been produced;—Surely GREAT IS THE POWER of all these concurrent considerations brought from every part of our Nature—from the Material and the Immaterial—from the Intellectual and Moral—from the Individual and the Social—from that which respects our existence on this side of the grave, and that which respects our existence beyond it—from that which looks down upon the Earth, and that which looks up towards Heaven.

DIES BOREALES.

No. V.

CAMP AT CLADICH. SCENE—*The Pavilion.*

TIME—*After breakfast.*

NORTH—TALBOYS—SEWARD—BULLER.

North. I begin to be doubtful of this day. On your visits to us, Talboys, you have been most unfortunate in weather. This is more like August than June.

Talboys. The very word, my dear sir. It is indeed most august weather.

North. Five weeks to-day since we pitched our camp—and we have had the Beautiful of the Year in all its varieties; but the spiteful Season seems to owe you some old grudge, Talboys —and to make it a point still to assail your arrival with "thunder, lightning, and with rain."

Talboys. "I tax not you, ye Elements! with unkindness." I feel assured they mean nothing personal to me—and though this sort of work may not be very favorable to Angling, 'tis quite a day for tidying our Tackle—and making up our Books. But don't you think, sir, that the Tent would look nothing the worse with some artificial light in the obscuration of the natural?

North. Put on the gas. Pretty invention, the Gutta Percha tube, isn't it? The Electric Telegraph is nothing to it. Tent illuminated in a moment, at a pig's whisper.

Talboys. Were I to wish, sir, for anything to happen now to the weather at all, it would be just ever so little toning down of that one constituent of the orchestral harmony of the Storm which men call—howling. The thunder is perfect—but that one Wind Instrument is slightly out of tune—he is most anxious to do his best—his motive is unimpeachable; but he has no idea how much more impressive—how much more popular—would be a somewhat subdued style. There again—that's positive discord—does he mean to disconcert the Concert—or does he forget that he is not a Solo?

Buller. That must be a deluge of—hail.

Talboys. So much the better. Hitherto we have had but rain. "Mysterious horrors! HAIL!"

> "'Twas a rough night.
> My young remembrance cannot parallel
> A fellow to it."

North. Suppose we resume yesterday's conversation?

Talboys. By all manner of means. Let's sit close—and speak loud—else all will be dumb show. The whole world's one waterfall.

North. Take up Knight on Taste. Look at the dog-ear.

Talboys. "The most perfect instance of this kind is the Tragedy of Macbeth, in which the character of an ungrateful traitor, murderer, usurper, and tyrant, is made in the highest degree interesting by the sublime flashes of generosity, magnanimity, courage, and tenderness, which continually burst forth in the manly but ineffective struggle of every exalted quality that can dignify and adorn the human mind, first against the allurements of ambition, and afterwards against the pangs of remorse and horrors of despair. Though his wife has been the cause of all his crimes and sufferings, neither the agony of his distress, nor the fury of his rage, ever draw from him an angry word, or upbraiding expression towards her; but even when, at her instigation, he is about to add the murder of his friend and late colleague to that of his sovereign, kinsman, and benefactor, he is chiefly anxious that she should not share the guilt of his blood:—'Be innocent of the knowledge, dearest chuck! till thou applaud the deed.' How much more real grandeur and exaltation of character is displayed in one such simple expression from the heart, than in all the labored pomp of rhetorical amplification."

North. What think you of that, Talboys?

Talboys. Why, like much of the cant of criticism, it sounds at once queer and common-place. I seem to have heard it before many thousand times, and yet never to have heard it at all till this moment.

North. Seward?

Seward. Full of audacious assertions, that can be forgiven but in the belief that Payne Knight had never read the tragedy, even with the most ordinary attention.

North. Buller?

Buller. Cursed nonsense. Beg pardon, sir—sink cursed—mere nonsense—out and out nonsense—nonsense by itself nonsense.

North. How so?

Buller. A foolish libel on Shakspeare. Was he the man to make the character of an ungrateful traitor, murderer, usurper, and tyrant, interesting by sublime flashes of generosity, magnanimity, courage, and tenderness, and—do I repeat the words correctly?—of every exalted quality that can dignify and adorn the human mind?

North. Buller—keep up that face—you are positively beautiful—

Buller. No quizzing—I am ugly—but I have a good figure—look at that leg, sir!

North. I prefer the other.

Talboys. There have been Poets among us who fain would—if they could—have so violated nature; but their fabrications have been felt to be falsehoods—and no quackery may resuscitate drowned lies.

North. Shakspeare nowhere insists on the virtues of Macbeth—he leaves their measure indeterminate. That the villain may have had some good points we are all willing to believe—few people are without them;—nor have I any quarrel with those who believe he had high qualities, and is corrupted by ambition. But what high qualities had he shown before Shakspeare sets him personally before us to judge for ourselves? Valor—courage—intrepidity—call it what you will—Martial Virtue.

> "For brave Macbeth, (well he deserves that name,)
> Disdaining fortune, with his brandished steel,
> Which smoked with bloody execution
> Like valor's minion,
> Carved out his passage till he faced the slave;
> And ne'er shook hands, nor bade farewell to him,
> Till he unseam'd him from the nave to the chaps,
> And fixed his head upon our battlements."

The "bleeding Serjeant" pursues his panegyric till he grows faint—and is led off speechless; others take it up—and we are thus—and in other ways—prepared to look on Macbeth as a paragon of bravery, loyalty, and patriotism.

Talboys. So had seemed Cawdor.

North. Good. Shakspeare sets Macbeth before us under the most imposing circumstances of a warlike age; but of his inner character as yet he has told us nothing—we are to find that out for ourselves during the Drama. If there be sublime flashes of generosity, magnanimity, and every exalted virtue, we have eyes to see, unless indeed blinded by the lightning—and if the sublime flashes be frequent, and the struggle of every exalted quality that can adorn the human mind, though ineffectual, yet strong—why, then, we must not only pity and forgive, but admire and love the "traitor, murderer, usurper, and tyrant," with all the poetical and philosophical fervor of that amiable enthusiast, Mr. Payne Knight.

Buller. Somehow or other I cannot help having an affection for Macbeth.

North. You had better leave the Tent, sir.

Buller. No. I won't.

North. Give us then, my dear Buller, your Theory of the Thane's character.

Buller. "Theory, God bless you, I have none to give, sir." Warlike valor, as you said, is marked first and last—at the opening, and at the end. Surely a good and great quality, at least for poetical purposes. High general reputation won and held. The opinion of the wounded soldier was that of the whole army; and when he himself says, "I have bought golden opinions from all sorts of people, which would be worn now in their newest gloss, not thrown aside so soon," I accept that he then truly describes his position in men's minds.

North. All true. But we soon gain, too, this insight into his constitution, that the pillar upon which he has built up life is Reputation, and not Respect of Law—not Self-Respect; that the point which Shakspeare above all others intends in him, is that his is a spirit not self-stayed—leaning upon outward stays—and therefore—

Buller. Liable to all—

North. Don't take the words out of my mouth, sir; or rather, don't put them into my mouth, sir.

Buller. Touchy to-day.

North. The strongest expression of this charactor is his throwing himself upon the illicit divinings of futurity, upon counsellors known for infernal; and you see what subjugating sway the Three Spirits take at once over him. On the contrary, the Thaness is self-stayed; and this difference grounds the poetical opposition of the two personages. In Macbeth, I suppose a certain splendor of character—magnificence of action high—a certain impure generosity—mixed up of some kindliness and sympathy, and of the pleasure from self-elation and self-expansion in a victorious career, and of that ambition which feeds on public esteem.

Buller. Ay—just so, sir.

North. Now mark, Buller—this is a character which, if the path of duty and the path of personal ambition were laid out by the Sisters to be one and the same path, might walk through life in sunlight and honor, and invest the tomb with proud and revered trophies. To show such a spirit wrecked and hurled into infamy—the ill-woven sails rent into shreds by the whirlwind—is a lesson worthy the Play and the Poet—and such a lesson as I think Shakspeare likely to have designed—or, without preaching about lessons, such an ethical revelation as I think likely to have caught hold upon Shakspeare's intelligence. It would seem to me a dramatically-poetical subject. The mightiest of temptations occurs to a mind, full of powers, endowed with available moral elements, but without set virtue —without principles—"and down goes all before it." If the essential delineation of Macbeth be this conflict of Moral elements—of good and evil—of light and darkness—I see a very poetical conception; if merely a hardened and bloody hypocrite from the beginning, I see none. But I need not say to you, gentlemen, that all this is as far as may be from the exaggerated panegyric on his character by Payne Knight.

Talboys. Macbeth is a brave man—so is Banquo—so are we Four, brave men—they in their way and day—we in ours—they as Celts and Soldiers—we as Saxons and Civilians—and we had all need to be so—for hark! in the midst of ours, "Thunder and Lightning, and enter Three Witches."

Buller. I cannot say that I understand distinctly their first Confabulation.

North. That's a pity. A sensible man like you should understand everything. But what if Shakspeare himself did not distinctly understand it? There may have been original errata in the report, as extended by himself from notes taken in short-hand on the spot—light bad—noise worse—voices of Weird Sisters worst—matter obscure—manner uncouth—why really, Buller, all things considered, Shakspeare has shown himself a very pretty Penny-a-liner.

Buller. I cry you mercy, sir.

Seward. *Where* are the Witches on their first appearance, at the very opening of the Wonderful Tragedy?

North. An open Place, with thunder and lightning.

Seward. I know that—the words are written down.

North. Somewhere or other—anywhere—nowhere.

Buller. In Fife or Forfar? Or some one or other of your outlandish, or inlandish, Lowland or Highland Counties?

North. Not knowing, can't say. Probably.

Seward.

> "When the Hurly Burly's done,
> When the Battle's lost and won."

What Hurly Burly? What Battle? That in which Macbeth

is then engaged? And which is to be brought to issue ere "set of sun" of the day on which "enter Three Witches?"

North. Let it be so.

Seward.

> "Upon the heath,
> There to meet with Macbeth."

The Witches, then, are to meet with Macbeth on the heath on the evening of the Battle?

North. It would seem so.

Seward. They are "posters over sea and land"—and, like whiffs of lightning, can outsail and outride the sound of thunder. But Macbeth and Banquo must have had on their seven-league boots.

North. They must.

Seward.

> "A drum, a drum!
> Macbeth doth come."

Was he with the advance guard of the Army?

North. Not unlikely—attended by his staff. Generals, on such occasions, usually ride—but perhaps Macbeth and Banquo, being in kilts, preferred walking in their seven-league boots. Thomas Campbell has said, "When the drum of the Scottish Army is heard on the wild heath, and when I fancy it advancing with its bowmen in front, and its spears and banners in the distance, I am always disappointed with Macbeth's entrance at the head of a few kilted actors." The army may have been there—but they did not see the Weirds—nor, I believe, did the Weirds see them. With Macbeth and Banquo alone had they to do; we see no Army at that hour—we hear no drums—we are deaf even to the Great Highland Bagpipe, though He, you may be sure, was not dumb—all "plaided and plumed in their tartan array" the Highland Host ceased to be—like vanished shadows—at the first apparition of "those so withered and so wild in their attire"—not of the earth though on it, and alive somewhere till this day—while generations after generations of mere Fighting Men have been disbanded by dusty Death.

Seward. I wish to know *where* and *when* had been the Fighting? The Norwegian—one Sweno, had come down very handsomely at Inchcolm with ten thousand dollars—a sum in those days equal to a million of money in Scotland——

North. Seward, speak on subjects you understand. What do you know, sir, of the value of money *in* those days in Scotland?

Seward. But *where* had been all the Fighting? There would seem to have been two hurley-burleys.

North. I see your drift, Seward. *Time and place,* through the First Scene of the First Act, are past finding out. It has been asked—Was Shakspeare ever in Scotland? Never. There is not one word in this Tragedy leading a Scotsman to think so—many showing he never had that happiness. Let him deal with our localities according to his own sovereign will and pleasure, as a Prevailing Poet. But let no man point out his dealings with our localities as proofs of his having such knowledge of them as implies personal acquaintance with them gained by a longer or shorter visit in Scotland. The Fights at the beginning seem to be in Fife. The Soldier, there wounded, delivers his relation at the King's Camp before Forres. He has crawled, in half an hour, or an hour—or two hours—say seventy, eighty, or a hundred miles or more—crossing the ridge of the Grampians. Rather smart. I do not know what you think here of Time; but I think that Space is here pretty well done for. The TIME of the Action of Shakspeare's Plays has never yet, so far as I know, been, in any one Play, carefully investigated—never investigated at all; and I now announce to you Three—don't mention it—that I have made discoveries here that will astound the whole world, and demand a New Criticism of the entire Shakspearean Drama.

Buller. Let us have one now, I beseech you, sir.

North. Not now.

Buller. No sleep in the Tent till we have it, sir. I do dearly love astounding discoveries—and at this time of day, an astounding discovery in Shakspeare! May it not prove a Mare's Nest!

North. The tragedy of Macbeth is a *prodigious* Tragedy, because in it the Chariot of Nemesis *visibly* rides in the lurid thunder-sky. Because in it the ill motions of a human soul, which Theologians account for by referring them all to suggestions of Beelzebub, are expounded in visible, mysterious, tangible, terrible shape and symbolization by the Witches. It is great by the character and person, workings and sufferings, of Lady Macbeth—by the immense poetical power in doing the Witches—mingling for once in the world the Homely, Grotesque and the Sublime—extinguishing the Vulgar in the Sublime—by the bond, whatsoever it be, between Macbeth and his wife —by making us tolerate her and him——

Buller. Didn't I say that in my own way, sir? And didn't you reprove me for saying it, and order me out of the Tent?

North. And what of the Witches?

Buller. Had you not stopt me. I say now, sir, that nobody understands Shakspeare's HECATE. Who is she? Each of the Three Weirds is = one Witch + one of the Three Fates —therefore the union of two incompatible natures—more than in a Centaur. Oh! sir! what a hand that was which bound the two into one—inseverably! There they are for ever as the Centaurs *are.* But the gross Witch prevails; which Shakspeare needed for securing belief, and he has it, full. Hecate, sir, comes in to balance the disproportion—she lifts into Mythology

—and strengthens the mythological tincture. So does the "Pit of Acheron." That is classical. To the best of my remembrance, no mention of any such Pit in the Old or New Statistical Account of Scotland.

North. And, in the incantation Scene, those Apparitions! Mysterious, ominous, picturesque—and self-willed. They are commanded by the Witches, but under a limitation. Their oracular power is their own. They are of unknown orders—as if for the occasion created in Hell.

North. Talboys, are you asleep—or are you at Chess with your eyes shut?

Talboys. At Chess with my eyes shut. I shall send off my move to my friend Stirling by first post. But my ears were open—and I ask—when did Macbeth first design the murder of Duncan? Does not everybody think—in the moment *after* the Witches have first accosted and left him? Does not—it may be asked—the whole moral significancy of the Witches disappear, unless the invasion of hell into Macbeth's bosom is first made by their presence and voices?

North. No. The whole moral significancy of the Witches only then appears, when we are assured that they address themselves only to those who already have been tampering with their conscience. "Good sir! why do you start, and seem to fear things that do sound so fair?" That question put to Macbeth by Banquo turns our eyes to his face—and we see Guilt. There was no start at "Hail to thee, Thane of Cawdor,"—but at the word "King," well might he start; for——eh?

Talboys. We must look up the Scene.

North. No need for that. You have it by heart—recite it.

Talboys.

"*Macbeth.* So foul and fair a day I have not seen.
Banquo. How far is't called to Forres?—What are these,
So wither'd, and so wild in their attire;

That look not like the inhabitants of the earth,
And yet are on't? Live you? or are you aught
That man may question? You seem to understand me,
By each at once her choppy finger laying
Upon her skinny lips:—You should be women,
And yet your beards forbid me to interpret
That you are so.

Macbeth. Speak, if you can;—What are you?

1st Witch. All hail, Macbeth! hail to thee, thane of Glamis!

2d Witch. All hail, Macbeth! hail to thee, thane of Cawdor!

3d Witch. All hail, Macbeth! that shalt be king hereafter.

Banquo. Good sir, why do you start; and seem to fear
Things that do sound so fair?—I' the name of truth,
Are ye fantastical, or that indeed
Which outwardly ye show? My noble partner
You greet with present grace, and great prediction
Of noble having, and of royal hope,
That he seems rapt withal; to me you speak not:
If you can look into the seeds of time,
And say which grain will grow, and which will not;
Speak then to me, who neither beg, nor fear
Your favors nor your hate.

1st Witch. Hail!

2d Witch. Hail!

3d Witch. Hail!

1st Witch. Lesser than Macbeth, and greater.

2d Witch. Not so happy, yet much happier.

3d Witch. Thou shalt get kings, though thou be none:
So, all hail, Macbeth and Banquo.

1st Witch. Banquo and Macbeth, all hail!

Macbeth. Stay, you imperfect speakers, tell me more;
By Sinel's death, I know, I am thane of Glamis:
But how of Cawdor? the thane of Cawdor lives,
A prosperous gentleman; and to be king,
Stands not within the prospect of belief,
No more than to be Cawdor. Say, from whence
You owe this strange intelligence? or why

Upon this blasted heath you stop our way
With such prophetic greeting?—Speak, I charge you.
[*Witches vanish.*

Bunquo. The earth hath bubbles, as the water has,
And these are of them:—Whither are they vanished?
Macbeth. Into the air, and what seem'd corporal, melted
As breath into the wind. Would they had staid!
Banquo. Were such things here, as we do speak about?
Or have we eaten of the insane root
That takes the reason prisoner.
Macbeth. Your children shall be kings.
Banquo. You shall be king.
Macbeth. And thane of Cawdor too; went it not so?
Banquo. To the self-same tune, and words."

North. Charles Kemble himself could not have given it more impressively.

Buller. You make him blush, sir.

North. Attend to that "start" of Macbeth, Talboys.

Talboys. He might well start on being told of a sudden, by such seers, that he was hereafter to be King of Scotland.

North. There was more in the start than that, my lad, else Shakspeare would not have directed our eyes to it. I say again—it was the start—of a murderer.

Talboys. And what if I say it was not? But I have the candor to confess, that I am not familiar with the starts of murderers—so may possibly be mistaken.

North. Omit what intervenes—and give us the Soliloquy, Talboys. But before you do so, let me merely remind you that Macbeth's mind, from the little he says in the interim, is manifestly ruminating on something bad, ere he breaks out into Soliloquy.

Talboys.

"Two truths are told,
As happy prologues to the swelling act

Of the Imperial theme.—I thank you, gentlemen.—
This supernatural soliciting
Cannot be ill—cannot be good:—If ill,
Why hath it given me earnest of success,
Commencing in a truth? I am Thane of Cawdor:
If good, why do I yield to that suggestion
Whose horrid image doth unfix my hair,
And make my seated heart knock at my ribs
Against the use of nature? Present fears
Are less than horrible imaginings:
My thought whose murder is yet but fantastical
Shakes so my single state of man, that function
Is smothered in surmise; and nothing is,
But what is not."

th. Now, my dear Talboys, you will agree with me in thinking that this first great and pregnant, although brief soliloquy, stands for germ, type, and law of the whole Play, and of its criticism—and for clue to the labyrinth of the Thane's character. "Out of this wood do not desire to go." Out of it I do not expect soon to go. I regard William as a fair Poet and a reasonable Philosopher; but as a supereminent Play-wright. The First Soliloquy *must* speak the nature of Macbeth, else the Craftsman has no skill in his trade. A Soliloquy *reveals.* That is its function. Therein is the soul heard and seen discoursing with itself—within itself; and if you carry your eye through—up to the First Appearance of Lady Macbeth—this Soliloquy is distinctly the highest point of the Tragedy—the tragic acme—or dome—or pinnacle—therefore of power indefinite, infinite. On this rock I stand, a Colossus ready to be thrown down by—an Earthquake.

Buller. Pushed off by—a shove.

North. Not by a thousand Buller-power. Can you believe, Buller, that the word of the Third Witch, "that shalt be KING

HEREAFTER," *sows* the murder in Macbeth's heart, and that it springs up, flowers, and fruits with such fearful rapidity?

Buller. Why—Yes and No.

North. Attend, Talboys, to the words "supernatural soliciting." What "supernatural soliciting" to evil is there here? Not a syllable had the Weird Sisters breathed about Murder. But now there is much soliloquizing—and Cawdor contemplates himself *objectively*—seen busy upon an elderly gentleman called Duncan—after a fashion that so frightens him *subjectively*—that Banquo cannot help whispering to Rosse and Angus—

"See how our partner's rapt!"

Talboys. "My thought whose murder's yet fantastical." I agree with you, sir, in suspecting that he must have thought of the murder.

North. It is from no leaning towards the Weird Sisters—whom I never set eyes on but once, and then without interchanging a word, leapt momentarily out of this world into that pitch-pot of a pond in Glenco—it is, I say, from no leaning towards the Weird Sisters that I take this view of Macbeth's character. No "sublime flashes of generosity, magnanimity, tenderness, and every exalted quality that can dignify and adorn the human mind," do I ever suffer to pass by without approbation, when coruscating from the character of any well-disposed man, real or imaginary, however unaccountable at other times his conduct may appear to be; but Shakspeare, who knew Macbeth better than any of us, has here assured us that he was in heart a murderer—for how long he does not specify—before he had ever seen a birse on any of the Weird Sisters' beards. But let's be canny. Talboys—pray, what is the meaning of the word "soliciting," "preternatural soliciting," in this Soliloquy?

Talboys. Soliciting, sir, is, in my interpreting, "an appealing, intimate visitation."

North. Right. The appeal is general—as that *challenge* of a trumpet—*Fairy Queen,* book III., canto xii., stanza 1—

"Signe of nigh battail or got victorye"—

which, all indeterminate, is notwithstanding *a challenge*—operates, and is felt as such.

Talboys. So a thundering knock at your door—which may be a friend or an enemy. It comes as a summoning. It is more than internal urging and inciting of me by my own thoughts—for mark, sir, the rigor of the word "supernatural," which throws the soliciting off his own soul upon the Weirds. The word is really undetermined to pleasure or pain—the essential thought being that there is a searching or penetrating provocative—a stirring up of that which lay dead and still. Next is the debate whether this intrusive, and pungent, and simulant assault of a presence and an oracle be good or ill?

North. Does the hope live in him for a moment that this home-visiting is not ill—that the Spirits are not ill? They have spoken truth so far—ergo, the Third "All hail!" shall be true, too. But more than that—they have spoken *truth.* Ergo, they are not spirits of Evil. That hope dies in the same instant, submerged in the stormy waves which the blast from hell arouses. The infernal revelation glares clear before him—a Crown held out by the hand of Murder. One or two struggles occur. Then the truth stands before him fixed and immutable —"Evil, be thou my good." He is dedicated: and passive to fate. I cannot comprehend this so feeble debate in the mind of a good man—I cannot comprehend any such debate at all in the mind of a previously settled and determined murderer; but I can comprehend and feel its awful significancy in the mind of a man already in a most perilous moral condition.

Seward. The "start" shows that the spark has caught—it has fallen into a tun of gunpowder.

Talboys. The touch of Ithuriel's spear.

North. May we not say, then, that perhaps the Witches have shown no more than this—the Fascination of Contact between Passion and Opportunity?

Seward. To Philosophy reading the hieroglyphic; but to the People what? To them they are a reality. They seize the imagination with all power. They come like "blasts from hell"—like spirits of Plague, whose breath—whose very sight kills.

> "Within them Hell
> They bring, and round about them; nor from Hell
> One step, no more than from themselves, can fly."

The contagion of their presence, in spite of what we have been saying, almost reconciles *my* understanding to what it would otherwise revolt from, the *suddenness* with which the penetration of Macbeth into futurity lays fast hold upon Murder.

Buller. Pretty fast—though it gives a twist or two in his handling.

Seward. Lady Macbeth herself corroborates your judgment and Shakspeare's on her husband's character.

Talboys. Does she?

Seward. She does. In that dreadful parley between them on the night of the Murder—she reminds them of a time when

> "*Nor time nor place*
> *Did then adhere, and yet you would make both;*
> They have made themselves, and that their fitness now
> Does unmake you."

This—mark you, sir—must have been before the Play began!

North. I have often thought of the words—and Shakspeare himself has so adjusted the action of the Play as that, *since the encounter with the Weirds,* no opportunity had occurred to Macbeth for the "making of time and place." Therefore it must, as you say, have been *before it.* Buller, what say you now?

Buller. Gagged.

North. True, she speaks of his being "full of the milk of human kindness." The words have become favorites with us, who are an affectionate and domestic people—and are lovingly applied to the loving; but Lady Macbeth attached no such profound sense to them as we do; and meant merely that she thought her husband would, after all, much prefer greatness unbought by blood; and, at the time she referred to, it is probable he would; but that she meant no more than that, is plain from the continuation of her praise, in which her ideas get not a little confused; and her words, interpret them as you will, leave nothing "milky" in Macbeth at all. Milk of human kindness, indeed!

Talboys.

"What thou would'st highly,
That would'st thou holily; would'st not play false,
And yet would'st wrongly win: thoud'st have great Glamis,
That which cries, 'Thus thou must do, if thou have it;
And that which rather thou dost fear to do,
Than wishest should be undone.'"

That is her Ladyship's notion of the "milk of human kindness!" "I wish somebody would murder Duncan—as for murdering him myself, I am much too tender-hearted and humane for perpetrating such cruelty with my own hand!"

Buller. Won't you believe a Wife to be a good judge of her Husband's disposition?

North. Not Lady Macbeth. For does not she herself tell us, at the same time, that he had formerly schemed how to commit Murder?

Buller. Gagged again.

North. I see no reason for doubting that she was attached

to her husband; and Shakspeare loved to put into the lips of women beautiful expressions of love—but he did not intend that we should be deceived thereby in our moral judgments.

Seward. Did this ever occur to you, sir? Macbeth, when hiring the murderers who are to look after Banquo and Fleance, cites a conversation in which he had demonstrated to them that the oppression under which they had long suffered, and which they had supposed to proceed from Macbeth, proceeded really from Banquo? My firm belief is that it proceeded from Macbeth—that their suspicion was right—that Macbeth is misleading them—and that Shakspeare means you to apprehend this. But why should Macbeth have oppressed his inferiors, unless he had been—long since—of a tyrannical nature? He oppresses his inferiors—they are sickened and angered with the world—by his oppression—he tells them 'twas not he but another who had oppressed them—and that other—at his instigation—they willingly murder. An ugly affair altogether.

North. Very. But let us keep to the First Act—and see what a hypocrite Macbeth has so very soon become—what a savage assassin! He has just followed up his Soliloquy with these significant lines—

> "Come what come may,
> *Time and the hour run through the roughest day;*"

when he recollects that Banquo, Rosse, and Angus are standing near. Richard himself is not more wily—guily—smily—and oily; to the Lords his condescension is already quite kingly—

> "Kind gentlemen, your pains
> Are registered where every day I turn
> The leaf to read them"—

Talboys. And soon after, to the King how obsequious!

> "The service and the loyalty I owe,
> In doing it, pays itself. Your Highness' part

> Is to receive our duties; and our duties
> Are to your throne and state, children, and servants;
> Which do but what they should by doing everything
> Safe toward you love and honor."

What would Payne Knight have said to all that? This to his King, whom he has resolved, first good opportunity, to murder?

North. Duncan is now too happy for this wicked world.

> "My plenteous joys,
> Wanton in fulness, seek to hide themselves
> In drops of sorrow."

Invaders—traitors—now there are none. Peace is restored to the Land—the Throne rock-fast—the line secure—

> "We will establish our estate upon
> Our eldest, Malcolm; whom we name hereafter,
> The Prince of Cumberland: which honor must
> Not, unaccompanied, invest him only,
> But signs of nobleness, like stars, shall shine
> On all deservers."

Now was the time for "the manly but ineffectual struggle of every exalted quality that can dignify and exalt the human mind"—for a few sublime flashes at least of generosity and tenderness, et cetera—now when the Gracious Duncan is loading him with honors, and, better than all honors, lavishing on him the boundless effusions of a grateful and royal heart. The Prince of Cumberland! Ha, ha!

> "The Prince of Cumberland!—That is a step
> On which I must fall down, or else o'erleap,
> For in my way it lies."

But the remorseless miscreant becomes poetical—

> "Stars, hide your fires!
> Let not light see my black and deep desires:
> The eye wink at the hand! yet let that be,
> Which the eye fears, when it is done, to see!"

The milk of human kindness has coagulated into the curd of inhuman ferocity—and all this—slanderers say—is the sole work of the Weird Sisters! No. His wicked heart—because it is wicked—believes in their Prophecy—the end is assured to him—and the means are at once suggested to his own slaughterous nature. No supernatural soliciting here, which a better man would not successively have resisted. I again repudiate—should it be preferred against me—the charge of a *tendresse* towards the Bearded Beauties of the Blasted Heath; but rather would I marry them all Three—one after the other—nay all three at once, and as many more as there may be in our Celtic Mythology—than see your Sophia, Seward, or Buller, your—

Buller. We have but Marmy.

North. Wedded to a Macbeth.

Seward. We know your affection, my dear sir, for your goddaughter. She is insured.

North. Well, this Milk of Human Kindness is off at a hand-gallop to Inverness. The King has announced a Royal Visit to Macbeth's own Castle. But Cawdor had before this despatched a letter to his lady, from which Shakspeare has given us an extract. And then, as I understand it, a special messenger besides, to say "the King comes here to-night." Which of the two is the more impatient to be at work 'tis hard to say; but the idea of the murder originated with the male Prisoner. We have his Wife's word for it—she told him so to his face—and he did not deny it. We have his own word for it—he told himself so to his own face—and he never denies it at any time during the play.

Talboys. You said, a little while ago, sir, that you believed Macbeth and his wife were a happy couple.

North. Not I. I said she was attached to him—and I say now that the wise men are not of the Seven, who point to her reception of her husband, on his arrival *at home*, as a proof of her want of affection. They seem to think she ought to have rushed into his arms—slobbered upon his shoulder—and so forth. For had he not been at the Wars? Pshaw! The most tender-hearted Thanesses of those days—even those that kept albums—would have been ashamed of weeping on sending their Thanes off to battle—much more on receiving them back in a sound skin—with new honors nodding on their plumes. Lady Macbeth was not one of the turtle-doves—fit mate she for the King of the Vultures. I am too good an ornithologist to call them Eagles. She received her mate fittingly—with murder in her soul; but more cruel—more selfish than he, she could not be—nor, perhaps, was she less; but she was more resolute—and resolution even in evil—in such circumstances as hers—seems to argue a superior nature to his, who, while he keeps vacillating, as if it were between good and evil, betrays all the time the bias that is surely inclining him to evil, into which he makes a sudden and sure wheel at last.

Buller. The Weirds—the Weirds!—the Weirds have done it all!

North. Macbeth—Macbeth!—Macbeth hath done it all!

Buller. Furies and Fates!

North. Who make the wicked their victims!

Seward. Is she sublime in her wickedness?

North. It would, I fear, be wrong to say so. But I was speaking of Macbeth's character—not of hers—and, in comparison with him, she may seem a great creature. They are now utterly alone—and of the two he has been the more familiar with murder. Between them, Duncan already is a dead man. But how pitiful—at such a time and at such a greeting—Macbeth's cautions

"My dearest love,
Duncan comes here to night!
Lady.—And when goes hence?

> *Macbeth.*—To-morrow, as he purposes.
> *Lady.*—Oh, never
> Shall sun that morrow see!"

Why, Talboys, does not the poor devil—

Talboys. Poor devil! Macbeth a poor devil?

North. Why, Buller, does not the poor devil—

Buller. Poor devil! Macbeth a poor devil?

North. Why, Seward, does not the poor devil—

Seward. Speak up—speak out? Is he afraid of the spiders? You know him, sir—you see through him.

North. Ay, Seward—reserved and close as he is—he wants nerve—*pluck*—he is close upon the coward—and that would be well, were there the slightest tendency towards change of purpose in the Pale Face; but there is none—he is as cruel as ever—the more close the more cruel—the more irresolute the more murderous—for to murder he is sure to come. Seward, you said well—why does not the poor devil speak up—speak out? Is he afraid of the spiders?

Talboys. Murderous-looking villain—no need of words.

North. I did not say, sir, there was any need of words. Why will you always be contradicting one?

Talboys. Me? I? I hope I shall never live to see the day on which I contradict Christopher North in his own Tent. At least—rudely.

North. Do it rudely—not as you did now—and often do—as if you were agreeing with me—but you are incurable. I say, my dear Talboys, that Macbeth so bold in a "twa-haun'd crack" with himself in a Soliloquy—so figurative—and so fond of swearing by the Stars and old Mother Night, who were not aware of his existence—should not have been thus tongue-tied to his own wife in their own secretest chamber—should have unlocked and flung open the door of his heart to her—like a man. I blush for him—I do. So did his wife.

Buller. I don't find that in the record.

North. Don't you? "Your face, my Thane, is as a book where men may read strange matters." She sees in his face self-alarm at his own murderous intentions. And so she counsels him about his face—like a self-collected, trustworthy woman. "To beguile the time, look like the time;" with further good stern advice. But—"We shall speak farther," is all she can get from him in answer to conjugal assurances that should have given him a palpitation at the heart, and set his eyes on fire—

> "He that's coming
> Must be provided for; and you shall put
> This night's great business into my despatch;
> Which shall, to all our nights and days to come,
> Give solely sovereign sway and Masterdom."

There spoke one worthy to be a Queen!

Seward. Worthy!

North. Ay—in that age—in that country. 'Twas not then the custom "to *speak* daggers but *use* none." Did Shakspeare mean to dignify, to magnify Macbeth by such demeanor? No—to degrade and minimize the murderer.

Talboys. My dear sir, I cordially agree with every word you utter. Go on—my dear sir—to instruct—to illumine—

Seward. To bring out "sublime flashes of magnanimity, courage, tenderness," in Macbeth—

Buller. "Of every exalted quality that can dignify and adorn the human mind"—the mind of Macbeth in his struggle with the allurements of ambition!

North. Observe, how this reticence—on the part of Macbeth—contrasted with his wife's eagerness and exultation, makes her, for the moment, seem the wickeder of the two—the fiercer and the more cruel. For the moment only; for we soon ask ourselves what means this unhusbandly reserve in him who had sent her *that letter*—and then a messenger to tell her the king was coming—and who had sworn to himself as savagely as she now does, not to let slip this opportunity of cutting his king's throat. He is well pleased to see that his wife is as bloody-minded as himself—that she will not only give all necessary assistance—as an associate—but concert the when, and the where, and the how—and if need be, with her own hand deal the blow.

Seward. She did not then know that Macbeth had made up his mind to murder Duncan that very night. *But we know it.* She has instantly made up hers—we know how; but being as yet unassured of her husband, she welcomes him home with a Declaration that must have more than answered his fondest hopes; and, therefore, he is almost mute—the few words he does utter seemed to indicate no settled purpose—Duncan may fulfil his intention of going in the morning, or he may not; but we know that the silence of the murderer now is because the murderess is manifestly all he could wish—and that, had she shown any reluctance, he would have resumed his eloquence, and, to convert her to his way of thinking, argued as powerfully as he did when converting himself.

Buller. You carry on at such a pace, sir, there's no keeping up with you. Pull up, that I may ask you a very simple question. On his arrival at his castle, Macbeth finds his wife reading a letter from her amiable spouse, about the Weird Sisters. Pray, when was that letter written?

North. At what hour precisely? That I can't say. It must, however, have been written before Macbeth had been presented to the king—for there is no allusion in it to the King's intention to visit their Castle. I believe it to have been written about an hour or so after the prophecy of the Weirds—either in some place of refreshment by the road-side—or in such a Tent as this—kept ready for the General in the King's

Camp at Forres. He despatched it by a Gilly—a fast one like your Cornwall Clipper—and then tumbled in.

Buller. When did she receive it?

North. Early next morning.

Buller. How could that be, since she is reading it, as her husband steps in, well on, as I take it, in the afternoon?

North. Buller, you are a blockhead. There had she, for many hours, been sitting, and walking *about* with it, now rumpled up in her fist—now crunkled up between her breasts—now locked up in a safe—now spread out like a sampler on that tasty little oak table—and sometimes she might have been heard by the servants—had they had the unusual curiosity to listen at the door—murmuring like a stock-dove—anon hooting like an owl—by-and-by barking like an eagle—then bellowing liker a hart than a hind—almost howling like a wolf—and why not?—now singing a snatch of an old Gaelic air, with a clear, wild, sweet voice, like that of a "human!"

> "Glamis thou art, and Cawdor; and shalt be
> What thou art promised."
> "Hie thee hither,
> That I may pour my spirits in thine ear.
> And chastise with the valor of my tongue,
> All that impedes thee from the golden round,
> Which Fate and metaphysical aid doth seem
> To have thee crown'd withal."

Buller. Grand indeed.

North. It *is* grand indeed. But, my dear Buller, was that all she had said to herself, think you? No—no—no. But it was all Shakspeare had time for on the Stage. Oh, sirs! The Time of the Stage is but a simulacrum of true Time. That must be done at one stroke, on the Stage, which in a Life takes ten. The Stage persuades *that* in one conversation, or soliloquy, which Life may do in twenty—you have not leisure or good will for the ambages and iterations of the Real.

Seward. See an artist with a pen in his hand, challenged; and with a few lines he will exhibit a pathetic story. From how many millions has he given you—One? The units which he abstracts, represent sufficiently and satisfactorily the millions of lines and surfaces which he neglects.

North. So in Poetry. You take little for much. You need not wonder, then, that on an attendant entering and saying, "The King comes here to-night," she cries, "Thou art mad to say it!" Had you happened to tell her so half an hour ago, who knows but that she might have received it with a stately smile, that hardly moved a muscle on her high-featured front, and gave a merciful look to her green eyes even when she was communing with Murder!

North. What hurry and haste had been on all sides to get into the House of Murder!

> "Where's the Thane of Cawdor?
> We coursed him, at the heels, and had a purpose
> To be his purveyor: but he rides well:
> And his great love, sharp as his spur, hath holp him
> To his home before us—Fair and noble Hostess,
> We are your guest to-night."

Ay, where is the Thane of Cawdor? I, for one, not knowing, can't say. The gracious Duncan desires much to see him as well as his gracious Hostess.

> "Give me your hand:
> Conduct me to mine host; we love him highly,
> And shall continue our graces towards him.
> By your leave, hostess."

Ay—where's the Thane of Cawdor? Why did not Shakspeare show him to us, sitting at supper with the King?

Talboys. Did he sup with the King?

Buller. I believe he sat down—but got up again—and left the Chamber.

Talboys. His wife seeks him out. "He has almost supped. Why have you left the Chamber?" "Has he asked for me?" "Know ye not he has?"

North. On Macbeth's Soliloquy, which his wife's entrance here interrupts, how much inconsiderate comment have not moralists made! Here—they have said—is the struggle of a good man with temptation. Hearken, say they—to the voice of Conscience! What does the good man, in this hour of trial, say to himself? He says to himself—"I have made up my mind to assassinate my benefactor in my own house—the only doubt I have, is about the consequences to myself in the world to come." Well, then—"We'd jump the world to come. But if I murder him—may not others murder me? Retribution even in this world." Call you that the voice of Conscience?

Seward. Hardly.

North. He then goes on to descant to himself about the relation in which he stands to Duncan, and apparently discovers for the first time, that "he's here in double trust;" and that as his host, his kinsman, and his subject, he should "against his murderer shut the door, not bear the knife myself."

Seward. A man of genius.

North. Besides, Duncan is not only a King, but a good King—

> "So clear in his great office, that his virtues
> Will plead like angels, trumpet-tongued, against
> The deep damnation of his taking off."

That is much better morality—keep there, Macbeth—or thereabouts—and Duncan's life is tolerably safe—at least for one night. But Shakspeare knew his man—and what manner of man he is we hear in the unbearable context, that never yet has been quoted by any one who had ears to distinguish between the true and the false.

> "And pity, like a naked new-born babe,
> Striding the blast, or heaven's cherubim, hors'd
> Upon the sightless couriers of the air,
> Shall blow the horrid deed in every eye,
> That tears shall drown the wind."

Cant and fustian. Shakspeare knew that cant and fustian would come at that moment from the mouth of Macbeth. Accordingly, he offers but a poor resistance to the rhetoric that comes rushing from his wife's heart—even that sentiment which is thought so fine—and 'tis well enough in its way—

> "I dare do all that may become a man;
> Who dares do more is none"—

is set aside at once by—

> "What beast was it, then,
> That made you break this enterprise to me?"

We hear no more of "Pity like a naked new-born babe"—but at her horrid scheme of the murder—

> "Bring forth men children only!
> For thy undaunted metal should compose
> Nothing but males!"

Shakspeare does not paint here a grand and desperate struggle between good and evil thoughts in Macbeth's mind—but a mock fight; had there been any deep sincerity in the feeling expressed in the bombast—had there been any true feeling at all—it would have revived and deepened—not faded and died almost—at the picture drawn by Lady Macbeth of their victim—

"When Duncan is asleep,
Whereto the rather shall this day's hard journey
Soundly invite him,"

the words that had just left his own lips—

"His virtues
Will plead like angels, trumpet-tongued, against
The deep damnation of his taking-off,"

would have re-rung in his ears; and a strange medley—words and music—would they have made—with his wife's

"When in swinish sleep
Their drenched natures lie, as in a death,
What cannot you and I perform upon
The unguarded Duncan?"

That is my idea of the Soliloquy. Think on it.

Talboys. The best critics tell us that Shakspeare's Lady Macbeth has a commanding Intellect. Certes she has a commanding Will. I do not see what a commanding Intellect has to do in a Tragedy of this kind—or what opportunity she has of showing it. Do you, sir?

North. I do not.

Talboys. Her Intellect seems pretty much on a par with Macbeth's in the planning of the murder.

North. I defy any human Intellect to devise well an atrocious Murder. Pray, how would you have murdered Duncan?

Talboys. Ask me rather how I would—this night—murder Christopher North.

North. No more of that—no dallying in that direction. You make me shudder. Shakspeare knew that a circumspect murder is an impossibility—that a murder of a King in the murderer's own house, with expectation of non-discovery, is the irrationality of infatuation. The poor Idiot chuckles at the poor Fury's device as at once original and plausible—and, next hour, what single soul in the Castle does not know who did the deed?

Seward. High intellect indeed!

Talboys. The original murder is bad to the uttermost. I mean badly contrived. What color was there in coloring the two Grooms? No two men kill their master, and then go to bed again in his room with bloody faces and poignards.

Buller. If this was really a very bad plot altogether, it is her Ladyship's as much—far more than his Lordship's. Against whom, then, do we conclude? Her? I think not—but the Poet. *He* is the badly-contriving assassin. He does not intend lowering your esteem for her Ladyship's talents. Am I, sir, to think that William himself, after the same game, would have hunted no better? I believe he would; but he thinks that this will carry the Plot through for the Stage well enough. The House, seeing and hearing, will not stay to criticise. The Horror persuades Belief. He knew the whole mystery of murder.

North. My dear Buller, wheel nearer me. I would not lose a word you say.

Buller. Did Macbeth commit an error in killing the two Grooms? And does his Lady think so?

Talboys. A gross error, and his Lady thinks so.

Buller. Why was it a gross error—and why did his lady think so?

Talboys. Because—why—I really can't tell.

Buller. Nor I. The question leads to formidable difficulties—either way. But answer me this. Is her swooning at the close of her husband's most graphic picture of the position of the corpses—real or pretended?

Seward. Real.

Talboys. Pretended.

Buller. Sir?

North. I reserve my opinion.

Talboys. Not a faint—but a *feint.* She cannot undo that which is done; nor hinder that which he will do next. She must mind her own business. Now distinctly her own business—is to faint. A high-bred, sensitive, innocent Lady, startled from her sleep to find her guest and King murdered, and the room full of aghast nobles, cannot possibly do anything else but faint. Lady Macbeth, who "all particulars of duty knows," faints accordingly.

North. Seward, we are ready to hear you.

Seward. She has been about a business that must have somewhat shook her nerves—granting them to be of iron. She would herself have murdered Duncan had he not resembled her Father as he slept; and on sudden discernment of that dreadful resemblance, her soul must have shuddered, if her body served her to stagger away from parricide. On the deed being done, she is terrified after a different manner from the doer of the deed; but her terror is as great; and though she says—

> "The sleeping and the dead
> Are but as pictures—'tis the eye of childhood
> That fears a painted Devil—"

believe me that her face was like ashes, as she returned to the chamber to gild the faces of the grooms with the dead man's blood. That knocking, too, alarmed the Lady, believe me, as much as her husband; and to keep cool and collected before him, so as to be able to support him at that moment with her advice, must have tried the utmost strength of her nature. Call her Fiend—she was Woman. Down stairs she comes—and stands among them all, at first like one alarmed only—astounded by what she hears—and striving to simulate the ignorance of the innocent—"What, in our house?" "Too cruel anywhere!" What she must have suffered then, Shakspeare lets us conceive for ourselves; and what on her husband's elaborate description of his inconsiderate additional murders. "The whole is too much for her"—she "is perplexed in the extreme"—and the sinner swoons.

North. Seward suggests a bold, strong, deep, tragical turn of the scene—that she faints actually. Well—so be it. I shall say, first, that I think it a weakness in my favorite; but I will go so far as to add that I can let it pass for a not unpardonable weakness—the occasion given. But I must deal otherwise with her biographer. Him I shall hold to a strict rendering of account. I will know of him what he is about, and what she is about. If she faints really, and against her will, having forcible reasons for holding her will clear, she must be shown fighting to the last effort of will, against the assault of womanly nature, and drop, vanquished, as one dead, without a sound. But the Thaness calls out lustily—she remembers, "as we shall make our griefs and clamors roar upon his death." She makes noise enough—takes good care to attract everybody's attention to her performance—for which I commend her. Calculate as nicely as you will—she distracts or diverts speculation, and makes an interesting and agreeable break in the conversation.—I think that the obvious meaning is the right meaning—and *that she faints on purpose.*

Talboys. Decided in favor of Feint.

Buller. You might have had the good manners to ask for *my* opinion.

North. I beg a thousand pardons, Buller.

Buller. A hundred will do, North. In Davies' *Anecdotes of the Stage*, I remember reading that Garrick would not trust Mrs. Pritchard with the Swoon—and that Macklin thought Mrs. Porter alone could have been endured by the audience. Therefore, by the Great Manager, Lady Macbeth was not allowed in the Scene to appear at all. His belief was, that with her Ladyship it was a feint—and that the Gods, aware of that, unless restrained by profound respect for the actress, would have *laughed*—as at something rather comic. If the Gods, in Shakspeare's days, were as the Gods in Garrick's, William, methinks, would not, on any account, have exposed the Lady to derision at such a time. But I suspect the Gods of the Globe would not have laughed, whatever they might have thought of her sincerity, and that she did appear before them in a Scene from which nothing could account for her absence. She was not, I verily believe, given to fainting—perhaps this was the first time she had ever fainted since she was a girl. *Now* I believe she did. She would have stood by her husband at all hazards, had she been able, both on his account and her own; she would not have so deserted him at such a critical juncture; her character was of boldness rather than duplicity; her business now—her duty—was to brazen it out; but she grew sick—qualms of conscience, however terrible, can be borne by sinners standing upright at the mouth of hell—but the flesh of man is weak, in its utmost strength, when moulded to woman's form—other qualms assail suddenly the earthly tenement—the breath is choked—the "distracted globe" grows dizzy—they that look out of the windows know not what they see—the body reels, lapses, sinks, and at full length smites the floor.

Seward. Well said—Chairman of the Quarter-sessions.

Buller. Nor, with all submission, my dear Sir, can I think you treat your favorite murderess, on this trying occasion, with your usual fairness and candor. All she says is, "Help me hence, ho!" Macduff says, "Look to the Lady"—and Banquo says "Look to the Lady"—and she is carried off. Some critic or other—I think Malone—says that Macbeth shows he knows "'tis a feint" by not going to her assistance. Perhaps he was mistaken—know it he could not. And nothing more likely to make a woman faint than that reveling and wallowing of his in that bloody description.

North. By the Casting Vote of the President—*Feint.*

Talboys. Let's to Lunch.

North. Go. You will find me sitting here when you come back.

SCENE II.—*The Pavilion.*

TIME—*after Lunch.*

NORTH—TALBOYS—BULLER—SEWARD.

North. Claudius, the Uncle-king in Hamlet, is perhaps the most odious character in all Shakspeare. But he does no unnecessary murders. He has killed the Father, and will the Son, all in regular order. But Macbeth plunges himself, like a drunken man, into unnecessary and injurious cruelties. He throws like a reckless gamester. If I am to own the truth, I don't know why he is so cruel. I don't think that he takes any in mere cruelty, like Nero—

Buller. What do we know of Nero? Was he mad?

North. I don't think that he takes any pleasure in mere cruelty, like Nero; but he seems to be under some infatuation that drags or drives him along. To kill is, in every difficulty, the ready resource that occurs to him—as if to go on murdering were, by some law of the Universe, the penalty which you must pay for having once murdered.

Seward. I think, Sir, that without contradicting anything we said before Lunch about his Lordship or his Kingship, we may conceive in the natural Macbeth considerable force of Moral Intuition.

North. We may.

Seward. Of Moral Intelligence?

North. Yes.

Seward. Of Moral Obedience?

North. No.

Seward. Moral Intuition, and Moral Intelligence breaking out, from time to time, all through—we understand how there is engendered in him strong self-dissatisfaction—thence perpetual goadings on—and desperate attempts to loose conscience in more and more crime.

North. Ay—Seward—even so. He tells you that he stakes soul and body upon the throw for a Crown. He has got the Crown—and *paid for it.* He *must* keep it—else he has bartered soul and body—for nothing! To make his first crime *good*—he strides gigantically along the road of which it opened the gate.

Talboys. An almost morbid impressibility of imagination is energetically stamped, and universally recognized in the Thane, and I think, sir, that it warrants, to a certain extent, a *sincerity* of the mental movements. He really sees a fantastical dagger—he really hears fantastical voices—perhaps he really sees a fantastical Ghost. All this in him is Nature—not artifice—and a nature deeply, terribly, tempestuously commoved by the near contact of a murder imminent—doing—done. It is more like a murder a-making than a murderer made.

Seward. See, sir, how precisely this characteristic is proposed.

Buller. By whom?

Seward. By Shakspeare in that first Soliloquy. The poetry coloring, throughout his discourse, is its natural efflorescence.

North. Talboys, Seward, you have spoken well.

Buller. And I have spoken ill.

North. I have not said so.

Buller. We have all Four of us spoken well—we have all

Four of us spoken ill—and we have all Four of us spoken but so-so—now and heretofore—in this Tent—hang the wind—there's no hearing twelve words in ten a body says. Honored sir, I beg permission to say that I cannot admit the Canon laid down by your Reverence, an hour or two ago, or a minute or two ago, that Macbeth's extravagant language is designed by Shakspeare to designate hypocrisy.

North. Why?

Buller. You commended Talboys and Seward for noticing the imaginative—the poetical character of Macbeth's mind. There we find the reason of his extravagant language. It may, as you said, be cant and fustian—or it may not—but why attribute to hypocrisy—as you did—what may have flowed from his genius? Poets may rant as loud as he, and yet be honest men. "In a fine frenzy rolling," their eyes may fasten on fustian.

North. Good—go on. Deduct.

Buller. Besides, sir, the Stage had such a language of its own; and I cannot help thinking that Shakspeare often, and too frankly, gave in to it.

North. He did.

Buller. I would, however, much rather believe that if Shakspeare meant anything by it in Macbeth's Oratory or Poetry, he intended thereby rather to impress on us that last noticed constituent of his nature—a vehement seizure of imagination. I believe, sir, that in the hortatory scene Lady Macbeth really vanquishes—as the scene ostensibly shows—his *ir*resolution. And if Shakspeare means *ir*resolution, I do not know why the *grounds* thereof which Shakspeare assigns to Macbeth should not be accepted as the true grounds. The Dramatist would seem to demand too much of me, if, *under* the grounds which he expresses, he requires me to discard these, and to discover and express others.

Seward. I do not know, sir, if that horrible Invocation of *hers* to the Spirits of Murder to unsex her, be held by many to imply that she has no need of their help!

North. It is held by many to prove that she was not a woman but a fiend. It proves the reverse. I infer from it that she does need their help—and, what is more, *that she gets it.* Nothing so dreadful, in the whole range of Man's Tragic Drama, as that Murder. But I see Seward is growing pale—we know his infirmity—and for the present shun it.

Seward. Thank you, sir.

North. I may, however, ask a question about Banquo's Ghost.

Seward. Well—well—do so.

Talboys. You put the question to me, sir? I am inclined to think, sir, that no real Ghost sits on the Stool—but that Shakspeare meant it as with the Daggers. On the Stage he appears—that is an abuse.

North. Not so sure of that, Talboys.

Talboys. Had Macbeth himself continued to believe that the first seen Ghost was a real Ghost, he would not, could not have ventured so soon after his disappearance to say again, "And to our dear friend Banquo." He does say it—and then again diseased imagination assails him at the rash words. Lady Macbeth reasons with him again, and he finally is persuaded that the Ghost, both times, had been but brain-sick creations.

> "My strange and self-abuse
> Is the initiate fear, that wants hard use:—
> I am but young in deed."

Buller. That certainly looks as if he did then know he had been deceived. But perhaps he only censures himself for being too much agitated by a real ghost.

Talboys. That won't do.

North. But go back, my dear Talboys, to the first enacting of the Play. What could the audience have understood to be happening, without other direction of their thoughts than the terrified Macbeth's bewildered words? He never mentions Banquo's name—and recollect that nobody sitting there then knew that Banquo had been murdered. The dagger is not in point. Then the spectators heard him say, "Is this a dagger that I see before me?" And if no dagger was there, they could at once see that 'twas fantasy.

Talboys. Something in that.

Buller. A settler.

North. I entirely separate the two questions—first, how did the Manager of the Globe Theatre have the King's Seat at the Feast filled; and second, what does the highest poetical Canon deliver? I speak now, but to the first. Now, here the rule is—"the audience *must understand, and at once,* what that which they see and hear means"—that Rule must govern the art of the drama in the Manager's practice. You allow that, Talboys.

Talboys. I do.

Buller. Rash—Talboys—rash; he's getting you into a net.

North. That is not my way, Buller. Well, then, suppose Macbeth acted for the first time to an audience, who are to establish it for a stock-play or to *damn it.* Would the Manager commit the whole power of a scene which is perhaps the most —singly—effective of the whole Play—

Buller. No—no—not the most effective of the whole Play—

North. The rival, then, of the Murder Scene—the Sleep-Walking stands aloof and aloft—to the chance of a true divination by the whole Globe audience? I think not. The argument is of a vulgar tone, I confess, and extremely literal, but it is after the measure of my poor faculties.

Seward. In confirmation of what you say, it has been

lately asserted that one of the two appearings at least is not Banquo's—but Duncan's. How is that to be settled but by a real Ghost—or Ghosts?

North. And I ask, what has Shakspeare himself undeniably done elsewhere? In Henry VIII., Queen Katharine sleeps and *dreams.* Her Dream enters, and performs various acts—somewhat expressive—minutely contrived and prescribed. It is a mute Dream, which she with shut eyes sees—which you in pit, boxes, and gallery see—which her attendants watching about her upon the stage, do *not* see.

Seward. And in Richard III.—He dreams, and so does Richmond. Eight Ghosts rise in succession and *speak* to Richard first, and to the Earl next—each hears, I suppose, what concerns himself—they seem to be present in the two Tents at once.

North. In Cymbeline, Posthumus dreams. His Dream enters—Ghosts and even JUPITER! They act and speak; and this Dream has a reality—for Jupiter hands or tosses a parchment-roll to one of the Ghosts, who lays it, as bidden, on the breast of the Dreamer, where he, on awaking, perceives it! I call all this physically strong, sir, for the representation of the metaphysically thought.

Buller. If Buller may speak, Buller would observe, that once or twice both Ariel and Prospero come forward "invisible." And in Spenser, the Dream of which Morpheus lends the use to Archimago, is—carried.

Seward. We all remember the Dream which Jupiter sends to Agamemnon, and which, while standing at his bed's-head, puts on the shape of Nestor and speaks;—the Ghost of Patroclus—the actual Ghost which stands at the bed's-head of Achilles, and *is* his Dream.

North. My friends, Poetry gives a body to the bodiless. The Stage of Shakspeare was rude, and gross. In my boyhood,

I saw the Ghosts appear to John Kemble in Richard III. Now they may be abolished with Banquo. So may be Queen Katherine's Angels. But Shakspeare and his Audience had no difficulty about one person's seeing what another does not—or one's *not* seeing, rather, that which another does. Nor had Homer, when Achilles alone, in the Quarrel Scene, sees Minerva. Shakspeare and his Audience had no difficulty about the bodily representation of Thoughts—the inward by the outward. Shakspeare and the Great Old Poets leave vague, shadowy, mist-shrouded, and indeterminate the boundaries between the Thought and the Existent—the Real and the Unreal. I am able to believe with you, Talboys, that Banquo's Ghost was understood by Shakspeare, the Poet, to be the Phantasm of the murderer's guilt-and-fear-shaken soul; but was required by Shakspeare, the Manager of the Globe Theatre, to rise up through a trap-door, mealy-faced and blood-boultered, and so make "the Table full."

Buller. Seward, do bid him speak of Lady Macbeth.

Seward. Oblige me, sir—don't now—after dinner, if you will.

North. I shall merely allude now, as exceedingly poetical treatment, to the discretion throughout used in the SHOWING of Lady Macbeth. You might almost say that she never takes a step on the stage, that does not *thrill the Theatre.* Not a waste word, gesture, or look. All at the studied fulness of sublime tragical power—yet all wonderfully tempered and governed. I doubt if Shakspeare could have given a good account of everything that he makes Macbeth say—but of all that She says he could.

Talboys. As far as I am able to judge, she but cnce in the whole Play loses her perfect self-mastery—when the servant surprises her by announcing the King's coming. She answers, "thou'rt mad to say it;" which is a manner of speaking used by those who cannot, or can hardly believe tidings that fill them with exceeding joy. It is not the manner of a lady to her servant who unexpectedly announces the arrival of a high—of the highest visitor. She recovers herself instantly. "Is not thy master with him, who, wer't so, would have informed for preparation?" This is a turn coloring her exclamation, and is spoken in the most self-possessed, argumentative, demonstrative tone. The preceding words had been torn from her; now she has passed, with inimitable dexterity, from the dreamed Queen, to the usual mistress of her household—*to the housewife.*

North. In the Fourth Act—she is not seen at all. But in the Fifth, lo! and behold! and at once we know why she had been absent—we see and are turned to living stone by the revelation of the terrible truth. I am always inclined to conceive Lady Macbeth's night-walking as the summit, or topmost peak of all tragic conception and execution—in Prose, too, the crowning of Poetry! But it must be, because these are the *ipsissima verba*—yea, the escaping sighs and moans of the bared soul. There must be nothing, not even the thin and translucent veil of the verse, betwixt her soul showing itself, and yours beholding. Words which your "hearing latches" from the threefold abyss of Night, Sleep, and Conscience! What place for the enchantment of any music is here? Besides, she speaks in a whisper. The Siddons did—audible distinctly, throughout the stilled immense theatre. Here music is not—sound is not—only an anguished soul's faint breathings—gaspings. And observe that Lady Macbeth carries—a candle—besides washing her hands—and besides speaking prose—three departures from the severe and elect method, to bring out that supreme revelation. I have been told that the great Mrs. Pritchard used to touch the palm with the tips of her fingers, for the washing, keeping candle in hand:—that the Siddons first set down her candle, that she might come forwards, and wash her hands in earnest, one over the other, as if she were at her wash-hand stand, with plenty of water in her basin—that when Sheridan got intelligence of her design so to do, he ran shrieking to her, and, with tears in his eyes, besought that she would not, at one stroke, overthrow Drury Lane—that she persisted, and turned the thousands of bosoms to marble.

Talboys. Our dear, dear Master.

North. You will remember, my friends, her *four rhymed lines*—uttered to herself in Act Third. They are very remarkable—

> "Nought's had, all's spent,
> Where our desire is got without content:
> 'Tis safer to be that which we destroy,
> Than, by destruction, dwell in doubtful joy."

They are her only *waking* acknowledgments of having *mistaken* life! So—they forbode the Sleep-Walking, and the Death—as an owl, or a raven, or vulture, or any fowl of obscene wing, might flit between the sun and a crowned but doomed head—the shadow but of a moment, yet ominous, for the augur, of an entire fatal catastrophe.

Seward. They do. But to say the truth, I had either forgot them or never discovered their significancy. O that William Shakspeare!

Talboys. O that Christopher North!

North. Speak so, friends—'tis absurd, but I like it.

Talboys. It is sincere.

North. At last they call him, "black Macbeth," and "this dead Butcher." And with good reason. They also call her "his fiend-like Queen," which last expression I regard as highly offensive.

Buller. And they call her so not without strong reason.

North. A bold, bad woman—not a Fiend. I ask—Did she,

or did she not, "with violent hand foredo her life?" They mention it as a rumour. The Doctor desires that all means of self-harm may be kept out of her way. Yet the impression on us, as the thing proceeds, is that she dies of pure remorse—which I believe. She is *visibly dying*. The cry of women, announcing her death, is rather as of those who stood around the bed watching, and when the heart at the touch of the invisible finger stops, shriek—than of one after the other coming in and finding the self-slain—a confused, informal, perplexing, and perplext proceeding—but the Cry of Woman is formal, regular for the stated occasion. You may say, indeed, that she poisoned herself—and so died in bed—watched. Under the precautions, that is unlikely—too refined. The manner of Seyton, "The Queen, my Lord, is dead," shows to me that it was hourly expected. How these few words would *seek* into you, did you first read the Play in mature age! She died a natural death—of remorse. Take my word for it—the rumor to the contrary was natural to the lip and ear of Hate.

Talboys. A question of primary import is—What is the relation of feeling between him and her? The natural impression, I think, is, that the confiding affection—the intimate confidence—is "there"—of a husband and wife who love one another—to whom all interests are in common, and are consulted in common. Without this belief, the Magic of the Tragedy perishes—vanishes to me. "My dearest love, Duncan comes here to-night." "Be innocent of the knowledge, *dearest chuck*," —a marvelous phrase for Melpomene. It is the full union—for ill purposes—that we know habitually for good purposes—that to me tempers the Murder Tragedy.

North. Yet believe me, dear Talboys—that of all the murders Macbeth may have committed, she knew beforehand but of ONE—Duncan's. The haunted somnambulist speaks the truth—the whole truth, and nothing but the truth.

Talboys. "The Thane of Fife had a wife." Does not that imply that she was privy to *that* Murder?

North. No. Except that she takes upon herself *all* the murders that are the offspring, legitimate or illegitimate, of that First Murder. But we *know* that Macbeth, in a sudden fit of fury, ordered the Macduff's to be massacred when on leaving the Cave Lenox told him of the Thane's flight.

Talboys. That is decisive.

North. A woman, she feels for a murdered woman. That is all—a touch of nature—from Shakspeare's profound and pitiful heart.

Talboys. "The Queen, my Lord, is dead." "She should have died hereafter; There would have been a time for such a word"—Often have I meditated on the meaning of these words—yet even now I do not fully feel or understand them.

North. Nor I. This seems to look from them—" so pressed by outward besiegings I have not capacity to entertain the blow as it requires to be entertained. With a free soul I could have measured it. Now I cannot."

Talboys. Give us, sir, a commentary on the Revelations of the Sleeping Spectre.

North. I dare not. Let's be cheerful. I ask this—when you see and hear Kemble-Macbeth—and Siddons-Macbeth—whom do you believe that you see and hear? I affirm that you at one and the same instant—or at the most in two immediately successive instants—yet I believe in one and the same instant,—*know* that you see and hear Kemble—or if that accomplished gentleman and admirable actor—Macready be performing the part—then Macready;—and yet *believe* that you see and hear Lord Macbeth. I aver that you entertain a mixt—confused—self-contradictory state of mind—that two elements of thought which cannot co-subsist do co-subsist.

Talboys. *De jure* they cannot—DE FACTO they do.

North. Just so.

Talboys. They co-subsist fighting, and yet harmonizing—there is half-belief—semi-illusion.

North. I claim the acknowledgment of such a state—which any one who chooses may better describe, but which shall come to that effect—for the lowest substratum of all science and criticism concerning POESY. Will anybody grant me this, then I will reason with him about Poesy, for we begin with something in common. Will anybody deny me this, then I will not argue with him about Poesy, for we set out with nothing in common.

Buller. We grant you all you ask—we are all agreed—"our unanimity is wonderful."

North. Leave out the great Brother and Sister, and take the Personated alone. I *know* that Othello and Desdemona never existed—that an Italian Novelist began, and an English Dramatist ended them—and there they are. But I do not *believe* in their existence, "their loves and woes?" Yes, I do *believe* in their existence, in their loves and woes—and I hate Iago accordingly with a vicious, unchristian, personal, active, malignant hatred.

Talboys. Dr. Johnson's celebrated expression, "all the belief that Poetry claims"——

Buller. Celebrated! Where is it?

Talboys. Preface to Shakspeare—is idle, and frivolous, and false?

North. It is. He belies his own experience. He cannot make up his mind to admit the *irrational thought* of belief which you at once reject and accept. But exactly the half acceptance, and the half rejection, separates poetry from—prose.

Talboys. That is, sir, the poetical from the prosaic.

North. Just so. It is the life and soul of all poetry—the lusus—the make-believe—the glamour and the gramarye. I do not know—gentlemen—I wish to be told, whether I am not throwing away words upon the setting up of a pyramid which was built by Cheops, and is only here and there crumbling a little, or whether the world requires that the position shall be formally argued and acknowledged. Johnson, as you remind me, Talboys, did not admit it.

Talboys. That he tells us in so many words. Has any more versed and profound master in criticism, before or since, authentically and authoritatively, luminously, cogently, explicitly, psychologically, metaphysically, physiosologically, psychogogically, propounded, reasoned out, legislated, and enthroned the Dogma?

North. I know not, Talboys. Do you admit the Dogma?

Talboys. I do.

North. Impersonation—Apostrophe—of the absent; every poetical motion of the Soul; the whole pathetic beholding of Nature—involve the secret existence and necessity of this irrational psychical state of grounding the Logic of Poesy.

Buller. Go on, sir.

North. I will—but in a new direction. Before everything else, I desire, for the settlement of this particular question, a foundation for, and some progress in the science of Murder Tragedies.

Seward. I know *properly* two.

Buller. Two only? Pray name.

Seward. This of Macbeth and Richard III.

Buller. The Agamemnon—the Choephoræ—the Electra—the Medea—

Seward. In the Agamemnon, your regard is drawn to Agamemnon himself and to Cassandra. However, it is after a measure a prototype. Clytemnestra has in it a principality. Medea stands eminent—but then she is in the right.

Buller. In the right?

Seward. Jason at least is altogether in the wrong. But we must—for obvious reasons—discuss the Greek drama by itself; and therefore not a word more about it now.

North. Richard III., and Macbeth and his wife, are in their Plays the principal people. You must go along with them to a certain guarded extent—else the Play is done for. To be kept abhorring and abhorring, for Five Acts together, you can't stand.

Seward. Oh! that the difference between Poetry and Life were once for all set down—and not only once for all, but every time that it comes in question.

Buller. My dear sir, do gratify Seward's very reasonable desire, and once for all set down the difference.

Seward. You bear suicides on the stage, and tyrannicides and other cides—all simple homicide—much murder. Even Romeo's killing Tybalt in the street, in reparation for Mercutio's death, you would take rather differently, if happening today in Pall Mall, or Moray Place.

North. We have assuredly for the Stage a qualified scheme of sentiment—grounded no doubt on our modern of every-day morality—but specifically modified by Imagination—by Poetry—for the use of the dramatist. Till we have set down what we *do* bear, and why, we are not prepared for distinguishing what we won't bear, and why.

Buller. Oracular!

Seward. Suggestive.

North. And if so, sufficient for the nonce. Hamlet's uncle, Claudius, seems to me to be the most that can be borne of one purely abhorrible. He is made disgusting besides—drunken and foul. Able he is—for he won the Queen by "witchcraft of his wit:" but he is made endurable by his diminished proportion in the Play—many others overpowering and hiding him.

Buller. Pardon me, sir, but I have occasionally felt, in

the course of this conversation, that you were seeking—in opposition to Payne Knight—to reduce Macbeth to a species of Claudius. I agree with you in thinking that Shakspeare would not give a Claudius so large a proportion of his drama. The pain would be predominant and insupportable.

North. I would fain hope you have misunderstood me, Buller.

Buller. Sometimes, sir, it is not easy for a plain man to know what you would be at.

North. I?

Buller. Yea—you.

North. Richard III. *is* a hypocrite—a hard, cold murderer from of old—and yet you bear him. I suppose, friends, chiefly from his pre-eminent intellectual Faculties, and his perfectly courageous and self-possessed Will. You do support your conscience—or traffic with it—by saying all along—we are only conducting him to the retribution of Bosworth Field. But, friends, if these motions in Macbeth, which look like revealings and breathings of some better elements, are sheer and vile hypocrisy—if it is merely his manhood that quails, which his wife has to virilify—a dastard and a hypocrite, and no more—I cannot abide him—there is too much of a bad business, and then I must think Shakspeare has committed an egregious error in poetry. Richard III. is a bold, heroic hypocrite. He knows he is one. He lies to man—never to his own Conscience, or to Heaven.

Talboys. What?

North. Never. There he is clear-sighted, and stands, like Satan, in open and impious rebellion.

Buller. But your Macbeth, sir, would be a shuffling Puritan—a mixture of Holy Willie and Greenacre. Forgive me——

Seward. Order—order—order.

Talboys. Chair—chair—chair.

Buller. Swing—Swing—Swing.

North. My dear Buller—you have misunderstood me—I assure you you have. Some of my expressions may have been too strong—not sufficiently qualified.

Buller. I accept the explanation. But be more guarded in future, my dear sir.

North. I will.

Buller. On that assurance I ask you, sir, how is the Tragedy of Macbeth morally saved? That is, how does the degree of complacency with which we consider the two murderers not morally taint ourselves—not leave us predisposed murderers?

North. That is a question of infinite compass and fathom—answered then only when the whole Theory of Poesy has been expounded.

Buller. Whew!

North. The difference established between our contemplation of the Stage and of Life.

Buller. I hardly expect that to be done this Summer in this Tent.

North. Friends! Utilitarians and Religionists shudder and shun. They consider the Stage and Life as of one and the same kind—look on both through one glass.

Buller. Eh?

North. The Utilitarian will settle the whole question of Life upon half its data—the lowest half. He accepts Agriculture, which he understands logically—but rejects Imagination which he does not understand at all—because, if you sow it in the track of his plough, no wheat springs. Assuredly not; a different plough must furrow a different soil for that seed and that harvest.

Buller. Now, my dear sir, you speak like yourself. You always do so—the rashness was all on my side.

Seward. Nobody cares—hold your tongue.

North. The religionist errs from the opposite quarter. He

brings measures from Heaven to measure things of the Earth. He weighs Clay in the balance of Spirit. I call him a Religionist who overruns with religious rules and conceptions things that do not come under them—completely distinct from the native simplicity and sovereignty of Religion in a piously religious heart. Both of them are confounders of the sciences which investigate the Facts and the Laws of Nature, visible and invisible—subduing inquiry under preconception.

Buller. Was that the Gong—or but thunder?

North. The Gong.

Talboys. I smell sea-trout.

SCENE III.—*Deeside.*

TIME—*after dinner.*

NORTH—BULLER—SEWARD—TALBOYS.

North. One hour more—and no more—to Shakspeare.

Buller. May we crack nuts?

North. By all means. And here they are for you to crack.

Buller. Now for some of your *astounding Discoveries.*

North. If you gather the Movement, scene by scene, of the Action of this Drama, you see a few weeks, or it may be months. There must be time to hear that Malcolm and his brother have reached England and Ireland—time for the King of England to interest himself in behalf of Malcolm, and muster his array. More than this seems unrequired. But the zenith of tyranny to which Macbeth has arrived, and particularly the manner of describing the desolation of Scotland by the speakers in England, conveys to you the notion of a long, long dismal reign. Of old it always used to do so with me; so that when I came to visit the question of the Time, I felt myself as if baffled and puzzled, not finding the time I had looked for, demonstrable. Samuel Johnson has had the same impression, but has not scrutinized the data. He goes probably by the old Chronicler for the actual time, and this, one would think, must have floated before Shakspeare's own mind.

Talboys. Nobody can read the Scenes in England without seeing long-protracted time.

> "*Malcolm.* Let us seek out some desolate shade, and there
> Weep our sad bosoms empty.
> *Macduff.* Let us rather
> Hold fast the mortal sword, and, like good men,
> Bestride our down-fallen birthdom: Each new morn,
> New widows howl; new orphans cry; new sorrows
> Strike heaven on the face, that it resounds
> As if it felt with Scotland, and yell'd out
> Like syllable of dolour."

North. Ay, Talboys, that is true Shakspeare. No Poet—before or since—has in so few words presented such a picture. No poet, before or since, has used *such* words. He writes like a man inspired.

Talboys. And in the same dialogue Malcolm says—

> "I think our country sinks beneath the yoke;
> It weeps, it bleeds; and each new day a gash
> Is added to her wounds."

North. Go on, my dear Talboys. Your memory is a treasury of all the highest Poetry of Shakspeare. Go on.

Talboys. And hear Rosse, on his joining Malcolm and Macduff in this scene, the latest arrival from Scotland;—

> "*Macduff.* Stands Scotland where it did?
> *Rosse.* Alas, poor country!
> Almost afraid to know itself! It cannot
> Be call'd our mother, but our grave: where nothing,
> But who knows nothing, is once seen to smile;

> Where sighs and groans, and shrieks that rent the air,
> Are made, not mark'd; where violent sorrow seems
> A modern ecstacy; the dead man's knell
> Is there scarce ask'd, for who; and good men's lives
> Expire before the flowers in their caps,
> Dying, or ere they sicken."

North. Words known to all the world, yet coming on the ear of each individual listener with force unweaken'd by familiarity, power increased by repetition, as it will be over all Scottish breasts *in secula seculorum.*

Talboys. By Heavens! he smiles! There is a sarcastic smile on that incomprehensible face of yours, sir—of which no man in this Tent, I am sure, may divine the reason.

North. I was not aware of it. Now, my dear Talboys, let us here endeavor to ascertain Shakspeare's Time. Here we have long time with a vengeance—*and here we have short time;* FOR THIS IS THE PICTURE OF THE STATE OF POOR SCOTLAND BEFORE THE MURDER OF MACDUFF'S WIFE AND CHILDREN.

Buller. What?

Seward. Eh?

North. Macduff moved by Rosse's words, asks him, you know, Talboys, "how does my wife?" And then ensues the affecting account of her murder, which you need not recite. Now, I ask, when was the murder of Lady Macduff perpetrated? Two days—certainly not more—after the murder of Banquo. Macbeth, incensed by the flight of Fleance, goes, the morning after the murder of Banquo, to the Weirds, to know by "the worst means, the worst." You know what they showed him—and that, as they vanished, he exclaimed—

> "Where are they? Gone?—Let this pernicious hour
> Stand aye accursed in the calendar!—
> Come in, without there!

Enter LENOX.

Len. What's your grace's will?
Macb. Saw you the weird sisters?
Len. No, my lord.
Macb. Came they not by you?
Len. No, indeed, my lord.
Macb. Infected by the air whereon they ride;
And damn'd all those that trust them!—I did hear
The galloping of horse: Who was't came by?
Len. 'Tis two or three, my lord, that bring you word,
MACDUFF IS FLED TO ENGLAND.
Macb. Fled to England?
Len. Ay, my good lord.
Macb. Time, thou anticipat'st my dread exploits:
The flighty purpose never is o'ertook,
Unless the deed go with it: from this moment,
The very firstlings of my heart shall be
The firstlings of my hand. And even now
To crown my thoughts with acts, be it thought and done:
The castle of Macduff I will surprise;
Seize upon Fife; give to the edge o' the sword
His wife, his babes, and all unfortunate souls
That trace his line. No boasting like a fool:
This deed I'll do, before this purpose cool."

And his purpose does not cool—for the whole Family are murdered. When, then, took place the murder of Banquo? Why, a week or two after the Murder of Duncan. A very short time indeed, then, intervened between the first and the last of these Murders. And yet from those pictures of Scotland, painted in England for our information and horror, we have before us a long, long time, all filled up with butchery over all the land! But I say there had been no such butchery—or anything resembling it. There was, as yet, little amiss with Scotland. Look at the *linking* of Acts II. and III. End of Act II., Macbeth is gone to Scone—to be invested. Beginning of Act III.,

Banquo says, in soliloquy, in Palace of Fores, "Thou hast it *now.*" I ask, when is *this* NOW? Assuredly just after the Coronation. The Court was moved from Scone to Fores, which, we may gather from finding Duncan there formerly, to be the usual Royal Residence. "Enter Macbeth as King." "Our great Feast"—our "solemn Supper"—"this day's Council"—all have the aspect of new taking on the style of Royalty. "Thou hast it NOW," is formal—weighed—and in a position that gives it authority—at the very beginning of an Act—therefore intended to mark time—a very pointing of the finger on the dial.

Buller. Good image—short and apt.

Talboys. Let me perpend.

Buller. Do, sir, let him perpend.

North. Banquo *fears* "Thou play'dst most foully for it:" he goes no farther—not a word of any tyranny done. All the style of an incipient, *dangerous* Rule—clouds, but no red rain yet. And I need not point out to you, Talboys, who carry Shakspeare unnecessarily in a secret pocket of that strange Sporting Jacket, which the more I look at it the greater is my wonder—that Macbeth's behavior at the Banquet, on seeing Banquo nodding at him from his own stool, proves him to have been *then* young in blood.

> "My strange and self abuse
> Is the initiate fear that wants hard use.
> We are yet but young in deed."

He had a week or two before committed a first-rate murder, Duncan's—that night he had, by hired hands, got a second-rate job done, Banquo's—and the day following he gave orders for a bloody business on a more extended scale, the Macduffs. But nothing here the least like Rosse's, or Macduff's, or Malcolm's Picture of Scotland—during those few weeks. For Shakspeare forgot what the true time was—his own time—*the short time;* and introduced *long time at the same time*—why, he himself no doubt knew—and you no doubt, Talboys, know also—and will you have the goodness to tell the "why" to the Tent?

Talboys. In ten minutes. Are you done?

North. Not quite. Meanwhile—Two Clocks are going at once—which of the two gives the true time of Day?

Buller. Short and apt. Go on, Sir.

North. I call that an ASTOUNDING DISCOVERY. Macduff speaks as if he knew that Scotland had been for ever so long desolated by the Tyrant—and yet till Rosse told him, never had he heard of the Murder of his own Wife! Here Shakspeare either forgot himself wholly, and the short time he had himself assigned—or, with his eyes open, forced in the *long time* upon the *short*—in wilful violation of possibility! All silent?

Talboys. After supper—you shall be answered.

North. Not by any man now sitting here—or elsewhere.

Talboys. That remains to be heard.

North. Pray, Talboys, explain to me *this.* The Banquet scene breaks up in most admired disorder—"stand not upon the order of your going—but go at once,"—quoth the Queen. The King, in a state of great excitement, says to her—

"I will to-morrow,
(Betimes I will,) unto the weird sisters:
More shall they speak; for now I am bent to know,
By the worst means, the worst: for mine own good,
All causes shall give way; I am in blood
Stept in so far, that, should I wade no more,
Returning were as tedious as go o'er."

One might have thought not quite so tedious; as yet he had murdered only Duncan and his grooms, and to-night Banquo. Well, he does go "to-morrow and by times" to the Cave.

"*Witch.* By the pricking of my thumbs,
Something wicked this way comes;
Open locks, whoever knocks.
Macbeth. How now, you secret, Black, and midnight Hags?"

It is a "dark Cave,"—dark at all times—and now "by times" of the morning! Now—observe—Lenox goes along with Macbeth—on such occasions 'tis natural to wish "one of ourselves" to be at hand. And Lenox had been at the Banquet. Had he gone to bed after that strange Supper? No doubt, for an hour or two—like the rest of "the Family." But whether he went to bed or not, *then and there* he and another Lord had a confidential and miraculous conversation.

Buller. Miraculous! What's Miraculous about it?

North. Lenox says to the other Lord—

"*My former speeches* have but hit your thoughts,
Which can interpret further; only, I say,
Things have been strangely borne: the gracious Duncan
Was pitied of Macbeth—marry he was dead.
And the right valiant Banquo walked too late;
Whom, you may say, if it please you, Fleance killed,
For Fleance fled."

Who told him all this about Banquo and Fleance? He speaks of it quite familiarly to the "other lord," as a thing well known in all its bearings. But not a soul but Macbeth, and the Three Murderers themselves, could possibly have known anything about it! As for Banquo, "Safe in a ditch he hides,"—and Fleance had fled. The body may, perhaps in a few days, be found, and, though "with twenty trenched gashes on its head," identified as Banquo's, and, in a few weeks, Fleance may turn up in Wales. Nay, the Three Murderers may confess. But now all is hush; and Lenox, unless endowed with second sight, or clairvoyance, could know nothing of the murder. Yet, from his way of speaking of it, one might imagine crowner's 'quest had sitten on the body—and the report been in the *Times* between supper and that after-supper confab! I am overthrown —everted—subverted—the contradiction is flagrant—the impossibility monstrous—I swoon.

Buller. Water—water.

North. Thank you, Buller. That's revivifying—I see now all objects distinctly. Where was I? O, ay. The "other Lord" seems as warlock-wise as Lenox—for he looks forward to times when

> "We may again
> Give to our tables meat, sleep to our nights;
> *Free from our feasts and banquets bloody knives.*"

An allusion, beyond doubt, to the murder of Banquo! A sudden thought strikes me. Why, not only must the real, actual, spiritual, corporeal ghost of Banquo *sat on the stool*, but "Lenox and the other Lord," as well as Macbeth, *saw him.*

Buller. Are you serious, sir?

North. So serious that I can scarcely hope to recover my usual spirits to-day. Have you, gentlemen, among you any more plausible solution to offer? All mum. One word more with you. Lenox tells the other Lord"

> "From broad words, and 'cause he fail'd
> His presence at the tyrant's feast, I hear,
> MACDUFF LIVES IN DISGRACE; SIR, CAN YOU TELL
> WHERE HE BESTOWS HIMSELF?"

And the "other Lord," who is wonderfully well informed for a person "strictly anonymous," replies that Macduff—

> "Is gone to pray the holy king, (Edward) on his aid
> To wake Northumberland, and warlike Siward."

Nay, he minutely describes Macduff's surly reception of the King's messenger, sent to invite him to the Banquet, and the happy style of that official on getting the Thane of Fife's "absolute, Sir, not I," and D. I. O.! and the same nameless "Lord in waiting" says to Lenox, that

> "*this report*
> *Hath so exasperate the king, that he*
> *Prepares for some attempt of war.*"

I should like to know first where and when these two gifted individuals picked up all this information? The king himself had told the Queen, that same night, that he had *not sent* to Macduff—but that he had heard "by the way" that he was not coming to the Banquet—and he only *learns* the flight of Macduff after the Cauldron Scene—that is at end of it:—

> "*Macbeth.* Come in, without there!
> *Enter Lenox.*
> *Lenox.* What's your Grace's will?
> *Macbeth.* Saw you the Weird Sisters?
> *Lenox.* No, indeed, my Lord.
> *Macbeth.* Infected be the air whereon they ride;
> And damn'd all those that trust them!—I did hear
> The galloping of horse: Who was't came by?
> *Lenox.* '*Tis two or three, my Lord, that bring you word,*
> MACDUFF IS FLED TO ENGLAND.
> *Macbeth.* FLED TO ENGLAND?"

For an Usurper and Tyrant, his Majesty is singularly ill-informed about the movements of his most dangerous Thanes! But Lenox, I think, must have been not a little surprised at that moment to find that, so far from the *exasperated* Tyrant having "*prepared for some attempt of war*" with England—he had not till then positively known that Macduff had fled! I pause, as a man pauses who has no more to say—not for a reply. But to be sure, Talboys will reply to anything—and were I to say that the Moon is made of green cheese, he would say —yellow—

Talboys. If of weeping Parmesan, then I—of the "cheese without a tear"—Double Gloster.

North. The whole Dialogue between Lenox and the Lord is *miraculous.* It abounds with knowledge of events that had not happened—and *could not* have happened—on the showing of Shakspeare himself; but I do not believe that there is another man now alive who knows that Lenox and the "other Lord" are caught up and strangled in that *noose of Time.* Did the Poet? You would think, from the way they go on, that one ground of war, one motive of Macduff's going, is the murder of Banquo—perpetrated since he is gone off!

Talboys. Eh?

North. Gentlemen, I have given you a specimen or two of Shakspeare's way of dealing with time—and I can elicit no reply. You are one and all dumb-foundered. What will you be—where will you be—when I—

Buller. Have announced "all my astounding discoveries!" and where, also, will be poor Shakspeare—where his Critics?

North. Friends, Countrymen, and Romans, lend me your ears! A dazzling spell is upon us that veils from our apprehension all incompatibilities—all impossibilities—for he dips the Swan-quill in Power—and Power is that which you must accept from him, and so to the utter oblivion, while we read or behold, of them all. To go to work with such inquiries is to try to articulate thunder. What do I intend? That Shakspeare is only to be *thus* criticised? Apollo forbid—forbid the Nine! I intend Prologemena to the Criticism of Shakspeare. I intend mowing and burning the brambles before ploughing the soil. I intend showing where we must not look for the Art and the Genius of Shakspeare, as a step to discovering where we must. I suspect—I know—that Criticism has oscillated from one extreme to another, in the mind of the country—from denying all art, to acknowledging consummated art, and no flaw. I would find the true Point. Stamped and staring upon the front of these Tragedies as a conflict. He, the Poet, beholds Life,—he, the Poet, is on the Stage. The littleness of the Globe Theatre mixes with the greatness of human affairs. You think of the Green-room and the Scene-shifters. I think that when we have stripped away the disguises and incumbrances of the Power, we shall see, naked, and strong, and beautiful, the statue moulded by Jupiter.

DIES BOREALES.

No. VI.

CAMP AT CLADICH. SCENE I.—*The Wren's Nest.*

TIME—*Six* A. M.

NORTH—TALBOYS—SEWARD.

North. You recollect the words of Edmund in Lear—

> "A credulous father, and a brother noble,
> Whose nature is so far from doing harm
> That he suspects none; on whose foolish honesty
> One's practices ride easy."

This is exactly Iago with Othello—believing in virtue, using, despising it. These idolators of self think the virtuous worship imaginary, unreal Gods. But they never doubt the sincerity of the worship; and therein show a larger intelligence, a clearer insight than those other idolators who, shut up in their own character, ascribe their own motives to all; and in virtues can see only different shapes of hypocrisy.

Talboys. The Devil himself knows better, sir. He knows that virtue exists; only he flatters himself that he can undermine its foundations. "And ofttimes does succeed"—seeking Evil "as contrary to His High Will whom we resist!"

North. The Evil principle at war with the Good.

Talboys. In what war soever, sir, you are once engaged, you soon feel yourself pledged to it. A few blows given on both sides settle you fast, and you no longer inquire about the cause.

North. To an evil soul all good is a reproach; therefore he wars on it. To the self-dissatisfied the happiness of the good is a reproach; therefore, if he be thoroughly selfish, he pulls it down.

Talboys. Every one's impulse is to throw off pain; and if no pity, no awe, no love be there to stay him, he pulls down of course.

North. My dear Talboys, believe me, that for a moment, every man has motives fit for a fiend. Perhaps he obeys—perhaps rejects them. The true fiend is constant.

Talboys. Every man has motives fit for a fiend! I beg you to speak for yourself, my dear sir.

North. I speak of myself, of you, and of Iago. What is the popular apprehension or theory of the malice disclosed in "mine Ancient"—not the Old One, but the Standard-bearer?

Talboys. Why, the prompt, apt, and natural answer will be, he is a Devil.

North. And pray what is a Devil?

Talboys. Iago.

North. Don't reason in a circle, sir.

Talboys. I'd rather reason in a circle, sir, than not reason at all. I like reasoning in a circle—it is pleasant pastime in a cold, raw morning—far preferable to ascending Cruachan; for you are never far from home, and when tired can leap out at your own pleasure, and take some reasoning in a straight line.

North. You are always so pleasant, Talboys, circular or zig-zag. Whence is the malice in the heart of a Devil?

Talboys. I want data, sir. Milton has given some historical elucidation of it; but the People reason less, and are no philosophers.

North. Hate in a devil is like Love in an Angel—uncaused, or self-causing; it is his natural function—his Essence, his Being. Herein the seraph is a seraph—the fiend is a fiend.

Talboys.

> "Evil! be Thou my good! By Thee at least
> Divided Empire with Heaven's King I hold,
> By Thee, and more perhaps than half will reign."

Reason—Motive—Cause.

North. Prospero calls Caliban a devil—a born Devil.

Talboys. Also a demi-Devil—as Othello calls Iago.

North. The Philosopher knows—*in humanity*—of no born devil. He follows, or tries to follow, the causes which have turned the imperfect nature into the worst. The popular sense takes things as it finds them, and acknowledges "born devils," Iago being one, and "of the prime." The *totality* of monster in the moral world seems to that unphilosophical, sincere, and much-to-the-purpose intuition, expressed under the image of a *nativity*. The popular sense recognizes a temper of man which elects evil for evil's sake—which inflicts pain, because it likes to see pain suffered—which destroys, because it revels in misery.

Talboys. Coleridge calls Iago's "a motiveless malignity." He hated Othello for not promoting him, but Cassio. That seems to me the real, tangible motive—a haunting, goading, fretting preference—an affront—an insult—a curbing of power—wounding him where alone he is sensitive—in self-esteem and pride. See his contempt for Cassio as a book-warrior—and "for a fair life"—simply like our notion of a "milksop."

Why Othello, who so prizes him for his honesty as to call him ever "honest Iago," keeps him down, I have not a guess—

North. Haven't you. And pray what right have you to interfere with the practice of promotion in the army of the Venetian State?

Talboys. I cannot approve of this particular instance—it looks like favoritism. Othello fancied Cassio—Cassio was the genteeler young fellow of the two—the better-born—Iago had risen from the ranks—and was a stout soldier—

North. You don't take your character of Cassio from Iago?

Talboys. I do. Iago was a liar—but here I think he spoke truth—there is nothing in the Play indicating that Cassio had seen much service—he had never been at Cyprus—nor anywhere else—he had never seen a Turk—he had never—

North. Hold your tongue.

Talboys. A more disgraceful Brawl—

North. Hold your tongue, I say.

Talboys. Don't keep pouring out your excuses for him, sir, with such overwhelming volubility—it won't do. He knew his own wretched head. "I have very poor and unhappy brains for drinking," yet drink he would,—"I have drunk but one cup to-night, and that was craftily qualified too"—worse than shirking—"behold what innovation it makes here,"—and yet he would not join the Teetotalers. Ou ton such a Lieutenant! Iago *was* an ill-used man.

North. Talboys—

Talboys. O that ceaseless volubility! Shakspeare afterwards makes Iago say that Cassio "has a daily beauty in his life." Where do we see it? In his *liaison* with that "fitchew?" From pleading with the Divine Desdemona on a question to him of life or death, to go straight to sup—and sleep with Bianca!

North. Othello's "Now thou art my Lieutenant," shows

the importance meant by Shakspeare to be attached to the previous oppression—or "holding down" of Iago. Alas! how that allocution instigating Iago to murder by more than a promise of promotion, sadly lowers Othello to me—I hardly know why. I feel a descent from his own passion to a sympathy with Iago's desire to step into his superior officer's shoes. I can fancy that Shakspeare meant this. Ay, that he did; for I believe that turbulent passion, in some of its moods, lowers —degrades—debases a great and generous nature.

Talboys. Iago was jealous of Othello. He says he was, and either believes it, or tries to believe it. His own words intimate the doubt, and the determination to believe. Malignity and hate indulge in giving acceptance to slight grounds—such he says, in his own coarse way, was the rumour—and perhaps it was true—

North. Certainly it was false. High characters, as Coriolanus, Hotspur, Othello, are, by a native majesty of spirit, saved and exalted from the pursuit of illicit pleasure.

Talboys. They are. But let his jealousy of Othello—sincere or assumed—or mixed or alternating—enter as an element into the hatred.

North. Let it. Iago was, you said truly, a stout Soldier—and I add, a hard, unfeeling, unprincipled Soldier. Of all trades in the world, that of a Soldier is the worst and the best —witness an Iago—an Othello. The same trade helped to make both. In Othello we almost see Wordsworth's *Happy Warrior*—in Iago one—

"Yet ill he lived, much evil saw,
'Mongst men to whom no better law
Nor better life was known;
Deliberately and undeceived,
Those bad men's vices he received
And gave them back his own!"

You are convinced, without a hint, that he is infidel—atheist: everything shaped like religion, like moral conscience—his mind shakes off and rejects with scorn. He does not, however, as I said, disbelieve in Virtues. He believes in them, and uses them to the destruction of the havers. What he disbelieves is the worth of Virtues. To that savage Idol, Self, the more bleeding and noble victims, the more grateful the sacrifice.

Talboys. A singular combination in him, sir, is his wily Italian wit—like Iachimo's—and his rough—soldierlike—plain, blunt, jovial manners—the tone of the Camp, and of the wild-living, *reckless* Camp—plenty of hardihood—fit for toil, peril, privation. You never for a moment doubt his courage—his presence of mind—his resources—he does not once quail in presence of Othello at his utmost fury. He does not stir up the Lion from without, through the bars of his cage, with an invisible rod of iron—that is, a whip of scorpions; he lashes up the Wild Beast, and flinches not an inch from paw that would smite, or tusk that would tear—a veritable Lion Queller and King.

North. I cannot but believe that the Othello of Shakspeare is black, and all black. I cannot conceive the ethnography of that age drawing—on the stage especially—the finer distinction which we know between a Moor and a Blackamoor or Negro. The opposition, entertained by nature, is between White and Black—not between White and Brown. You want the opposition to tell with all its power. "I saw Othello's visage in his mind" is nothing, unless the visible visage is one to be conquered—to be accepted by losing sight of it. I say again, that I cannot myself imagine the cotemporary audience of Shakspeare deciding color between a Moor and a Negro. The tradition of the Stage, too, seems to have made Othello jet black. Such, I opine, was the notion of the Moor, *then*, to the People, to the Court, to the Stage, to Shakspeare.

Talboys. Wooly-headed?

North. Why, yes—if you choose—in opposition to the "curled darlings."

Talboys. Yet Coleridge has said it would be "something monstrous to conceive this beautiful Venetian girl falling in love with a veritable Negro."

North. Coleridge almost always thought, felt, wrote, and spoke finely, as a Critic—but may I venture, in all love and admiration of that name, to suggest that the removal which the stage makes of a subject from reality must never be forgotten. In life you cannot bear that the White Woman shall marry the Black Man. You could not bear that an English Lady Desdemona—Lady Blanche Howard—should—under any imaginable greatness—marry General Toussaint or the Duke of Marmalade. Your senses revolt with offence and loathing. But on the Stage some consciousness that everything is not as literally meant as it seems—that symbols of humanity, and not actual men and women, are before you—saves the Play.

Talboys. I believe that Wordsworth's line—

"The gentle Lady married to the Moor,"

expresses explicitly the feeling of the general English heart—pity for the contrast, and a thought of the immense love which has overcome it.

North. White and Black is the utter antithesis—as, at intensity, Night and Day. Yes—Talboys—Every jot of soot you take from his complexion, you take an iota from the signified power of love.

Talboys. As you say, sir, the gap which is between the Stage and Reality must prevent, in our hearts, anything like loathing of the conjunction.

North. The touch of such an emotion would annul the whole Tragedy. A disparity, or a discrepency, vast as mysterious—but which love, at the full, is entitled to overlook—overstep! Whether Fate dare allow prosperity to a union containing so mighty an element of disruption, is another question. It seems like an attempt at overruling the "Æterna fœdera rerum."

Talboys. For half an hour after her death, Othello believes her guilty. You must take it for a representation of what his feelings would have been, if she had really been guilty.

North. Unless the fact of her innocence have a secret potency that reaches, through all appearance and evidence of her guilt, into his innermost soul. Be that as it may, he is, after the deed, perplexed and unmanned, totally unlike a man who has performed a great sacrifice to the offended gods. You may say that the convulsion of uptorn love is too fresh, and that he would in time have regained his strength—that had she been guilty, the first half-hour must have been just what it was. All I know is, that his mind first becomes clear, when he knows her innocent. Then he is, in a measure, himself, and sees his way. Had she been guilty, he would have lived two years with a stern, desolate soul—not harsh, perhaps, to honest folks, though—and have then fallen in battle.

Talboys. But how is Iago affected by the blackness? No doubt, with more hate and aversion at being commanded by and outshone by him. High military rank and command—high favor by the Senate—high power and esteem in the world—high royalty of spirit—happiness in marriage—all these in Othello are proper subjects of envy, and motives of hate in Iago. The Nigger!

North. Antipathy of bad to good—of base to noble—exacerbated by physical antipathy of color! But I never could fathom the hate and malice and revenge of Iago.

Talboys. It is unfathomable—and therefore fit agent in Tragedy.

North. Even so. I don't believe that Shakspeare always means you to be able to lay motives in the balance and weigh them. Far otherwise.

Talboys. Ay—Think how the Murder of Duncan leaps up, Hell-born, into the heart of Macbeth—at the breath of the Weird Sisters!

North. Perhaps. Poetry shaping out an action, distinguishes herself, amongst other points of distinction herein, from History, that while she shows lucidly and of her own clear knowledge, the concatenation of Cause and Effect, yet passion and imagination require the indefinite. There is then a conflict of claims and powers; and the part of logic is hence imperfectly rendered. You see the river sweeping by you, without knowing all the springs that have fed it.

Talboys. Say that again, sir.

North. *There* IS the hatred—a tragical power, which the Poet is principally concerned to use—less to explain.

Talboys. You said, sir, the noble Moor must have been much disennobled ere he could have cried to Iago, "Now thou art my lieutenant."

North. I did, and you think so too.

Talboys. I do. Othello and Iago are joint conspirators to two double murders. Can you conspire to a murder—a private assassination—without lowering yourself—even on the Stage? Othello takes on himself the murder of Desdemona—act, responsibility, consequences; but does he not seem to hire Iago to assassinate Cassio?

North. What did Othello intend to do—after all was accomplished? Consequences indeed! He was stone-blind to the future. What does he expect? that when he has killed his wife, everything is to go on as smoothly as before? That no notice will be taken of it? or that he will have to make another speech to the Senate? He has told them how he married her

—the counterpart will be to relate "a plain unvarnished tale of my whole course" of smothering and stabbing her with bolster and dagger. "Now thou art my lieutenant"—shows—if not stone-blindness—a singular confidence in the future.

Talboys. The Personages who come in at the End look at the matter contrariwise. Othello exalts the killing of his wife into a sacrifice to Justice. But Cassio? That is mere—pure Revenge. "O that the slave had forty thousand lives,—one is too poor, too weak for my revenge."

North. Upon what pedestal does Othello stand *now*—engaging another to kill Cassio in the dark, for his own revenge? I repeat it, surely the Noble Moor is now very much disennobled.

Talboys. I rejoice, my dear sir, that you have so completely got rid of that nasty cough—your voice is as clear as a bell. Lungs sound—

North. As those of a prize bagpiper. Talboys, I cannot help thinking that Shakspeare shows up in Othello foul passions—that you see in him two natures conjoined—the moral Caucasian White, and the animal tropical Black. In the Caucasian, the spiritual or angelical in us attains its manifestation. In the offspring of the tropics, amongst the sands, and under the suns of Africa, the animal nature takes domination. The sands and suns that breed Lions, breed Men with Lions' hearts in them. The Lion is for himself noble, but blood of the Irrational in the veins of the Rational is a contradiction. The noblest moral nature and the hot blind rage of animal blood!

Talboys. Ay, the noblest moral nature, and high above every other evidence of it, his love of HER—which, what it was, and what it would have remained, or become—and what he was and would have been, had Iago not been there—we may imagine! With all the Power of a warrior, and a ruler, he has the sensibility of a Lover—with all spontaneous dignity and nobility, he has the self-mastery of reason—before his overthrow.

North. Wherefore, my dear Sheriff, I prefer Othello as a specimen of the *Ethical Marvelous.* Like, as in another kingdom, a Winged Horse or a Centaur—the meeting of two natures which readily hold asunder. All this has under the Æthiop complexion its full force—less if you mitigate—if not mitigate merely, but take away, where are we all? The innate repugnance of the White Christian to the Black Moorish blood, is the ultimate tragic substratum—the "*must*" of all that follows. Else—*make* Othello White—and, I say again, see where we are!

Talboys. Shakspeare, sir, is not one to flinch from the utmost severity of a Case.

North. Not he, indeed—therefore I *swear* Othello is a Blackamoor.

Talboys. And I take it, sir, that Othello's natural demeanor is one of great gravity, to which the passionate moods induced are in extremity of contrast. I conceive that by these mixtures and contrasts, he is rendered picturesque and poetical.

North. I swear Othello was a Blackamoor—and that Desdemona was the Whitest Lady in Europe.

Talboys. Had he lived to be tried for murder, I think his counsel might have successfully set up the plea of insanity.

North. They might have successfully set it up—but I, the Judge, would have successfully put it down. Honestly, I don't think Othello mad; and for this reason, that the thought never before came into my head. An incident that appears to me most wonderful in dramatic invention is—the Swooning. Look at the precise words preceding his falling down. To me it has no other effect or sense, than that of the blood being driven up into the head, and oppressing with physical pressure that bodily organ

—the brain. The soul strikes the body like a hammer, and knocks it down.

Talboys. Ay, how his words waver—"That's not so good now"—from a man believing, or on the point of believing. There is to me a physical faintness in these words, and in the play upon the words "lie with her," &c., intellect reeling to fall.

North. Good. But I believe body and soul of Othello—or the relation between body and soul—to be physiologically right and sound. The swooning goes soon off—the accident of an hour—the mind is else in full vigor, sound, and misled. You must recollect that a mind of supereminent physical (may one say so?) and moral power—a mind that would have been strong and calm through the Russian Campaign of Napoleon—is not in a day stricken into a state which requires the medical skill and attention of Dr. Willis. Othello had an immensely strong physical constitution undoubtedly—had he not, the adventures related would long ago have extinguished him. This is one meaning of that sudden and strange narrative which children are taught by rote, and which men may not have quite fathomed; but a strong body and strong soul conjoined do not lightly admit of disjunction. Madness, properly so called is a disjunction, in some way or kind, of the natural union between soul and body. A few days disrupt the ties in the aged Lear. You may think that in Othello—I suppose Ætat. 40 or 45—the ties would bear some wrenching of the rack, ere snapping. I think that they held firm.

Talboys. True, sir, insanity would even detract from the moral majesty and splendor of Othello.

North. It would. The time comes back to me when I *did not care for the Play or the Man.* The Play now seems to me wonderful, more even than Hamlet or Lear—and the Man, in poetical invention, a match for Achilles or Satan.

Talboys. Sir--sir.

North. Passion in the blood like that of a Negro—and right in the soul as of Socrates or Epaminondas. Yes, Talboys, the Majesty of the Moral soul in Othello seems to me the most prophetic, or divining or inconceivable of Shakspeare's conceptions.

Talboys. Nay—nay—my dear sir.

North. Everything else might seem to offer its own reason—

Talboys. Nay—nay—my dear sir. Compare the gross Hamlet of Saxo Grammaticus with Ours.

North. Well, do—but Othello—you don't know whence he is derived. He is a tropical animal—kindred to the lion—the tiger—the dragon—and, on the other hand, he has the rational equipoise of the faculties that stamp the Philosopher—and he is everything between the two.

Talboys. An Eloge, indeed—perhaps a *leetle* too eulogistic.

North. No. What a simple sincerity colors the narrative of his love-making! Is your *imagination* bewitched by the wild story of his adventurous life? Hers, doubtless, was fascinated. But your *soul*, methinks, is won to approving the Venetian Maiden's choice by a profounder, a more legitimate charm. Who ever heard Othello relate, and hung back from believing him? He is honest, and she is honest. That is the bond whereby the Parcæ united their souls and their threads. Why they disunited both—how that infernal intervention of Lachesis and Atropos crossed their pure souls in their pure conjunction, let Clotho—if she can—tell.

Talboys. Let's be more cheerful.

North. Ay—let's.

Talboys. Othello shows that our Good—our excellence—our capacity of happiness—lies all in Love. That our light in which we walk—our light which we give forth—is Love. He declares this, by cleaving to this Good--by having it—by losing it—by recovering it. The self-consciousness of Othello returns to its unison with universal being—with heaven's harmony of the worlds. Iago denies this Good—never acknowledges it—although he serves involuntarily to demonstrate the truth—of which Othello perishes the self-sacrificed witness. It is great, sir, in the Tragedy, but in Him the House of Love is divided against itself. His jealousy, child of his love, lifts up a parricidal hand, wounds and is wounded—but only unto its own death. And what is the feeling left by the catastrophe?

North. Say, my friend, say.

Talboys. Peace—rest—repose—depth of tranquillity—like the sea stilled from storms.

North. The charmed calm that reflects heaven.

Talboys. Peace grounded in this proved thought—that LOVE IS BEST. Of all the Persons, whose stars will you accept to be your own? If you are a man, Othello's; if woman, the wronged and murdered Desdemona's. Study for ever the two closing and summing up verses—"I *kissed* thee ere I *killed* thee; no way but this—Killing myself to die upon a kiss!" To gather up all the terror that is past, as if not only the winds were upgathered like sleeping flowers, but upgathered into the sleeping flowers. I don't know how to avoid comparing—all alike as the characters are—the end of Romeo and Juliet—Lear and Cordelia—Othello and Desdemona. I never can separate them. LOVE the mightiest torn asunder in life—reunited in death. Love—the solace of lapsed and mortal humanity.

North. Lend the Old Hobbler your arm.

Scene II.—*Pavilion.*

Time—*After breakfast.*

North—Talboys—Seward—Buller.

North. NOW FOR THE GRAND INQUIRY.

How long think you was Othello Governor of Cyprus, and Desdemona the General's wife?

Talboys. How long? Why some weeks, or some months; quarter of a year, half a year, a year.

North. A most satisfactory answer indeed to a simple question. How long have I been Commander of the forces at Cladich!

Talboys. Tents pitched on the 14th May 1849—This is the 24th of June Ditto. You, like Michael Cassio, are "a great arithmetician"—and can calculate the Days.

North. That's precise. Let's have some small attempt at precision with respect to the time at Cyprus.

Talboys. Well then—a month—Two Months.

North. And you are a Student—a Scholar—in Shakspeare!

Talboys. What the ace do you mean?

North. Just Two Days.

Talboys. What the deuce do you mean? The Man has lost his Senses.

North. Who? Shakspeare?

Talboys. Really, sir, you are getting daily more and more paradoxical—and I begin to tremble for your wits.

North. See that your own have not gone a wool-gathering, Talboys. Two Months! For two Months read Two Days—I insist on it.

Talboys. Gentlemen, the case seems serious. What would you propose?

Seward. Let's hear the Sage.

North. Open Shakspeares. Act II.—Scene I.

Buller. All ready, sir.

North. A Sea-port Town in Cyprus—not Nicosia, the capital of the Island, which is inland—thirty miles from the Sea—but Famagusta.

Talboys. So says in a note Malone—what's that to the purpose?

North. I wish to be precise. Ship ahoy!

Talboys.

> "The ship is here put in,
> A Veronese; Michael Cassio,
> Lieutenant to the warlike Moor, Othello,
> Is come on shore."—

North.

> "A sail—a sail—a sail!
> My hopes do shape him for the Governor."

Buller.

> "Tis one Iago, Ancient to the General."

Talboys.

> "The riches of the ship is come on shore!"

Buller.

> "Ye men of Cyprus, let her have your knees.

North.

> The Moor! I know his trumpet."

There's the power of poetry for you—I do pity poor prose. The sea-beach—town—fortifications—all crowded with people on the gaze-out—*for hours.* For ships on the stormy sea. But not a ship to be seen. Obedient to the passion of the people, one ship after another appears in the offing—salutes and is saluted—is within the Bay—inside the Breakwater—drops anchor—the divine Desdemona has landed—Othello has her in his arms—

> "O my soul's joy!
> If after every tempest comes such calms,
> May the winds blow till they have waken'd death!
> And let the laboring bark climb hills of seas
> Olympus-high; and duck again as low
> As hell's from heaven!"

all *in five minutes*—in three minutes—in one minute—in no time—in less than no time.

Talboys. What's your drift?

North. Handle Shakspeares! Scene II.—A Street—On the day of Othello's arrival—the Proclamation is issued "that there is full liberty of feasting for this present hour of *Five*, till the bell has told Eleven"—For besides the mere perdition of the Turkish Fleet, it is the "celebration *of his nuptials.*"

Talboys. We all know that—go on.

Seward. His nuptials! Why, I thought he had been married at Venice!

North. Who cares what you think? Scene III.—A Hall in the Castle—and enter Othello, Desdemona, Cassio, and attendants. Othello says—

> "Good Michael, look you to the guard to-night;
> Let's teach ourselves that honorable stop,
> Not to outsport discretion."

And before retiring for the night with Desdemona, he says—

> "Michael, good night; *To-morrow with our earliest,*
> *Let me have speech with you.*"

Talboys. Why lay you such emphasis on these unimportant words?

North. They are not unimportant. Then comes the Night Brawl—as schemed by Iago. Othello, on the spot, cashiers Cassio—and at that very moment, Desdemona entering disturbed, with attendants, he says—

> "Look if my gentle love is not rais'd up.—
> Come, Desdemona; 'tis the soldiers' life,
> To have their balmy slumbers wak'd with strife."

Iago advises the unfortunate Cassio to "confess himself freely" to Desdemona—who will help to put him in his place again—and Cassio replies—"*betimes in the morning I will beseech the virtuous Desdemona to undertake for me:* I am desperate of *my fortunes, if they check me here;*—and the Scene concludes with these words of Iago's—

> "Two things are to be done.—
> My wife must move for Cassio to her mistress;
> I'll set her on;
> Myself, the while, *to draw the Moor apart,*
> *And bring him jump when he may Cassio find*
> *Soliciting his wife: Ay, that's the way;*
> *Dull not device by coldness and delay.*"

"By the mass, 'tis morning," quoth Iago—and Act II. closes with the dawn of the Second Day at Cyprus. You don't deny that?

Talboys. Nobody denies it—nobody ever denied it—nobody ever will deny it.

North. Act Third. Now for Act III.

Talboys. Our six eyes and our six ears are all wide awake, sir.

North. It opens before the Castle—as the *same morning* is pretty well advanced—and Cassio is ordering some musicians to play "Good-morrow, General."

Talboys. On the same morning? I am not sure of that, sir.

North. Nobody denies it—nobody ever did deny it—nobody ever will deny it.

Talboys. Not so fast, sir.

North. Why, you slow coach! Cassio says to the Clown, who is with the Musicians, "There's a poor piece of gold for thee: if the Gentlewoman that attends the General's wife be stirring, tell her, there's one Cassio entreats her a little favor of speech;"—and as the Clown goes off, Iago enters and says to Cassio—

"*You have not been a-bed, then?*"

And Cassio answers—

"Why, no; *the day had broke*
Before we parted. I have made bold, Iago,
To send in to your wife. My suit to her
Is, that she will to virtuous Desdemona
Procure me some access.
Iago. I'll send her to you presently;
And I'll devise a mean to draw the Moor
Out of the way, that your converse and business
May be more free."

Emilia then enters, and tells Cassio that all will soon be well —"the General and his Wife are talking of it—and she speaks for you stoutly."—

Talboys. All this does not positively imply that the preceding night was the night of the Brawl. Cassio, though originally intending it, on reflection may have thought it to precipitate to apply to Desdemona the very next day; and there is nothing improbable in his having been with Iago till daybreak on some subsequent night. It is not quite clear, then, that the Third Act commences on the morning after Cassio's dismissal.

North. O rash and inconsiderate man!

Talboys. Who is?

North. You. It is not quite clear! I say 'tis clear as mud or amber. Iago has with such hellish haste conceived and executed his machinations, that Cassio has been cashiered some few hours after landing in Cyprus. In the pride of success, he urges on Cassio to apply without delay to Desdemona in the morning. We see the demi-devil determined to destroy—"By the mass, 'tis morning—pleasure and action make the hours seem short." Iago may have gone to bed for a few hours—Cassio had not—"You have not been a-bed, then." "Why, no; the day had broke before we parted." The time of the end of Second Act, and of the beginning of Third Act, are thus connected as firmly as words and deeds can connect. You say there is nothing improbable in Cassio's having been with Iago till daybreak on some subsequent night? Why, who the devil cares to know that Cassio had not been to bed on some other night? His not having been to bed on *this* night is an indication of *his* anxiety, and Iago's question is a manifestation of *his* malevolence cloaked with an appearance of concern. In each case an appropriate trait of character is brought before us; but the main purpose of the words is to fix the time, which they do without the possibility of a doubt. They *demonstrate* that the Third Act opens on the morning immediately subsequent to the night on which Act Second closes. This morning dovetails into that night with an exactness which nothing could improve.

Talboys. Why so fierce, my good sir?

North. Fierce! I may well be fierce. What! Cassio's desire to see Desdemona cool before morning—Iago's desire to drive him on to his destruction cool too—and both walk away without further heed—and when next seen, after an interval of some weeks or months, talking about not having been in bed during some other night on which nothing particular has happened! Bah!

Talboys. Sir, I do not like to see you so much excited. You mistake me—I was merely, at your bidding, assisting you in your expiscation of the Time—we are at one about it.

North. My dear Talboys, forgive me—my irascibility is a disease—

Talboys. Health—health—exuberant health of mind and body—May you live a thousand years.

North. The Third Act, then, you allow, opens on the morning of the day following the night on which the Second Act closes.

Talboys. I not only allow, my dear sir, I insist on it. Let me hear any man deny it, and I will knock the breath out of his body. Proceed, sir.

North. Obstinate? I never called you obstinate, my dear Talboys. Well—let me proceed, with you for an ally. In this same scene, First of Act Third, Cassio says to Emilia,

> "Yet, I beseech you,
> If you think fit, or that it may be done,
> Give me advantage of some brief discourse
> With Desdemona alone."

And Emilia says to him,

> "Pray you, come in;
> *I will bestow you where you shall have time*
> *To speak your bosom freely.*
> *Cassio.* I am much bound to you."

And off they go to sue to the gentle Desdemona.

Talboys. Alas! somewhat too gentle.

North. Then follows Scene II. of Act III.—a very short one—let me read it aloud.

"*A Room in the Castle.*"

Enter OTHELLO, IAGO, *and Gentlemen.*

Othello. These letters give, Iago, to the pilot;
And, by him, do my duties to the State;
That done, I will be walking on the works;
Repair there to me.
Iago. Well, my good Lord, I'll do't.
Othello. This fortification, gentlemen,—shall we see't?
Gent. We'll wait upon your lordship. [*Exeunt.*"

That this Scene is on the same day as Scene Second—and with little intermission of time—is too plain to require proof. Othello here sends off his first dispatches to Venice by the pilot who had brought him safely to Cyprus, and then goes out to inspect the fortification. That is in the natural course of things—such a scene at any subsequent time would be altogether without meaning.

Talboys. I cannot see that, sir.

North. None so blind as they who will not see.

Talboys. There again.

North. What do you want, Talboys?

Talboys. Have the goodness, my dear sir, to pause a moment—and go back to the close of the Scene preceding this short one. Then and there, Cassio, as we saw, goes into the Castle with Emilia, "*to be bestowed*" that he may have an opportunity of asking Desdemona to intercede for him with Othello. But "to be bestowed" may mean to have apartments there—and he may have been living in the Castle for several days, with or without Othello's knowledge, before that short Scene which you have just now quoted.

North. Living in the Castle for several days! With or without Othello's knowledge! Prodigious! All that Cassio asked was, "the advantage of some *brief discourse;*" and, that he might have that advantage, Emilia gave him apartments in the Castle! And there we may suppose him living at rack and manger, lying *perdu* in the Governor's House! Emilia was a queer customer enough, but she could hardly have taken upon herself the responsibility of secreting a man under the same roof with Desdemona, without the sanction of her Mistress—and if with her sanction, what must we think of the "gentle Lady married to the Moor?" Talboys, you are quizzing the old Gentleman.

Talboys. I give it up.

North. The short Scene I quoted, then, *immediately* follows the preceding—in time; and that short Scene is manifestly introduced by Shakspeare, merely to get Othello out on the ramparts with Iago, *that* Iago may bring the Moor "plump on Cassio soliciting his wife." SCENE THIRD OF ACT III. Unfurl.

Talboys. Ay, ay, sir. *Scene Third of Act III.* That is the Scene of Scenes.

North. Scene Third of Act III., accordingly, shows us Desdemona, Cassio, and Emilia before the Castle—and while Cassio is "soliciting his wife"—"enter Othello and Iago at a distance."

"*Emilia.* Madam, here comes
My Lord.
Cassio. Madam, I'll take my leave.
Desdemona. Why stay,
And hear me speak.
Cassio. Madam, *not now: I am very ill at ease*—
Unfit for my own purposes.
Desdemona. Well—well—
Do your discretion. [*Exit* CASSIO."

Down to this exit of Cassio, we are on the morning or forenoon of the Second Day at Cyprus. Every word said proves we are. Cassio's parting words prove it. "Madam, *not now*—I'm very ill at ease—unfit for my own purposes." He had been up all night—had been drunk—cashiered. He sees Othello coming—his heart sinks—and he retreats in shame and fear—"unfit for his own purposes."

Talboys. Eh?

North. In Scene First of Act III., Emilia tells Cassio that she will do a particular thing—do it of course—*quam primum*—as a thing that requires no delay, and demands haste—and in Scene III. she appears having done it. In Scene First she tells Cassio that she will bring him to speak with Desdemona about his replacement—and in Scene Third, before the Castle, we find that she has done this. The opportunity came immediately—it was made to her hand—all that was necessary was that Othello should not be present—and he was not present. He had gone out on business. Now was just the nick of time for Cassio to bespeak Desdemona's intercession, and now was just the nick of time on which that intercession was by him bespoken. Nothing could be more nicely critical or opportune.

Talboys. Between us, sir, we have tied down Scene III. of Act Third to the Forenoon of the Second Day at Cyprus.

North. We have tied down Shakspeare thus far to SHORT TIME AT CYPRUS—and to Short Time we shall tie him down till the Catastrophe. OTHELLO MURDERED DESDEMONA THAT VERY NIGHT.

Talboys. No—no—no. Impossible.

North. Inevitably—and of a dead certainty.

Talboys. How—how, sir?

North. Why will an Eagle be an Owl?

Talboys. A compliment and a banter—

North. Why, you Owl! we have just seen Cassio slink

away—all is plain sailing now—Talboys—for Iago by four words seals her doom.

> "*Ha! I like not that!*
> *Othello.* What dost thou say?
> *Iago.* Nothing, my lord: or if—I know not what.
> *Othello.* Was not that Cassio parted from my wife?
> *Iago.* Cassio, my Lord? No, sure; I cannot think it,
> That he would steal away *so guilty like*
> *Seeing you coming.*"

Mark what follows—there is not a moment of intermission in the Action down to end of this Scene Third of Act Third, which you well call the Scene of Scenes, by which time Othello has been convinced of Desdemona's guilt, and has resolved on her Death and Cassio's.

Talboys. Not a moment of intermission! Let's look to it —if it indeed be so—

North. See—hear Desdemona pleading for Cassio—see, hear Othello—saying—"Not now, sweet Desdemona;" and then again—"Prythee, no more: let him come when he will I—will deny thee nothing." And again—

> "I will deny thee nothing.
> Whereon, I do beseech thee, grant me this,
> To leave me but a little to myself.
> *Des.* Shall I deny you? no: Farewell, my lord.
> [*Exit with Emilia.*"

Turn over leaf after leaf—without allowing yourself to read that dreadful colloquy between the Victim and his Destroyer—but letting it glimmer luridly by—till Desdemona comes back—and Othello, under the power of the Angel Innocence, exclaims—

> "If she be false, O, then heaven mocks itself!—
> I'll not believe it."

Talboys. I behold her! I hear her voice—"gentle and low, an excellent thing in woman."

> "Why is your speech so faint? are you not well?
> *Oth.* I have a pain upon my forehead here."

She drops that fatal handkerchief—

> "I am very sorry that you are not well."

What touching words! They go out together—ignorant she that her husband hath heartache, worse than any headache—

North. Both to be effectually cured *that night* by—bleeding.

Talboys. By bleeding?

North. You Owl—yea.

Talboys. A sudden thought strikes me, sir. Desdemona has said to Othello—

> "Your dinner, and the generous Islanders
> By you invited, do attend your presence."

How's this? This looks like long time—

North. It may look what it chooses—but we have *proved* that we are now on the forenoon of the Second Day at Cyprus.

Talboys. Would it not have been treating them too unceremoniously to have sent round the cards of invitation only the night before? As far as I have been able to learn, they have long been in the habit of giving not less than a week's invitation to dinner at Cyprus. In Glasgow it is commonly three weeks. And why "*generous?*" Because they, the Islanders, have given a series of splendid entertainments to Othello and his Bride.

North. No nonsense, sir. Othello had done what you or I would have done, had either of us been Governor of Cyprus. He had invited the "generous Islanders," immediately on his landing, to dine at the Castle "next day." Had he not done so, he had been a hunks. "Generous," you know, as well as I do, means high-born—men of birth—not generous of entertainments.

Talboys. True, too. But how comes it to be the dinner hour?

North. People dined in those days all England over, about eleven A. M.—probably they dined still earlier in the unfashionable region of Cyprus. You are still hankering after the heresy of long time—but no more of that *now*—let us keep to our demonstration of short time—by-and-by you shall see the Gentleman with the Scythe—the Scythian at full swing—as long as yourself.

Talboys. I sit corrected. Go on.

North. Othello and Desdemona have just gone out—to do the honors at the Dinner Table to the generous Islanders. He must have been a strange Chairman—for though not yet absolutely mad, his soul was sorely changed. Perhaps he made some apology, and was not at that Dinner at all—perhaps it was never eaten—but we lose sight of him for a little while; and Emilia, who remains behind, picks up the fatal hankerchief, and, with a strange wilfulness, or worse, says—

"I'll have the work ta'en out,
And give't Iago."

Iago snatches it from her—and in soliloquy says—

"I will in Cassio's lodgings lose this napkin,
And let him find it."
"This may do something,—
The Moor already changes with the poison:
Dangerous conceits are, in their natures, poisons,
Which at the first, are scarce found to distaste;
But, with a little, act upon the blood,
Burn like the mines of sulphur.—I did say so:—
Enter OTHELLO.
Look! where he comes! Not poppy, nor mandragora,
Nor all the drowsy syrups of the world,
Shall ever medicine *thee to that sweet sleep*
Which thou ow'dst yesterday."

Then follows, without break, all the rest of this dreadful Third Scene. The first dose of the poison—the second, and third, and fourth—are all given on one and the same day. The mineral has gnawed through all the coats of the stomach—and *He has sworn to murder Her*—all in one day. We have Iago's word for it. *Yesterday* his sleep was sweet—how happy he was then we can imagine—how miserable he is *now* we see—"what a difference to *him*," and *in* him, between Saturday and Sunday!

> "O, blood! Iago, blood!
> * * *
> Now by yond' marble heaven,
> In the due reverence of a sacred vow,
> I here engage my words.
> *Iago.* Do not rise yet. *Kneels.*
> Witness, you ever-burning lights above!
> You elements, that clip us round about!
> Witness, that here Iago doth give up,
> The execution of his wit, hands heart,
> To wrong'd Othello's service! Let him command,
> And to obey shall be in me remorse,
> What bloody work soever."

Talboys. Thou Great original Short-Timeist! Unanswerable art Thou. But let us look at the close of this dreadful Third Act.

> "*Othello.* I greet thy love,
> Not with vain thanks, but with acceptance bounteous,
> And will upon the instant put thee to't:
> Within *these three days* let me hear thee say
> That Cassio's not alive.
> *Iago.* My friend is dead; 'tis done at your request:
> But let *her* live.
> *Othello.* Damn her, lewd minx! O, damn her!
> Come, go with me apart; I will withdraw,

26

> To furnish me with some swift means of death
> To the fair devil. Now art thou my lieutenant.
> *Iago.* I am your own for ever."

In three days—at the longest—for Cassio;—but Iago understood, and did it that very night. And swift means of death for the fair devil were in Othello's own *hands*—ay—he smothered her that night to a dead certainty—a dead certainty at last—though his hands seem to have faltered.

North. In the next Scene—Scene IV.—we find Desdemona anxious about the loss of the handkerchief, but still totally unapprehensive of the Moor's jealousy—

> "Who—he? I think the sun, where he was born,
> Drew all such humors from him."

Othello enters, saying, "Well, my good Lady,"—and mutters aside, "Oh! hardness to dissemble,"—and very ill he does dissemble, for he leaves Desdemona and Emilia amazed at his mad deportment, the latter exclaiming—"Is not this man jealous?" Iago had told Othello of Cassio's possessing the handkerchief in the previous Scene, and Othello takes the first opportunity, *that same afternoon,* to ascertain for himself whether she had parted with it. Would he have let an hour elapse before making the inquiry? Can it be for a moment imagined that he passed days and nights with Desdemona without attempting to sound her regarding this most pregnant proof of her guilt? This Scene concludes the Third Act—*and the time is not long after dinner.*

Talboys. All this being *proved,* it is unnecessary to scrutinize the consecution of the Scenes of Acts Fourth and Fifth. —*Iago's work is done—one day* has sufficed—and what folly to bring in long time after this—when his presence would have been unsupportable—had it not been impossible. Death must follow doom.

North. Death must follow doom. In these four words you

have settled the question of time. Long time seemed necessary to change Othello into a murderer—and all the world but you and I believe that long time there was; but you and I know better—and have demonstrated short time—for at the end of the "dreadful Third Act" Othello is a murderer—and what matters it now *when* he really seized the pillow to smother her, or unsheathed the knife?

Talboys. It matters not a jot. But he did the deed that same night—or he had not been Othello.

North. There again—*or he "had not been Othello."* In these four words, you have settled the question of time—now and for ever.

Talboys. It would be a waste of words, sir, to seek to prove by the consecution of the Scenes in Acts Fourth and Fifth—though nothing could be easier—that he *did* murder her that very night.

North. Very few will suffice. Act IV. begins a little before supper-time. Bianca enters in Scene I. inviting Cassio to supper—"An you'll come to supper to-night, you may." If anything were wanting to connect the closing Scene of Act III. with this opening Scene of Act IV., it is fully supplied by Bianca, who at the end of Act III. gets the handkerchief, in order that she may copy it, and in the scene of this IVth Act, comes back in a fury. "Let the devil and his dam haunt you—what did you mean by that same handkerchief you gave me *even now?* I was a fine fool to take it." Cassio had given it to her a little after dinner, and Bianca, inviting him to supper, says he had given it to her EVEN NOW. This Scene I. of Act IV. ends with Othello's invitation to the newly-arrived Lodovico—"I do intreat that we may sup together." Scene II. comprehends the interview between Othello and Emilia; Othello and Desdemona—Desdemona, Emilia and Iago. The whole do not occupy an hour of time—they follow one another naturally, and the action is continuous. Scene III. shows Lodovico and the Noble Venetians still at the Castle—but now it is *after* supper. Lodovico is departing—

> "I do beseech you, sir, trouble yourself no farther.
>
> *Othello.* O pardon me; 'twill do me good to walk,
> O Desdemona!
>
> *Desdemona.* My Lord?
>
> *Othello.* *Get you to bed on the instant, I will be returned forthwith.*"

Desdemona obeys—the bed-scene follows—and *she is murdered.* What say you, Seward?

Seward. "I say ditto to Mr. Burke."

North. Buller?

Buller. I say ditto to Mr. North.

North. Why have both of you been so silent?

Seward. I knew it all before.

Talboys. What a bouncer!

Buller. I never speak when I am busking Flies. There's a Professor for you—(six red and six black)—pretty full in the body—long-winged—liker eagle than insect—sharper than needle—and with barb "inextricable as the gored Lion's bite." Lunch-gong. To the Deeside.

North. Verdict: DESDEMONA MURDERED BY OTHELLO ON THE SECOND NIGHT IN CYPRUS.

SCENE III.—*Deeside.*

TIME—*At and after Lunch.*

NORTH—TALBOYS—SEWARD—BULLER.

North. Having demonstrated SHORT TIME AT CYPRUS, let us now, if it please you, gentlemen, show forth LONG TIME AT CYPRUS.

Talboys. With all our heart. We have *demonstrated* the one, let us *show forth* the other.

North. And as, in our Demonstration of Short Time, we kept Long Time out of sight—excluded him from the Tent—

Buller. Pardon me, sir. I for one was beginning to feel his influence.

North. How?

Buller. In that contraction and expansion of the jaws denoted by that most expressive and characteristic word YAWN; for Seward and I were but listeners.

North. I don't believe you heard one word.

Buller. I did—several; and spoiled a promising Palmer in idly trying to audit your discourse at the interesting point of quarrel—just as you, sir, threw yourself back on your Swing, with an angry jerk, and Talboys started up, "like Teneriffe or Atlas removed," endangering the stability of the Tent.

North. My dear Talboys, I was saying to you, when rudely interrupted by Buller, that as in our demonstration of Short Time at Cyprus, we, purposely and determinedly, and wisely kept Long Time out of sight, on account of the inextricable perplexity and confusion that would otherwise have involved the argument, so now let us, in showing forth Long Time at Cyprus, keep out of sight Short—and then shall we finally have before our ken TWO TIMES at Cyprus, each firmly established on its own ground—and imperiously demanding of the Critics of this great Tragedy—Reconcilement. Reconcilement it may be beyond their power to give—but let them first see the GREAT FACT which not one of the whole set have seen—HAND IN HAND ONE DAY AND UNASSIGNED WEEKS! The condition is altogether anomalous—

Talboys. A DAY OF THE CALENDAR, AND A MONTH OF THE CALENDAR! No human soul ever dreams of the dreadful sayings and doings all coming off IN A DAY! till he looks—till he is made to look—as we have made Seward and Buller to look—for they heard every word we said—and finds himself nailed by Act and Scene.

North. To some FIFTEEN HOURS.

Buller. I thought you were going to show forth Long Time at Cyprus.

North. Why, there it is, staring you in the face everywhere—you may see it with your eyes shut—and as most people read with their eyes shut, they see it—and they see it only—while—

Buller. Why, sir, since you won't get on a little faster, Talboys and I must be Ushers to Long Time.

North. Be—do.

Talboys. Long time cunningly insinuates itself, serpentwise, throughout Desdemona's first recorded conversation with Cassio, at the beginning of Scene III., Act III.—the "Dreadful Scene." Thus—

> "Assure thee,
> If I do vow a friendship, I'll perform it
> To the last article: my lord shall never rest;
> I'll watch him tame, and talk him out of patience;
> His bed shall seem a school, his board a shrift;
> I'll intermingle everything he does
> With Cassio's suit; Therefore be merry, Cassio;
> For thy solicitor shall rather die
> Than give thy cause away."

This points to a protracted time in the future—and thoug announcing an intention merely, yet somehow it leaves an impression that Desdemona carries her intention into effect—that she does, "watch him tame," does make his "bed seem a school"—does "intermingle everything she does with Cassio's suit." The passage recurred to my mind, I recollect, when you first hinted to me the question of time; and no doubt it tells so on the minds of many—

North. Inconsiderate people.

Talboys. All people are more or less inconsiderate, sir.

North. True.

Talboys. Then Desdemona says—

> "How now, my lord?
> I have been talking with a suitor here,
> A man *that languishes in your displeasure.*"

I cannot listen to that line, even now, without a feeling of the heart-sickness of protracted time—"hope deferred maketh the heart sick"—*languishes!* even unto death. I think of that fine line in Wordsworth—

> "So fades—*so languishes*—grows dim, and dies."

Seward. Poo!

North. Seward, the remark is a fine one.

Talboys. Far in this Scene, Othello says to Iago—

> "If more thou dost perceive, let me no more:
> Set on thy wife to observe."

Iago has not said that he had perceived anything, but Othello, greatly disturbed, speaks as if Iago had said that he had perceived a good deal; and we might believe that they had been a long time at Cyprus. Othello then says—

> "This honest creature, doubtless,
> Sees and knows more, much more, than he unfolds."

In all this, sir, we surely have a feeling of longish time.

Seward. Poo!

North. Heed him not—English manners. We have—

Talboys.

> "O curse of marriage!
> That we can call those delicate creatures ours—
> And not their appetites."

This is the language of a some time married man—not of a man the morning after his nuptials.

North. The Handkerchief.

Talboys. Ay—Emilia's words.

> "I am glad I have found this napkin;
> This was her first remembrance from the Moor—
> My wayward husband hath a hundred times
> Woo'd me to steal it; but she so loves the token,
> (For he conjured her she would ever keep it,)
> That she reserves it evermore about her,
> To kiss, and talk to."

Here we have long time, and no mistake. Iago has wooed her to steal it a hundred times? When and where? Since their arrival at Cyprus.

Seward. I don't know that.

Talboys. Nor do I. But I say the words naturally give us the impression of long time. In none of his soliloquies at Venice, or at Cyprus on their first arrival, has Iago once mentioned that Handkerchief as the chief instrument of his wicked design—and therefore Emilia's words imply weeks at Cyprus—

> "What will you give me now
> For that same handkerchief?
> *Iago.* What handkerchief?
> *Emilia.* Why, that the Moor first gave to Desdemona;
> That which so often you did bid me steal."

North. Go on.

Talboys.

> "What sense had I of her stolen hours of lust!
> I saw it not—thought it not—it harm'd not me—
> *I slept the next night well*—was free and merry;
> I found not Cassio's kisses on her lips."

Next night—night after night—many nights—many *wedded* nights—long time at Cyprus.

North. And then Cassio's dream.

Talboys. "I lay with Cassio—*lately*." Where, but at Cyprus? "Cursed fate! that *gave thee to the Moor*."

Seward. Of that by-and-by.

Talboys. Of that now. What?

Seward. By-and-by.

North. Better be a dumb dog, Seward, than snarl so.

Talboys. And on Othello going off in a rage about the handkerchief—what saith Desdemona?

> "*I ne'er saw this before.*"

These few words are full charged with long time.

North. They are. And Emilia's—"Tis not a year or two shows us a man." True, that is a kind of general reflection—but a most foolish general reflection, indeed, if made to a Wife weeping at her husband's harshness the day after marriage.

Talboys. Emilia's "year or two" cannot mean one day—it implies weeks—or months. Desdemona then says—

> "Something, sure, of state,
> *Either from Venice*, or some unhatch'd practice," &c.

Does not *that* look like long time at Cyprus? Unlike the language of one who had herself arrived at Cyprus from Venice but the day before. And in continuation, Desdemona's

"Nay, we must think, men are not gods;
Nor of them look for such observances
As fit the bridal."

And that thought brings sudden comfort to poor Desdemona, who says sweetly—

"Beshrew me much, Emilia,
I was (unhandsome warrior as I am),
Arraigning his unkindness with my soul;
But now, I find, I had suborn'd the witness,
And he's indicted falsely."

That is—why did I, a married woman some months old, forget that the honey-moon is gone, and that my Othello, hero as he is, is now not a Bridegroom—but a husband? "Men are not gods."

North. And Bianca? She's a puzzler.

Talboys. A puzzler, and something more.

"*Bianca.* Save you, friend Cassio!
Cassio. What make you from home?
How is it with you, my most fair Bianca?
I'faith, sweet love, I was coming *to your house.*
Bianca. And I was going to your lodging, Cassio.
What! keep a week away? seven days and nights?
Eight score eight hours? And lovers' absent hours,
More tedious than the dial eight score times?
O weary reckoning!
Cassio. Pardon me, Bianca;
I have this while with leaden thoughts been press'd;
But I shall, in a more continuate time,
Strike off the score of absence."

Here the reproaches of Bianca to Cassio develop long time. For, besides his week's absence from her house, there is implied the preceding time necessary for contracting and habitually carrying on the illicit attachment. Bianca is a Cyprus householder; Cassio sups at her house; his intimacy, which has various expressions of continuance, has been formed with her there; he has found her, and grown acquainted with her there, not at Venice. I know it has been suggested that she was his mistress at Venice—that she came with the squadron from Venice; and that her last cohabitation with Cassio had taken place in Venice about a week ago—but for believing this there is here not the slightest ground. "What! keep a week away?" would be a strange exclamation, indeed, from one who knew that he had been but a day on shore—had landed along with herself yesterday from the same ship—and had been a week cooped up from her in a separate berth. And Bianca, seeing the handkerchief, and being told to "take me this work out," cries—

> "O Cassio! whence came this?
> This is some token from a newer friend.
> *To the felt absence now I feel a cause.*"

"To the felt absence," Eight score eight hours! the cause? Some new mistress at Cyprus—not forced separation at sea.

North. Then, Talboys, in Act. IV., Scene I., Othello is listening to the conversation of Iago and Cassio, which he believes relates to his wife. Iago says—

> "She gives it out that you shall marry her;
> Do you intend it!
> *Cassio.* Ha! ha! ha!
> *Othello.* Do you triumph, Roman? Do you triumph?
> *Iago.* Faith! the cry goes, *that you shall marry her.*
> *Cassio.* Pr'ythee, say true.
> *Iago.* I am a very villain else.
> *Othello.* Have you SCORED ME? Well."

That is, have you marked me for destruction, in order that you may marry my wife? Othello believes that Cassio is said to entertain an intention of marrying Desdemona, and infers that, as a preliminary, he must be put out of the way. This on the first day after marriage? No, surely—long time at Cyprus.

Talboys. Iago says to Cassio,

> "My Lord is fallen into an epilepsy;
> This is his second fit: *he had one yesterday.*
> *Cassio.* Rub him about the temples.
> *Iago.* No, forbear;
> The lethargy must have his quiet course:
> If not, he foams at mouth; and, by-and-by,
> Breaks out to savage madness."

This is a lie—but Cassio believes it. Cassio could not have believed it, and therefore Iago would not have told it, had "yesterday" been the day of the triumphant, joyful, and happy arrival at Cyprus. Assuredly, Cassio knew that Othello had no fit *that* day; that day he was Othello's lieutenant—Iago but his Ancient—and Iago could know nothing of any fits that Cassio knew not of—therefore—Long Time.

North.

> "For I will make him tell the tale anew,
> Where, how, how oft, how long ago, and when,
> He hath—and is again to—"

He does so—and Othello believes what he hears Cassio tell of Bianca to be of Desdemona. Madness any way we take it—but madness possible only—on long time at Cyprus.

Talboys. Then, sir, the trumpet announcing the arrival of Lodovico from Venice, at the close of Iago's and Othello's murderous colloquy, and Lodovico giving Othello a packet containing—his recall!

> "They do command him home,
> Deputing Cassio in his government."

What are we to make of that?

North. The Recall, except after considerable time, would make the policy of the Senate frivolous—a thing Shakspeare never does, for the greatness of political movements lies everywhere for a support to the strength and power of his tragical fable. Half that we know of Othello out of the Scenes is, that he is the trusted General of the Senate. What gravity his esteem with you derives hence, and can we bear to think of him superseded without cause? Had Lodovico, who brings the new commission, set off the day after Othello from Venice? No. You imagine an intercourse, which has required time, between Othello, since his appointment, and the Senate. Why, in all the world, do they thus suddenly depose him, and put Cassio in his place? You cannot very well think that the next measure of the Senate, after entrusting the command of Cyprus, their principal Island, to their most tried General, in most critical and perilous times, was to displace him ere they hear a word from him. They have not had time to know that the Turkish fleet is wrecked and scattered, unless they sit behind Scenes in the Green-room.

Talboys. We must conclude that the Senate must give weeks or months to this New Governor ere interfering with him.—To recall him before they know he has reached Cyprus —nay, to send a ship after him next day—or a day or two following his departure—would make these "most potent, grave, and reverend Signors," enigmas, and the Doge an Idiot. What though a steamer had brought tidings back to Venice that the Turks had been "banged" and "drowned?" That was not a sufficient reason to order Othello back before he could have well set his foot on shore, or taken more than a look at the state of the fortifications, in case the Ottoman should fit out another fleet.

North. Then mark Lodovico's language. He asks, seeing Othello strike his wife—as well he may—"Is it his use?" Or did the letters "work upon his blood, and new-create this fault?" And Iago answers, "It is not honesty in me to speak *what I have seen and known.*" Lodovico says, "The noble Moor, whom our Senate call all in all sufficient?" Then they have not quarreled with him, at least—nor lost their good opinion of him! Iago answers, "He is much changed?" What, in a day? And again—"It is not honesty in me to speak what I have seen and known." What, in a day? Lodovico comes evidently to Othello after a long separation—such as affords room for a moral transformation; and Iago's words—lies as they are—and seen to be lies by the most unthinking person—yet to refer to much that has passed in an ample time—to a continued course of procedure.

North. But in all the Play nothing is so conclusive of long time as the Second Scene of the Third Act.

"*Othello.* You have seen nothing then?
Emilia. Nor ever heard; nor ever did suspect.
Othello. Yes, you have seen Cassio and she together.
Emilia. But then I saw no harm; and then I heard
Each syllable, that breath made up between them.
Othello. What, did they never whisper?
Emilia. Never, my Lord.
Othello. Nor send you out o' the way?
Emilia. Never.
Othello. To fetch her fan, her gloves, her mask, nor nothing?
Emilia. Never, my Lord.
Othello. That's strange."

If all this relates to their residence at Cyprus, it indicates many weeks.

Seward. Ay—IF.

North. What wicked whisper was that? Did you whisper, Buller?

Buller. No. I have not once whispered for a quarter of a century—My whispering days have long been over.

North. Then a word about Emilia. "I prythee, let thy wife attend on her," says Othello, going on board at Venice, to Iago. In the slight way in which such arrangements can be touched, this request is conclusive evidence to Emilia's being then *first* placed about Desdemona's person. It has no sense else; nor is there the slightest ground for supposing a prior acquaintance, at least intimacy. What had an Ensign's wife to do with a Nobleman's daughter? and now she is attached as an Attendant. Now, consider, first, Emilia's character. She seems not very principled, not very chaste. She gives you the notion of a tolerably well-practiced Venetian Wife. Hear Iago's opinion, who suspects her with two persons, and one on general rumor. Yet how strong her affection for Desdemona, and her faith in her purity! She witnesses for her, and she dies for her! I ask, how long did that affection and that opinion take to grow? a few days at Venice, and a week while they were sea-sick aboard ship? No. Weeks—months. A gentle lady once made to me that fine remark,—"Emilia has not much worth in herself, but is raised into worth by her contact with Desdemona—into heroic worth!" "I care not for thy sword—I'll make thee known, though I lost twenty lives." And that bodeful "Perchance, Iago, I will ne'er go home!" what does it mean? but a dim surmise, or a clear, that what she will disclose will bring the death upon her from his dagger, which it brings. The impure dying a voluntary martyr for the pure is to the highest degree affecting—is the very manner of Shakspeare, to express a principal character by its influence on subordinate ones—has its own moral sublimity; but more than all, for our purpose, it witnesses time. Love and Faith, and Fidelity, won from her in whom these virtues are to be first created!

Seward. Very fine. My dear sir, you are not angry with me?

Talboys. Angry. Not he. Look on his face—how mild!

North. Othello in his wrath, calls Emilia "a closet-lock-and-key of villanous secrets: and yet she'll kneel and pray; I have seen her do't." Where and when? It could only have been at Cyprus; and such language denotes a somewhat long attendance there on Desdemona.

Seward. Ingenious—and better than so.

North. "Some of your function, mistress," renewed to Emilia—when, after conversing with Desdemona, Othello is going out—is his treatment of one whom he supposes to have been serviceable to his wife's and Cassio's amour. Where? There, only there, in Cyprus, by all witnessing, palpably. *She* could not before. He speaks to her as *professional* in such services, therefore long dealing in them; but this all respects this one intrigue, not her previous life. The wicked energy of the forced attribution vanishes, if this respects anything but her helpfulness to his wife and her paramour, and at Cyprus—there—only there. Nothing points to a farther back looking suspicion. Iago's "thousand times committed" can only lengthen out the stay at Cyprus. Othello still believes that she once loved him—that she has fallen to corruption.

Buller. Antenuptial?

North. Faugh! Could he have the most horrible, revolting, and loathsome of all thoughts, that he wedded her impure? and not a hint given of that most atrocious pang? Incredible—impossible! I can never believe, if Shakspeare intended an infidelity taking precedency of the marriage, that he would not by word or by hint have said so. Think how momentous to our intelligence of the jealousy the *date* is; not as to Tuesday or Wednesday, but as to before or after the nuptial knot—before or after the first religious loosing of the virgin zone. That a man's wife has turned into a wanton—hell and horror! But that he wedded one—Pah! Faugh! Could Iago, could

Othello, could Shakspeare have left *this* point in the chronology of guilt to be argued out doubtfully? No. The greatest of Poets for pit, boxes, and gallery, must have written intelligibly to pit, boxes, and gallery; and extrication, unveiled, after two hundred and fifty years, by studious men, in a fit of perplexity, cannot be the thunderbolt which Shakspeare flung to his audience at the Globe Theatre.

Talboys. You remember poor, dear, sweet Mrs. Henry Siddons—*the* Desdemona—how she gave utterance to those words

"It was his bidding—therefore, good Emilia,
Give me my nightly wearing, and adieu;
We must not now displease him.
Emilia. I would you had never seen him!
Desdemona. So would not I; my love doth so approve him,
That even his stubbornness, his checks, and frowns,—
Pr'ythee unpin me,—have grace and favor in them.
Emilia. I have laid those sheets you bade me on the bed.
Desdemona. All's one: Good father! how foolish are our minds!
If I do die before thee—pr'ythee shroud me
In one of those same sheets."

The wedding sheets were *reserved.* They had been laid by for weeks—months—time long enough to give a saddest character to the bringing them out again—a serious, ominous meaning—disturbed from the quietude, the sanctity of their sleep by a wife's mortal presentiment that they may be her shroud.

North. *Long time established at Cyprus.*

Verdict—DESDEMONA MURDERED BY OTHELLO HEAVEN KNOWS WHEN.

SCENE IV.—*The Grove.*

TIME—*After Lunch.*

NORTH—TALBOYS—SEWARD—BULLER.

Seward. On rising sir, to——

North. Sit down—no gentleman speaks on his legs before, at, or after meals in a private Party.

Seward. Except in Scotland. On sitting down, sir, to state MY THEORY, I trust that I shall not lay myself open to the im——

North. Speak with your natural tone as if you were sitting, Seward, and not with that Parliamentary sing-song in which Statesmen, with their coat-tails perked up behind, declaim on the state of Europe—

Seward. I IMAGINE, SIR, THAT SHAKSPEARE ASSUMED THE MARRIAGE TO HAVE TAKEN PLACE SOME TIME BEFORE THE COMMENCEMENT OF THE PLAY SUFFICIENTLY LONG TO ADMIT THE POSSIBILITY OF A COURSE OF GUILT BEFORE THE PLAY OPENS. I imagine that, with this general idea in his mind, he gave his full and unfettered attention to the working out of THE PLOT, which has no reference to the time, circumstances, or history of the Marriage, but relates exclusively to the Moor's Jealousy. Therefore the indications of past time at Venice are vague, and rarely scattered through the dialogue.

Talboys. A more astounding discovery indeed, Seward, than any yet announced by that stunner, Christopher North. Pardon me, sir.

North. We have said our say, Shirra; let the Lord-Lieutenant of his County say his—

Talboys. And the Chairman of the Quarter Sessions, and President of the Agricultural Society of the Land's End say his.

Buller. I can beat you at chess.

Talboys. You!!!

North. Gentlemen, let there be no bad blood.

Seward. Supposing that this was Shakspeare's general idea of the Plot, I would first beg your attention to the fact that the marriage has taken place—none of us know how long—*before the beginning of the Play.*

Talboys. The same night—the same night.

Seward. I said—none of us know how long; and as you are a Lawyer, Mr. Talboys—

Talboys. For goodness' sake, my dear Seward, don't mister me—

Seward. The only evidence, my dear Talboys, as to the history of the marriage is that given by Roderigo in the First Scene. He, with the most manifest anxiety to prove himself an honest witness, declares that now, at midnight, Desdemona had eloped—NOT WITH *the Moor,* but with no "worse nor better guard, but with a knave of common hire, a gondolier, *to,*" &c. &c. She has fled *alone* from her father's house; and Roderigo, being interrogated, "Are they married, think ye?" answers, "Truly I think they are."

Talboys. What do you say to Iago's saying to Cassio—

> "Faith he *to-night* has boarded a land Carrack;
> If it prove lawful prize, he's made for ever.
> *Cassio.* I do not understand.
> *Iago.* He's married."

Seward. It cannot be inferred, from these words, that this was the first occasion on which Desdemona and Othello had come together as man and wife. The words are quite consistent with the supposition that their marriage had taken place some time before; also quite consistent with Iago's knowledge of that event. It was not his cue or his humor to say more than he did. Why should he?

Talboys. It cannot be inferred! It can—I infer it. And pray, how do you account for Othello saying to Desdemona, on the day of their arrival at Cyprus,

> "The purchase made—the fruits are to ensue;
> That profits yet to come 'twixt me and you."

Seward. "The purchase made"—refers to the price which Othello had paid for connubial delight with Desdemona awaiting him at Cyprus. That price was the peril which he had undergone during his stormy voyage. In his exuberant satisfaction, simply expressing a self-evident truth, that his happiness was *yet* before him. Had Desdemona been then a virgin bride, Othello would hardly have used such language. Iago speaks in his usual characteristic coarse way—so no need to say a word more on the subject.

Talboys. Very well. Be it so. But why should such a private marriage have been resorted to; and if privacy was desirable at first, what change had occurred to cause the public declaration of it?

Seward. Othello had been nine months unemployed in war—the Venetian State was at peace—and he had been in constant intercouse with Brabantios—

> "Her father lov'd me—oft invited me;"

and he "took *once* a pliant hour" to ask Desdemona to be his wife. That "once" cannot refer to the day on which the Play commences; and that their marriage took place some time before, is alike reconcileable with the character of the "gentle Lady," and with that of the impetuous Hero.

Talboys. Truly!

Seward. Still, a private marriage is, under any circum

stances, a questionable proceeding; and our great Dramatist was desirous that as little of the questionable as possible should either be or appear in the conduct of the "Divine Desdemona;" and therefore he has left the private marriage very much in the shade.

Talboys. Very much in the shade indeed.

Seward. Her duplicity must be admitted, and allowance must be made for it. It was wrong, but not in the least unnatural, and perfectly excusable—

Talboys. No.

Seward. And grievously expiated.

Talboys. It was indeed. Poor dear Desdemona!

Seward. It is, you know, part of the proof of her capacity for guilt, that she ingeniously deceived her father.

Talboys. But why reveal it now?

Seward. Circumstances are changed. The Cyprus wars have broke out, and Othello is about to be commissioned to take the command of the Venetian force.

> "I do know, the State
> Cannot with safety cast him, for he's embarked
> With such loud reason to the Cyprus wars,
> Which even now stand in act, that for their souls
> Another of his fathom have they not
> To lead this business."

It was therefore necessary that the marriage should be declared, if Desdemona was to accompany her husband to Cyprus. And the elopment from her father to her husband did take place just in time.

Talboys. Is that what people call plausible?

Seward. All the difficulties of Time are thus removed in a moment. In a blaze of light we see LONG TIME AT VENICE—SHORT TIME AT CYPRUS.

Buller. LONG TIME AT VENICE—SHORT TIME AT CYPRUS.

That's the Ticket. You Scotsmen are not wholly without insight; but for seeing into the heart of the hole—or of the stone—

Talboys. Give me a Devonshire Cider-swiller or a Cornish Miner.

North. What! Can't we discuss a Great Question in the Drama without these unseemly personal and national broils. For shame, Talboys.

Talboys. You Scotsmen indeed!

> "Nay, but he prated,
> And spoke such scurvy and provoking terms
> Against YOUR HONOR."

North. My dear Seward, let's hear how you support your Theory.

Seward. A great deal of weight, my dear Mr. North, is to be attached to the calm tone—the husband-like and matron-like demeanor of Othello and Desdemona when confronted with the Senate. That scene certainly impresses one with the conviction that they had been man and wife for a considerable period of time.

North. Very good, Seward—very good.

Seward. I do indeed think, sir, that the bride and bridegroom show much more composure throughout the whole of that Scene, than is very reconcileable with the idea that this was their nuptial night. Othello's "natural and prompt alacrity" in undertaking the wars was scarcely complimentary to his virgin Spouse upon this supposition; and Desdemona's cool distinguishings between the paternal and marital claims on her duty seem also somewhat too matronly for the occasion.

North. Very good—very good—my dear Seward, I like your observation much, that the demeanor of the married pair before the Senate has a stamp of composure. That is finely felt; but I venture to aver, my dear friend, that we must otherwise understand it. The dignity of their spirits it is that holds them both composed. Invincible self-collectedness is by more than one person in the Play held up for a characteristic quality of Othello. To a mind high and strong, which Desdemona's is, the exigency of a grand crisis, which overthrows weaker and lower minds, produces composure; from a sense of the necessity for self-possession; and involuntarily from the tension of the powers—their sole direction to the business that passes—which leaves no thought free to stray into disorder, and the inquietude of personal regards. Add, on the part of Othello, the gravity, and on that of Desdemona the awe of the Presence in which they stand, speak, and act; and you have ennobling and sufficing tragical, that is loftily and pathetically poetical, motives for that elate presence of mind which both show. Now all the greatness and grace vanish, if you suppose them calm simply because they have been married these two months. That is a reason fit for Thalia, not for Melpomene.

Talboys. Let any one English among all the two of you answer that.

Seward. The Duke says—

> "You must hence to-night.
> *Desdemona.* To-night, my Lord?
> *Othello.* With all my heart."

This faint expression of Desdemona's slight surprise and reluctance, and no more—is, I allow—natural and delicate in her—whether wife, bride, or Maid—But Othello's "with all my heart" is—

Talboys. Equally worthy of Othello. You know it is.

North. My dear Seward—do the Doge—Brabantio—the Senate understand and believe what Othello has been telling them—and that he has now disclosed to them the fact of a private marriage with Desdemona, of some weeks' or months' standing? Is that their impression?

Seward. I cannot say.

North. I can. Or has Othello been reserved—cautious—crafty in all his apparent candor—and Desdemona equally so? Are they indeed oldish-married folk?

Talboys. Shocking—shocking. That Scene in the Council Chamber of itself deals your "Theory!" its death-blow.

Seward. I look on it in quite another light. I shall be glad to know what you think is meant by Desdemona's to the Duke

> "If I be left behind
> *The rites for which I love him are denied me.*"

What are the *rites* which are thus all comprehensive of Desdemona's love for Othello? The phrase is, to the habit of our ears, perhaps somewhat startling; yet five lines before she said truly "I saw Othello's visage in his mind"—a love of spirit for spirit. And Again—

> "To his honor and his valiant parts
> Did I my soul and fortunes consecrate."

I think they had been married some time.

Talboys. The word *rites* is the very word most fitting the Lady's lips—used in a generous, free, capacious sense—as of the solace entire which the wife of a soldier has, following him; as to dress his wounds, wind his laurels, hear his councils, cheer his darker mood, smile away the lowering of the Elements—

Seward. You won't understand me.

North. No—no—no. It won't go down. I have opened my mouth far and wide, and it won't go down. Our friend Isaac Widethroat himself could not bolt it. The moral impossibility would choke him—that Othello would marry Desdemona to leave her at her Father's House, for which most perilous and entangling proceeding quite out of his character, no motive is offered, or imaginable. The love-making might go on long—and I accept a good interval since he drew from her the prayer for his history. The pressure of the war might give a decisive moment for the final step, which must have been in agitation for some time on Desdemona's behalf and part, who would require some persuasion for a step so desperate, and would not at once give up all hope of her father's consent, who "loved" Othello.

Talboys. If they were married, how base and unmanly *to steal one's Wedded wife out of one's Father-in-law's house!* The only course was to have gone in the middle of the day to Brabantio and say, "this we have done"—or "this I have done. Forgive us, if you can—we are Man and Wife." Men less kingly than Othello have often done it. To steal in order to marry was a temptation with a circumstantial necessity—a gallant adventure in usual estimation.

North. The thing most preposterous to me in a long marriage at Venice, is the continued lying position in which it places Othello and Desdemona towards her father. Two months—say—or three or four—of difficult deception! when the uppermost characteristic of both is clear-souledness—the most magnanimous sincerity. By that, before anything else, are they kindred and fit for one another. On that, before anything else, is the tragedy grounded—on his suspicious openness which is drawn against its own nature, to suspect her purity that lies open as earth's bosom to the sun. And she is to be killed for a dissembler! In either, immense contrast between the person and fate. That These Two should truckle to a domestic lie!

Talboys. No. The Abduction and Marriage were of one stroke—one effort—one plot. When Othello says, "That I have ta'en away—that I have married her"—he tells literally and simply that which has happened as it happened, in the order of events.

Seward. Why should not Othello marry Desdemona, and keep her at her father's, as theorised?

North. It is out of his character. He has the spirit of command, of lordship, of dominion—an *animus imperiosus.* This element must be granted to fit him for his place; and it is intimated, and is consistent with and essential to his whole fabric of mind. Then, he would not put that which belonged to him out of his power, in hostile keeping—his wife and not his wife. It is contrary to his great love, which desires and would feed upon her continual presence. And against his discretion, prudence or common sense, to risk that Brabantio, discovering, might in fury take sudden violent measures—shut her up in a convent, or turn her into the streets, or who knows what—kill her.

Talboys. Then the insupportable consideration and question, how do they come together as man and wife? Does she come to his bed-room at his private Lodgings, or his quarters at the Sagittary? Or does he go to hers at her father's, climbing a garden wall every night like Romeo, bribing the porter, or trusting Ancilla? You cannot figure it out any way without *degradation*, and something ludicrous; and a sense of being entangled in the impracticable.

North. The least that can be said is, that it invests the sanctimony of marriage with the air of an illicit amour.

Talboys. Then the high-minded Othello running the perpetual and imminent risk of being caught thieving—slipping through loop-holes—mouse-holes—key-holes. What in Romeo and Juliet is romance, between Othello and Desdemona is almost pollution.

North. What a desolating of the MANNERS of the Play! Will you, then, in order to evade a difficulty of the mechanical construction, clog and whelm the poetry, and moral greatness of the Play, with a preliminary debasement? Introduce your Hero and Heroine under a cloud?

Talboys. And how can you show that Othello could not at any moment have taken her away, as at last you suppose him to do, having a motive? Mind—he knows that the wars are on—he does not know he shall be sent for that night. He does not know that he may not have to keep her a week at his quarters.

North. My dear Seward—pray, meditate but for a moment on these words of Desdemona in the Council Chamber—

> "My noble Father,
> I do perceive here a DIVIDED DUTY:
> My life and education both do learn me
> How to respect you; you are the LORD OF DUTY,
> I am hitherto your Daughter: BUT HERE'S MY HUSBAND;
> And so *much duty as my mother showed*
> *To you*, preferring you before her Father,
> So much I challenge that I may profess
> Due to the Moor, my Lord."

These are weighty words—of grave and solemn import—and the time has come when Desdemona the Daughter is to be Desdemona the Wife. She tells simply and sedately—affectionately and gratefully—the great primal Truth of this our human and social life. Hitherto her Father has been to her the Lord of Duty—the Lord of Duty henceforth is to be her Husband. Othello, up to that night, had been but her Lover; and up to that night—for the hidden wooing was nothing to be ashamed of or repented—there had been to her no "divided Duty"—to her Father's happiness had been devoted her whole filial heart. But had she been a married woman for weeks or months before, how insincere—how hypocritical had that appeal been felt by herself to be, as it issued from her lips! The Duty had, in that case, been "divided" before—and in a way not pleasant for us to think of—to her Father violated or extinct.

Talboys. I engage, Seward, over and above what our Master has made manifest, to show that though this Theory of yours would remove some difficulties attending the time in Cyprus, it would leave others just where they are—and create many more.

North. Grant that Othello and Desdemona must be married for two months before he murders her—that our hearts and imaginations require it. The resemblance to the ordinary course of human affairs asks it. We cannot bear that he shall extinguish her and himself—both having sipped only, and not quaffed from the cup of hymeneal felicity. Your soul is outraged by so harsh and malignant a procedure of the Three Sisters. Besides, in proper poetical equilibration, he should have enjoyed to the full, with soul and with body, the happiness which his soul annihilates. And men do not kill their wives the first week. It would be too exceptional a case. Extended time is required for the probability—the steps of change in the heart of Othello require it—the construction and accumulation of proofs require it—the wheel of events usually rolls with something of leisure and measure. So is it in the real World—so must it seem to be on the Stage—else no versimilitude—no "veluti in speculum." "Two months shall elapse between marriage and murder," says Shakspeare—going to write. They must pass at Venice, or they must pass at Cyprus. Place Shakspeare in this position, and which will he choose? If at Venice, a main requiring condition is not satisfied. For in the fits and snatches of the clandestine marriage, Othello has never possessed with full embrace, and heart overflowing, the happiness which he destroys. If an earthquake is to ruin a palace, it must be built up to the battlements and pinnacles; furnished, occupied, made the seat Pleasure, Pomp, and Power; and then shaken into heaps—or you have but half a story. Only at Cyprus Othello *possesses* Desdemona. There where he is Lord of his Office, Lord over the Allegiance of soldier and civilian—of a whole population—Lord of the Island, which, sea-surrounded, is as a world of itself—Lord of his will—Lord of his wife.

Talboys. I feel, sir, in this view much poetical demonstration —although mathematical none—and in such a case Poetry is your only Principia.

North. Your hand. But if, my dear Seward, Shakspeare elects time at Venice, he wilfully clouds his two excellent Persons with many shadows of indecorum, and clogs his Action with a procedure and a state of affairs, which your Imagination loses itself in attempting to define—with improbabilities—with impracticabilities—with impossibilities. If he was resolute to have a well-sustained logic of Time, I say it was better for him to have his Two Months distinct at Cyprus. I say that, with his creative powers, if he was determined to have Two Calendar Months, from the First of May to the First of July, and then in one Day distinctly the first suspicion sown and the murder done, nothing could have been easier to him than to have imagined, and indicated, and hurried over the required gap of time; and that he would have been bound to prefer this course to that inexplicable marriage and no marriage at Venice.

Buller. How he clears his way!

North. But Shakspeare, my dear Boys, had a better escape. Wittingly or unwittingly, he exempted himself from the obligation of walking by the Calendar. He knew—or he felt that the fair proportionate structure of the Action required liberal time at Cyprus. He took it; for there it is, recognized in the consciousness of every sitting or standing spectator. He knew, or he felt, that the passionate expectation to be sustained in the bosoms of his audience required a rapidity of movement in his Murder-Plot, and it moves on feet of fire.

Seward. Venice is beginning to fade from my ken.

North. The first of all necessities towards the Criticism of he Play, Seward, is to convince yourself that there was not— ould not be a time of concealed marriage at Venice—that it is ot hinted, and is not inferable.

Buller. Shall we give in, Seward?

Seward. Yes.

North. You must go to the TREMENDOUS TROUBLE TIME AT YPRUS, knowing that the solution is to be had there, or no- here. If you cast back a longing lingering look towards Venice, ou are lost. Put the mountains and waves between you and he Queen of the Sea. Push yourself through at Cyprus, or perish in the adventure.

Talboys. Through that Mystery, you alone, sir, are the Man to help us through—and you must.

North. Not now—to-morrow. Till then, be revolving the subject occasionally in your minds.

Talboys. Let's off to the Pike-ground at Kilchurn.

DIES BOREALES.

No. VII.

CAMP AT CLADICH. SCENE—*The Wren's Nest.*

TIME—*Three o'clock* A. M.

NORTH—TALBOYS.

North. PERTURBED SPIRIT! why won't you rest? Wha
brings thee here?

Talboys. Seward snores.

North. Why select Seward?

Talboys. I do not select him—he selects himself—singles himself out from the whole host; so that you hear his Snore loud over that of the Camp—say rather his Snore alone—like Lablache singing a Solo in a chorus.

North. It must be Buller.

Talboys. Buller began it——

North. List!—How harmonious in the hush the blended Snore of Camp and Village! How tuned to unison—as if by pitch-pipe—with the dreamy din of our lapsing friend here, who by and by will awake into a positive Waterfall.

Talboys. The Snore of either army stilly sounds. At this

distance, the Snore disposes to sleep. Seward must have awakened himself—there goes Buller——

North. Where?

Talboys. Shriller than Seward—quite a childish treble—liker the Snore of a female—

North. Females never snore.

Talboys. How dow you know? I won't answer for some of them. Lionesses do—not perhaps in their wild state—but in Zoological Gardens.

North. Not quite so loud, Chanticleer—you will disturb my people.

Talboys. Disturb your people! Why, he has already stirred up the Solar System.

> "The Cock that is the Trumpet of the Morn,
> Doth with his lofty and shrill-sounding throat,
> Awake the God of Day."

Taking the distance of the Earth from the Sun, in round numbers, at Ninety-Five Millions of Miles, pretty well for a bird probably weighing some six pounds not merely to make himself heard by the God of Day, but by one single crow to startle Dan Phœbus from his sleep, and force him *nolens volens* to show his shining morning face at Cladich.

North. Out of Science, we seldom think of the vastness of the System of the Universe. Our hearts and imaginations diminish it for the delight of love. In our usual moods we are all Children with respect to Nature; and gather up Stars as if they were flowers of the field—to form a coronet for Neæra's hair.

Talboys. What ailed poor dear Doctor Beattie at Cocks in general? I never could understand the Curse.

> "Proud harbinger of Day,
> Who scarest my visions with thy clarion shrill,

Fell Chanticleer! who oft hath reft away
My fancied good, and brought substantial ill!
Oh, to thy cursed scream discordant still
Let Harmony aye shut her gentle ear;
Thy boastful mirth let jealous rivals spill,
Insult thy crest, and glossy pinions tear,
And ever in thy dreams the ruthless fox appear."

You poets, in your own persons, are a savage set.

North. I am not a poet, sir; nor will I allow any man with impunity to call me so.

Talboys. But Doctor Beattie was, and a Professor of Moral Philosophy to boot, at Aberdeen or St. Andrews, or some other one of our ancient Universities—for every stone-and-lime building in Scotland is ancient; and goodness me! hear him cursing cocks, and dooming the whole Gallic race to every variety of cruel and ignominious deaths, in revenge for having been disturbed from his morning dreams by a Gentleman with Comb and Wattles crowing on his own Dunghill, in red jacket, speckled waistcoat, and gray beaks, the admiration of Earochs and How-Towdies.

North. Doctor Beattie was a true Poet—and had an eye and an ear for Nature. Yet now and then he shut both—

"Hence the sacred owl on pinions gray
Breaks from the rustling boughs;
And down the lone vale sails away
To more profound repose."

I have seen that Stanza quoted many thousand times as exquisite. It is criminal. An owl was never heard, scared or unscared, to "break from the rustling boughs." Silently as a leaf he leaves his perch; you hear no rustle, for he makes none—any more than a ghost.

Talboys. Nor are the other lines good—for they present the image of a long rectilinear flight, which that of an owl in no circumstances is; and, in a fright, he would take the first blind shelter.

North. Poets seldom err so—yet I remember a mistake of Coleridge's about that commonest of all birds, the Rook.

"My gentle-hearted Charles! when the last Rook
Bent its straight path along the dusky air
Homewards, I blest it! deeming its black wing
(Now a dim speck, now vanishing in light)
Had crossed the mighty orb's dilated glory,
When thou stood'st gazing; or, when all was still,
Flew creaking o'er thy head; and had a charm
For thee, my gentle-hearted Charles, to whom
No sound is dissonant which tells of life."

Talboys. There is much stillness in the Sibylline Leaves. For Charles read Charlotte. 'Tis more like love than friendship—effeminate exceedingly; and, "no sound is dissonant which tells of life," reminds one of the Sunday Jackasses on Blackheath.

North. "'*Flew creaking.*' Some months after I had written this line," says Coleridge, in a note, "it gave me pleasure to find that Bartram had observed the same circumstance of the Savanna Crane. 'When these birds move their wings in flight, their strokes are slow, moderate, and regular; and even when at a considerable distance, or high above us, we plainly hear the quill-feathers; their shafts and webs, upon one another, creak as *the joints or working of a vessel in a tempestuous sea.*'" That a Rook may fly "creaking" when moulting, or otherwise out of feather, I shall not take upon me to deny; but in ordinary condition, he does not fly "creaking." Coleridge was wont, in his younger days, to mistake exceptions for general rules. In such a case as this, a moment's reflection would have sufficed to tell him that there could not have been "creaking" without let or hindrance to flight—and that the flight of a rook is easy and equable—"The blackening train o' craws to their repose." What creaking must have been there! But Burns never heard it.

Talboys. One Burns, as an observer of nature, is worth fifty Coleridges.

North. Not an arithmetical question. Why, even dear Sir Walter himself occasionally makes a slip in this way.

"Beneath the broad and ample bone,
That buckled heart to fear unknown,
A feeble and a tim'rous guest
The field-fare framed her lowly nest!"

The field-fare is migratory—and does not build here; in Norway, where it is native, it builds in trees—often high up on lofty trees—and in crowds.

Talboys. I believe, sir, they have been known to breed in this country—and perhaps here they build on the ground.

North. Don't be nonsensical. Our Great Minstrel knew wood-craft well; and hill-craft and river-craft; yet in his fine picture of Coriskin and Coolin,

"The wildest glen but this can show
Some touch of nature's genial glow:
On high Benmore green mosses grow,
And heath-bells bud in deep Glencroe,
And Copse on Cruachan Ben;
But here, above, around, below,
In mountain or in glen,
Nor tree, nor shrub, nor plant, nor flower,
Nor aught of vegetative power
The weary eye may ken.
For all is rocks at random strewn,
Black waves, bare crags, and banks of stone,
As if were here denied
The summer's sun, the spring's sweet dew,

That clothe with many a varied hue
The bleakest mountain's head;"

would you believe it, that he introduces Deer—*fallow* Deer!

Talboys.

"Call it not vain; they do not err
Who say that, when the Poet dies,
Mute nature mourns her worshiper,
And celebrates his obsequies;
Who say tall cliff and cavern lone
For the departed bard make moan;
That mountains meet in crystal rill,
That flowers in tears of balm distil;
Through his loved groves that breezes sigh,
And oaks in deeper groan repiy,
And rivers teach their rushing wave
To murmur dirges round his grave."

North. And there the last Minstrel should have ceased. What follows spoils all—fanciful, fantastic—not imaginative, poetical. The Minstrel is at pains to let us know that

"Mute nature does *not* mourn her worshiper!"

that not

"O'er mortal urn
These things inanimate can mourn."

What, then, is the truth? To explain the mystery of flowers distilling tears of balm, we are told that

"The maid's pale shade, who wails her lot,
That love, true love, should be forgot,
From rose and heather shakes the tear
Upon the gentle Minstrel's bier—"

The Phantom Knight shrieks upon the wild blast—and the Chief, from his misty throne on the mountains, fills the lonely caverns with his groans—while his

Tears of rage impel the rill!
All mourn the minstrel's harp unstrung,
Their name unknown, their praise unsung!"

Had Sir Walter been speaking in his own person he never would have written thus—nor thus contradicted and extinguished the Passion in the stanzas you so feelingly recited. But he puts the words into the lips of an old Harper improvising at a Feast—on which occasion anything will pass for poetry—even to the mind of the true Poet himself—but, believe me, it is sheer nonsense—and by the power of contrast recalls Wordsworth's profound saying—

"The Poets, in their elegies and lays
Lamenting the departed, call the groves—
They call upon the hills and streams to mourn,
And senseless rocks: nor idly; for they speak
In these their invocation, with a voice
Obedient to the strong creative power
Of human passion. Sympathies there are
More tranquil, yet perhaps of kindred birth,
That steal upon the meditative mind,
And grow with thought. Beside yon spring I stood,
And eyed its waters, till we seemed to feel
One sadness, they and I. For then a bond
Of brotherhood is broken; time has been
When, every day, the touch of human hand
Dislodged the natural sleep that blnds them up
In mortal stillness; and they ministered
To human comfort."

Talboys. Are all these the Cladich Cock and his echoes? No, surely. Farm Crows to Farm, from Auchlian to Sonnachan. You might also believe them bagpipes. And so it is—that is a bagpipe. On which side of the Loch? Why, on neither—beg pardon—on both; forgive me—on the Water;—incredible—in the Camp! No snore can long outlive that—the People are up and doing. In my mind's eye I see women slipping easily into petticoats—men laboriously into breeches——

North. My more Celtic imagination sees chiefly kilts. But pray, may I ask again, Talboys, what brought you here at this untimeous hour of the Morn?

Talboys. I feel that I ought to apologize for my unwelcome intrusion on your privacy, sir; but on my honor I believed you were in the Van. Yesterday I was so engrossed by you and Shakspeare, that during our colloquy I had not a moment to look at the Wren's Nest.

North. Its existence is believed in by few of the natives. I know no such place for a murder. There would be no need to bury the body—here at this Table he might be left sitting for centuries—a dead secret in a Safe.

Talboys. No need to bury the body! You have no antipathy, I trust, sir, to me?

North. We are not responsible for our antipathies——

Talboys. I allow that—but we are for every single murder we commit; and though there may be no need to bury the body, murder will spank out——

North. We are willing to run the risk. What infatuation to seek the Lion in his Den—the Wren in his Nest! Sit down, sir, and let us have, in the form of dialogue, your last speech and dying words on Othello.

Talboys. Hamlet, sir?

North. Othello.

Talboys. Romeo and Juliet?

North. Othello.

Talboys. Well—Lear let it be.

North. Mind what are you about, Talboys. There are limits to human forbearance. Swear that after this morning's breakfast you will never again utter the words Othello—Iago—Cassio—Desdemona——

Talboys. I swear. Meanwhile, let us recur to the Question of Short and Long Time.

North. When Shakspeare was inditing the scenes of the "the Decline and Fall"—"The Temptation"—"The Seduction"—or whatsoever else you choose to call it—the Sequence of Cause and Effect—the bringing out into prominence and power the successive ESSENTIAL MOVEMENTS of the proceeding transformation were intents possessing his whole spirit. We can easily conceive that they might occupy it absolutely and exclusively—that is to say, excluding the computation and all consideration of actual time. If this be an excessive example, yet I believe that a huddling up of time is a part of the poetical state; that you must, and, what is more, may, crowd into a Theatrical or Epic Day, far more of transaction between parties, and of changes psychological, than a natural day will hold—ay, ten times over. The time on the Stage and in Verse is not literal time. Not it, indeed; and if it be thus with time, which is so palpable, so self-evidencing an entity, what must be the law, and how wide-ranging, for everything else, when we have once got fairly into the Region of Poetry?

Talboys. The usefulness of the Two Times is palpable from first to last—of the Short Time for maintaining the tension of the passion—of the long for a thousand general needs. Thus Bianca must be used for convincing Othello very potently, positively, unanswerably. But she cannot be used without supposing a protracted intercourse between her and Cassio. Iago's dialogue with him falls to the ground, if the acquaintance began yesterday. But superincumbent over all is the *necessity of our not knowing* that Iago begins the Temptation, and that Othello extinguishes the Light of his Life all in one day.

North. And observe, Talboys, how this concatenation of the passionate scenes operates. Marvellously! Let the Entrances of Othello be four—A, B, C, D. You feel the close connection of A with B, of B with C, of C with D. You feel the coherence, the nextness; and all the force of the impetuous Action and Passion resulting. But the logically-consequent near connection of A with C, and much more with D, as again of B with D, you *do not feel.* Why? When you are at C, and feeling the pressure of B upon C, you have lost sight of the pressure of A upon B. At each entrance you go back one step—you do not go back two. The suggested intervals continually keep displacing to distances in your memory the formerly felt connections. This could not so well happen in real life, where the relations of time are strictly bound upon your memory. Though something of it happens when passion devours memory. But in fiction, the conception being loosely held, and shadowy, the feat becomes easily practicable. Thus the Short Time tells for the support of the Passion, along with the Long Time, by means of virtuous installations from the hand or wing of Oblivion. From one to two you feel no intermission—from two to three you feel none—from three to four you feel none; but I defy any man to say that from one to four he has felt none. I defy any man to say honestly, that "sitting at the Play" he has kept count from one to four.

Talboys. If you come to that, nobody keeps watch over the time in listening to Shakspeare. I much doubt if anybody knows at the theatre that Iago's first suggestion of doubt occurs the day after the landing. I never knew it till you made me look for it—

North. For which boon I trust you are truly grateful.

Talboys. 'Tis folly to be wise.

North. Why, Heaven help us! if we did not go to bed, and did not dine, which of us could ever keep count from Monday to Saturday! As it is, we have some of us hard work to know what happened yesterday, and what the day before. On Tuesday I killed that Salmo Ferox?

Talboys. No—but on Wednesday I did. You forget yourself, my dear sir, just like Shakspeare.

North. Ay, Willy forgets himself. He is not withheld by the chain of time he is linking, for he has lost sight of the previous links. Put yourself into the transport of composition, and answer. But besides, every past scene—or to speak more suitably to the technical distribution of the Scenes, in our Editions—every past *changed occupation of the Stage by one coming in or one going out,* (which different occupation, according to the technicality of the French stage, of the Italian, of the Attic, of Plautus, of Terence, constitutes a Scene)—every such past marked moment in the progress of the Play has the effect for the Poet, as well as for you, of protracting the time in retrospect—throwing everything that has passed further back. As if, in traveling fifty miles, you passed fifty Castles, fifty Churches, fifty Villages, fifty Towns, fifty Mountains, fifty Valleys, and fifty cataracts—fifty Camels, fifty Elephants, fifty Caravans, fifty Processions, and fifty Armies—the said fifty miles would seem a good stretch larger to your recollection, and the five hours of traveling a pretty considerable deal longer, than another fifty miles and another five hours in which you had passed only three Old Women.

Talboys. My persuasion is, sir, that nobody alive knows—of the auditors—that the first suggestion of doubt and the conclusion to kill are in one scene of the Play. I do, indeed, believe, with you, sir, that the goings-out and re-enterings of Othello have a strangely deluding effect—that they disconnect the time more than you can think—and that all the changes of persons on the stage—all shiftings of scenes and droppings of curtains, break and dislocate and dilate the time to your imagination, till you do not in the least know where you are. In this laxity of your conception, all hints of extended time sink in and spring up, like that fungus which, on an apt soil, in a night grows to a foot diameter.

North. You have hit it there, Talboys. Shakspeare, we have seen, in his calmer constructions, shows, in a score of ways, weeks, months; that is therefore the true time, or call it the historical time. Hurried himself, and hurrying you on the torrent of passion, he forgets time, and a false show of time, to the utmost contracted, arises. I do not know whether he did not perceive this false exhibition of time, or perceiving he did not care. But we all must see a reason, and a cogent one, why he should not let in the markings of protraction upon his dialogues of the Seduced and the Seducer. You can conceive nothing better than that the Poet, in the moment of composition, seizes the views which at that moment offer themselves as effective—unconscious or regardless of incompatibility. He is whole to the present; and as all is feigned, he does not remember how the foregone makes the ongoing impracticable. Have you ever before, Talboys, examined time in a play of Shakspeare? Much more, have you ever examined the treatment of time on the Stage to which Shakspeare came, upon which he lived, and which he left?

Talboys. A good deal.

North. Not much, I suspect.

Talboys. Why, not at all—except t'other day along with you—in Macbeth.

North. He came to a Stage which certainly had not cultivated the logic of time as a branch of the Dramatic Art. It appears to me that those old people, when they were enwrapt in the transport of their creative power, totally forgot all regard, lost all consciousness of time. Passion does not know the clock or the calendar. Intimations of time, now vague, now positive, will continually occur; but also the Scenes float, like the Cyclades in a Sea of Time, at distances utterly indeterminate—

Most near? Most remote? That is a Stage of Power, and not of Rules—Dynamic, not Formal. I say again at last as at first, that the time of Othello, tried by the notions of time in *our Art*, or tried if you will, by the type of prosaic and literal time, is—INSOLUBLE.

Talboys. To the first question, therefore, being What is the truth of the matter? the answer stands, I conceive without a shadow of doubt or difficulty, "The time of Othello is—as real time—INSOLUBLE."

North. By heavens, he echoes me!

Talboys. Or, it is proposed incongruously, impossibly. Then arises the question, How stood the time in the mind of Shakspeare?

North. I answer, I do not know. The question splits itself into two—first, "How did he *project* the time?" Second, "How did he conceive it in the progress of the Play?" My impression is, that he projected extended time. If so, did he or did he not know that in managing the Seduction he departed from that design by contracting into a Day? Did he deliberately entertain a double design? If he did, how did he excuse this to himself? Did he say, "A stage necessity, or a theatrical or dramatic necessity"—namely, that of sustaining at the utmost possible reach of altitude the tragical passion and interest —"requires the precipitation of the passion from the first breathing of suspicion—the 'Ha! Ha! I like not that,' of the suggesting Fiend to the consecrated 'killing myself, to die upon a kiss!'—all in the course of fifteen hours—and this tragical vehemency, this impetuous energy, this torrent of power I will have; at the same time I have many reasons—amongst them the general probability of the action—for a dilated time; and I, being a magician of the first water, will so dazzle, blind, and bewilder my auditors, that they shall accept the double time with a double belief—shall feel the unstayed rushing on of action and passion, from the first suggestion to the cloud of deaths —and yet shall remain with a conviction that Othello was for months Governor of Cyprus—they being on the whole unreflective and uncritical persons?"

Talboys. And, after all, who willingly criticises his dreams or his pleasures?

North. And the Audience of the Globe Theatre shall not —for "I hurl my dazzing spells into the spungy air," and "the spell shall sit when the curtain has fallen." Shakspeare might, in the consciousness of power, say this. For this is that which he has—knowingly or unknowingly—done. Unknowingly? Perhaps—himself borne on by the successively rising waves of his work. For you see, Talboys, with what prolonged and severe labor we two have arrived at knowing the reality of the case which now lies open to us in broad light. We have needed time and pains, and the slow settling of our understandings, to unwind the threads of delusion in which we were encoiled and entoiled. If a strange and unexplained power could undeniably so beguile us—a possibility of which, previously to this examination, we never have dreamt—how do we warrant that the same dark, nameless mysterious power shall not equally blind the "Artificer of Fraud?" This is matter of proposed investigation and divination, which let whoever has will, wit, and time presently undertake.

Talboys. Why, we are doing it, sir. He will be a bold man who treats of Othello—after Us.

North. Another question is—What is the Censure of Art on the demonstrated inconsistency in Othello? I propose, but now deal not with it. Observe that we have laid open a new and starling inquiry. We have demonstrated the double time of Othello—the Chronological Fact. That is the first step set in light—the first required piece of the work—*done.* Beyond this, we have ploughed a furrow or two, to show and lead further direction of the work in the wide field. We have touched on the gain to the work by means of the duplicity—we have proposed to the self-consciousness of all hearers and readers the psychological fact of their own unconsciousness of the guile used towards them, or of the success of the fallacy; and we have asked the solution of the psychological fact. We have also asked the Criticism of Art on the government of the time in Othello—supposing the Poet in pride and audacity of power to have designed that which he has done. Was it High Art?

Talboys. Ay—was it High Art?

North. I dare hardly opine. Effect of high and most defying art it has surely; but you ask again—did he know? I seem to see often that the spirit of the Scene possessed Skakspeare, and that he fairly forgot the logical ties which he had encoiled about him. We know the written Play, and we may, if we are capable, know its power upon ourselves. There *are* the Two Times, the Long and the Short; and each exerts upon you its especial virtue. I can believe that Shakspeare unconsciously did what Necessity claimed—the impetuous motion on, on, on of the Passion—the long time asked by the successive events; the forces that swayed him, each in its turn, its own way.

Talboys. Unconsciously?

North. Oh heavens! Yes—yes—no—no. Yes—no. No—yes. What you will.

"Willingly my jaws I close,
Leave! oh! leave me to repose."

Talboys. Consciously or unconsciously?

North. Talboys, Longfellow, Perpetual Præses of the Seven Feet Club, we want Troy, Priam, Achilles, Hector, to have been. Perhaps they were—perhaps they were not. We must be ready for two states of mind—simple belief, which is the temper of childhood and youth—recognition of illusion with self-surrender, which is the attained state of criticism wise and childlike. At last we voluntarily take on the faith which was in the goldener age. The child believed; and the man believes. But the child believes *this;* and the man who perceives how *this* is a shadow, believes *that* beyond. *This* he believes in play—*that* in earnest. The child mixed the two—the tail of the fairies and the hope of hereafter. Union, my dear Boys, is the faculty of the young, but division of the old. I speak of Shakspeare at five years of age; not of Us, whom, ere we can polysyllable men's names, dominies instruct how to do old men's work and to distinguish.

Talboys. My dear sir, I do so love to hear your talkee talkee; but be just ever so little a little more intelligible to ordinary mortals—

North. You ask what really happened? The Play bewilders you from answering—accept it as it rushes along through your soul, reading or sitting to hear and see. The main and strange fact is, that these questions of Time, which, reading the Play backwards, force themselves on us, never occur to us leaning straight forwards. Two Necessities lie upon your soul.

Talboys. Two Necessities, sir?

North. Two Necessities lie upon your soul. You cannot believe that Othello, suspecting his Wife, folds his arms night after night about her disrobed bosom. As little can you believe that in the course of twelve hours the spirit of infinite love has changed into a dagger-armed slayer. The Two Times —marvelous as it is to say—take you into alternate possession. The impetuous motion forwards, in the scenes and in the tenor of action, which belong to the same Day, you feel; and you ask no questions. When Othello and Iago speak together, you lose the knowledge of time. You see power and not form. You feel the aroused Spirit of Jealousy: you see, in the field of belief, a thought sown and sprung—a thought changed into a doubt—a doubt into a dread—a dread into the cloud of death. Evidences press, one after the other—the spirit endures change—you feel succession—as cause and effect must succeed—you do not compute hours, days, weeks, months;—yet confess I must, and confess you must, and confess all the world and his wife must, that the condition is altogether anomalous—that a time which is at once a day of the Calendar and a month of the Calendar, does not happen anywhere out of Cyprus.

Talboys. It has arisen just as you say, sir—because Two Necessities pressed. The passion must have its torrent, else *you* will never endure that Othello shall kill Desdemona. Events must have their concatenation, else—but I stop at this the incredible anomaly, that for *Othello* himself you require the double time! You cannot imagine him embracing his wife, misdoubted false; as little can you his Love measureless, between sunrise and sunset turned into Murder.

North. Even so.

Talboys. My dear sir, what really happened?

North. Oh! Talboys, Talboys. Well then—*not* that Othello killed her upon the first night after the arrival at Cyprus. The Cycle could not have been so run through.

Talboys. How then in reality did the Weeks pass?

North. That's a good one! Why I was just about to ask you—and 'tis your indisputable duty to tell me and the anxious world—how.

Talboys. I do not choose to commit myself in such a serious affair.

North. Suppose the framing of the tale into a Prose Romance. Surely, surely, surely, no human romancer, compounding the unhappy transactions into a prose narrative, could, could could have put the first sowing of doubt, and the smothering under the pillows, for incidents of one day. He would have made Othello for a time laugh at the doubt, toss it to the winds. Iago would have wormed about him a deal slowlier. The course of the transactions in the Novel would have been much nearer the course of reality.

Talboys. In Cinthio's Novel—

North. Curse Cinthio.

Talboys. My Lord, I bow to your superior politeness.

North. Confound Chesterfield. My dear friend, Reality has its own reasons—a Novel its own—and its own a Drama. Every work of art brings its own conditions, which divide you from the literal representation of human experience. Ask Painter, Sculptor, and Architect. Every fine art exercises its own sleights.

Talboys. In the Novel, I guess or admit that they would have been a month at Cyprus ere Iago had stirred. What hurry? He would have watched his time—ever and anon would have thrown in a hundred suggestions of which we know nothing. Let any man, romancer or other, set himself to conceive the Prose Novel. He cannot, by any possibility, conceive that he should have been led to make but a day of it. Ergo, the Drama proceeds upon its own Laws. No representation in art is the literal transcript of experience.

North. The question is, what deviations—to what extent—does the particular Art need? And why? The talked Attic Unity of Time instructs us. But Sophocles and Shakspeare must have one view of the Stage, in essence. You must sit out your three or four hours. You must listen and see with expectation *intended*, like a bow drawn. To which intent Action and Passion must press on.

Talboys. Compare, sir, the One Day of Othello to the Sixteen Years of Hermione! There, intensest Passion sustained; here, the unrolling of a romantic adventnre. Each true to the temper imposed on the hearing spectator.

North. Good. The Novel is not a Transcript—the Play is not a Transcript. Ask not for a Transcript, for not one of those who could give it you, will. A *conditional imitation we desire* and demand—and we have it in Othello.

Talboys. And put up we must with Two Times—one for your sympathy with his tempest of heart—one for the verisimilitude of the transaction.

North. Think on the facility with which, in the Novel, Iago could have strewn an atom of arsenic a-day on Othello's platter, to use him to the taste; and how, in the Play, this representation is impossible. Then, the original remaining the same, each manner of portraiture *leaves it,* and each after *its own Laws.*

Talboys. Did not Shakspeare know as much about the Time which he was himself making *as we do,* as much and more?

North. I doubt it. I see no necessity for believing it. We judge him as we judge ourselves. He came to his Art as it was, and created—improving it—from that point. An Art grows in all its constituents. The management of the Time is a constituent in the Art of "feigned history," as Poetry is called by Lord Bacon. But I contend that on our Stage, to which Shakspeare came, the management of Time was in utter neglect—an undreamed entity; and I claim for the first foundation of any Canon respective to this matter acute sifting of all Plays *previous.*

Talboys. Not so very many—

North. Nor so very few. Shakspeare took up the sprawling, forlorn infant, dramatic Time. He cradled, rocked, and fed it. The bantling throve, and crawled vigorously about on all-fours. But since then, thou Tallometer, imagine the study that *we* have made. Count not our Epic Poems—not our Metrical Romances—not our Tragedies. Count our Comedies, and count above all our Novels. I do not say that you can settle Time in these by the Almanac. They are the less poetical when you can do so; but I say that we have with wonderful and immense diligence studied the working out of a Story. Time being here an essential constituent, it cannot be but that, in our more exact and critical laying-out of the chain of occurrences, we have arrived at a tutored and jealous respect of Time—To say nothing of our Aristotelian lessons—totally unlike anything that existed under Eliza and James, as a general proficiency of the Art—as a step gained in the National Criticism.

Talboys. Ay, it must be difficult in the extreme for us so to divest ourselves of our own intellectual habits and proficiency as to take up, and into our own, the mind of that age. But, unless we do so, we are unable to judge what might or might not happen to any one mind of that age; and when we affirm that Shakspeare must have known what he was doing in regard to the Time of Othello, we are suffering under the described difficulty or disability—

North. Why, Talboys, you are coming day after day, to talk better and better sense—take care you get not too sensible—

Talboys. We must never forget, sir, that the management of the Time was on that Stage a slighted and trampled element—that what Willy gives us of it is gratuitous, and what we must be thankful for—and finally that he did not distinctly scheme out, in his own conception, the Time of Othello—very far from it.

North. I verily believe that if you or I had shown him the Time, tied up as it is, he would have said, "Let it go hang. They won't find it out; and, if they do, let them make the best, the worst, and the most of it. The Play is a good Play, and I shall spoil it with mending it." Why, Talboys, if Queen Elizabeth had required that the Time should be set straight, it could not have been done. One—two—six changes would not have done it. The Time is an entangled skein that can only be disentangled by breaking it. For the fervor of action on the Stage, Iago could not have delayed the beginning beyond the next day. And yet think of the Moral Absurdity—to begin—really as if the day after Marriage, to show Jealousy! The thing is out of nature the whole diameter of the globe. His project was "after a time t' abuse Othello's ear," which is according to nature, and is *de facto* the impression made—strange to say—from beginning to end. But the truth is, that the Stage three hours are so soon gone, that you submit yourself to everything to come within compass. Your imagination is bound to the wheels of the Theatre Clock.

Talboys. Yet, in your conversation on Macbeth, you called your discovery an "astounding discovery"—and it is so. The Duplicity of Time in Othello is a hundred times more astounding—

North. And the discovery of it will immortalize my name. I grieve to think that the Pensive Public is sadly deficient in Imagination. I remember or invent that she once resisted me, when I said that "Illusion" is one constituent of Poetry. Illusion, the Pensive Public must be made to know, is WHEN THE SAME THING IS, AND IS NOT. Pa—God bless him!—makes believe to be a Lion. He roars and springs upon his prey. He at once believes himself to be a Lion, and knows himself to be Pa. Just so with the Shakspeare Club—many millions strong. The two times at Cyprus *are there;* the reason for the two times—to wit, probability of the Action, storm of the Passion *is there;* and if any wiseacre should ask, "How do we manage to stand the *known* together-proceeding of two times?" The wiseacre is answered—"We don't stand it—for we know nothing about it. We are held in a confusion and a delusion about the time." We have effect of both—distinct knowledge of neither. We have suggestions to our Understanding of extended time—we have movements of our Will by precipitated time.

Talboys. We have—we have—we have. Oh, sir! sir! sir!

North. Does any man by possibility ask for a scheme and an exposition, by which it shall be made luminous to the smallest capacity, *how* we are able distinctly all along to know, and bear in mind, that the preceding transactions are accomplished in a day, and at the same time and therewithal, distinctly all along to know and bear in mind that the same transactions proceeding before our eyes take about three months to accomplish? Then, I am obliged—like the musicians, when they are told that, if they have any music that may not be heard, Othello desires them to play it—to make answer, "Sir, we have none such." It is to ask that a deception shall be not only seemingly but really a truth! Jedediah Buxton, and Blair the Chronologist would, "sitting at *this* play," have broken their hearts. You need not. If you ask me—which judiciously you may—what or how much did the Swan of Avon intend and know of all this astonishing legerdemain, when he sang thus astonishingly? Was he the juggler juggled by aërial spirits—as Puck and Ariel? I put my finger to my lip, and nod on him to do the same; and if I am asked, "Shall a modern artificer of the Drama, having the same pressure from within and from without, adopt this resource of evasion?" I can answer, with great confidence, "He had better look before he leap." If any spectator, upon the mere persuasion and power of the Representation, ends with believing that the seed sown and the harvest reaped are of one day, I believe that he may yet have the belief of extended time at Cyprus. I should say by *carrying the one day with him on forwards from day to day!* Or if you wish this more intelligibly said, that he shall continually *forget* the past notices. Once for all, he shall *forget* that the *first suggestion was on the day after the arrival.*

Talboys. Inquire, sir, what intelligent auditors, who have not gone into the study, have thought; for that, after all, is the only testimony that means anything.

North. Well, Talboys, suppose that one of them should actually say, "Why, upon my word, if I am to tell the truth, I did take note that Iago began 'abusing Othello's ear, the day after the arrival. I did, in the course of the Play, gather up an impression that some good space of time was passing at Cyprus—and I did, when the murder came, put it down upon the same day with the sowing of the suspicion, and I was not aware of the contradiction. In short, now that you put me upon it, I see that I did that which thousands of us do in thousands of subjects—keep in different corners of the brain two beliefs—of which, if they had come upon the same ground, the one must have annihilated the other. But I did not at the time bring the data together. *I suppose that I had something else to think of.*"

Talboys. Assume, sir, for simplicity's sake, that Shakspeare knew what he was doing.

North. Then the Double Time is to be called—an Imposture.

Talboys. Oh, my dear sir—oh, oh!

North. A good-natured Juggler, my dear Talboys, has cheated your eyes. You ask him to show you how he did it. He does the trick slowly—and you see. "Now, good Conjuror, *do it slowly, and cheat us.*" "I can't. I cheat you by doing it quickly. To be cheated, you must *not* see what I do; but you must *think* that you see." When we inspect the Play in our closets, the Juggler does his tricks slowly. We sit at the Play, and he does it quick. When you see the trick again done the right way—that is quick—you cannot conceive how it is that you no longer see that which you saw when it was done slowly! Again the impression returns of a magical feat.

Talboys. I doubt if we saw Othello perfectly acted, whether all our study would preserve us from the returning imposture.

North. I will defy any one most skillful theatrical connoisseur, even at the tenth, or twentieth, or fiftieth Representation, so to have followed the comings-in and the goings-out, as to satisfy himself to demonstration, that interval into which a month or a week or a day can be dropped—*there is none.*

Talboys. When do you propose publishing this your "astounding Discovery?"

North. Not till after my death.

Talboys. I shall attend to it.

North. In comparing Shakspeare and the Attic Three, we seem to ourselves, but really do not, to exhaust the Criticism of the Drama. Is Mr. Sheriff Alison right, when he said that the method of Shakspeare is justified only by the genius of Shakspeare? That less genius needs the art of antiquity? Our own art inclines to a method between the two; and we should have to account for the theatrical success, during a century or more, of such Plays as the Fair Penitent, Jane Shore, &c.

Talboys. Why, sir, does Tragedy displace often from our contemplation, Comedy? Not when we are contemplating Shakspeare. To me his method, in reading him, appears justified by the omnipotent Art, which, despite refractoriness, binds together the most refractory times, things, persons, events *in Unity.*

North. Most true. We feel, in reading, the self-compactness and self-completeness of each Play. Thus in Lear—

Talboys. In Lear the ethical ground is the Relation of Parent to Child, specifically Father and Daughter. If the treatment of that Relation is full to your satisfaction, that may effect you as a Unity. Full is not exhaustive; but one part of treatment demands another. Thus the violated relation requires for its complement the consecrated relation.

North. In Hamlet?

Talboys. The ethical ground in Hamlet, sir, is the relation of Father and Son, very peculiarly determined, or specialtied. Observe, sir, how the *like* relation between Father and Daughter, the *same* between Father and Son occurs in Polonius's House. Here too, a slain Father—a part of the specialty. Compare, particularly, the dilatory revenge of Hamlet, and the dispatchful of Laertes. Again, the relation of Gertrude the Mother and Hamlet the Son—so many differences! And the strange discords upon the same relation—my Uncle-Father and Aunt-Mother—the tragic grotesque.

North. Eh?

Talboys. Then in Lear the House of Gloster counterparts Lear's. And compare the ill-disposed Son-in-law Cornwall, and the well-disposed Son-in-law Albany. The very Fool has a sort of *filial* relation to Lear—"Nuncle"—and "come on, my Boy." At least the relation is in the same direction—old to young—protecting to dependent—spontaneous love to grateful, requiting love, and an intimate, fondling familiarity. Compare in Hamlet, Ophelia's way of taking her father's death—madness and unconscious suicide—the susceptible girl,—and the brother to kill the slayer, "to cut his throat i' the church"—the energetic youthy man, *ferox juvenis*—fiery—full of exuberant strength;—all variations of the grounding thought—relation of Parent and Child.

North. Of Othello?

Talboys. The moral Unity of Othello can be nothing but the Connubial Relation. How is this dealt with? Othello and Desdemona deserve one another—both are excellent—both impassioned, but very differently—both frank, simple, confiding—both unbounded in love. But they have married against the father's wish—privily, and—he dies—so here is from another sacred quarter an influence thwarting—a law violated, and of which the violation shall be made good to the uttermost.

So somebody remarks that Brabantio involves the fact in the Nemesis, "She has deceived her Father, and may thee." Then the pretended corrupt love of her and Cassio is a reflection in divers ways of the prevailing relation—for a corrupt union of man and woman images *ex opposito* the true union—and then it comes as the wounding to the death. Again, Rodrigo's wicked pursuit of her is an imperfect, false reflection. And then there is the false relation—in Cassio and Bianca—woven in essentially when Iago, talking to Cassio, of Bianca, makes Othello believe that they are speaking of Desdemona. Then the married estate of Iago and Emilia is another image—an actual marriage, and so far the same thing, but an inwardly unbound wedlock—between heart and heart no tie—and so far not the same thing—the same with a difference, exactly what Poetry requires. Note that this image is also participant in the Action, essentially, penetratively to the core; since hereby Iago gets the handkerchief, and hereby too, the knot is resolved by Emilia's final disclosures and asseverations sealed by her death. Observe that each husband kills, and indeed stabs his wife—motives a little different—as heaven and hell.

North. The method of Shakspeare makes his Drama the more absolute reflection of our own Life, wherein are to be considered two things——

Talboys. First—if the innermost grounding feeling of all our other feelings is and must be that of Self—the next, or in close proximity, Sympathy with our life—then by the overpowering similitude of those Plays to our Lives—of the method of the Plays to the method of our life—that Sympathy is by Shakspeare seized and possessed as by no other dramatist—the persuasion of reality being immense and stupendous. Elements of the method are, the mixture of comic and tragic—the crossing presentment of different interests—presentment of the same interests from divided places and times—multiplying of agents, that is number and variety—being of all ranks, ages, qualities, offices—coming in contact—immixt in Action and Passion. This frank, liberal, unreserved, spontaneous and natural method of imitation must ravish our sympathy—and we know that the plays of Shakspeare are to us like another world of our own in its exuberant plenitude—a full second humanity.

North. Opposed to this is the severe method of the Greek Stage—selecting and simplifying.

Talboys. Of the modern craftsmen, to my thinking Alfieri has carried the Attic severity to the utmost; and I am obliged to say, sir, that in them all—those Greeks and this Italian—the severity oppresses me—I feel the rule of Art—not the free movement of human existence. That I feel overpoweringly, only in Shakspeare.

North. Ay.

Talboys. Alfieri says that the constitueut Element of Tragedy is Conflict—as of Duty and Passion—as of conscious Election in the breast of Man and Fate.

North. He does—does he?

Talboys. There is Conflict—or Contrast—or Antithesis—the Jar of Two Opposites—a Discord—a Rending—in Lear; between his misplaced confidence and its requital—between his misplaced displeasure and the true love that is working towards his weal. And, again, between the Desert and the Reward of Cordelia—with more in the same Play.

North. Schiller says of Tragic Fate,

> "The great gigantic Destiny
> That exalts Man in crushing him."

Welcker has, I believe, written on the Fate of the Greek Tragedy, which I desire to see.

Talboys. Are Waves breaking against a Rock the true image of Tragedy?

North. Hardly; any more than a man running his head

against a post, or stone wall is. The two antagonistic Forces, Talboys, must each of them have, or seem to have, the possibility of yielding; the Conflict or Strife must have a certain play. Therefore I inquire—Is the Greek Fate the most excellent of Dramatic means? and is the Greek Fate inflexible? And, granting that the Hellenic Fate is thoroughly sublime and fitting to Greek Tragedy, and withal inflexible—does it follow that Modern Tragedy must have a like overhanging tyrannical Necessity?

Talboys. No.

North. No. The Greek Tragedy representing a received religious Mythology, we may conceive the poetical, or esthetical *hardness* of a Fate known for unalterable, to have been tempered by the inherent Awe—the Holiness. There is a certain swallowing-up of human interests, hopes, passions—this turmoiling, struggling life—in a revealed Infinitude. Our Stage is human—built on the Moral Nature of Man, and on his terrestrial Manner of Being. It stands *under* the Heavens—*upon* the Earth. In Hamlet, the Ghost, with his command of Revenge, represents the Impassive, inflexible—with a breath freezing the movable human blood into stillness—everything else is in agitation.

Talboys. Say it again, sir.

North. Beg my pardon and your own, fully and unconditionally, Talboys, this very instant, for talking slightingly of the Greek Drama.

Talboys. Not guilty, my Lord. Of all Dramas that ever were dramatized on the Stage of this unintelligible world, the Greek Drama is the most dramatic, saving and excepting Shakspeare's.

North. Ay, wonderful, my dear Talboys, to see the holy affections demonstrated mighty on the heathen Proscenium.

Antigone! Daughter and Sister. Or in another House, Orestes, Electra.

Talboys. Macbeth murders a King, who happens to be his kinsman; but Clytemnestra murders her husband, who happens to be a King—the profounder and more interior crime.

North. We see how grave are the undertakings of Poetry, which engages itself to please, that it may accomplish sublimer aims. By pleasure she wins you to your greater good—to Love and Intelligence. The heathen Legislator, the heathen Philosopher, the heathen Poet, looks upon Man with love and awe. He desires and conceives his welfare—his wellbeing—HIS HAPPINESS.

Talboys. And the Poet, you believe, sir, with intenser love —with more solemn awe—with more penetrant intuition.

North. I do. And he has his way clearer before him.

Talboys. The Legislator, sir, will alchemize the most refractory of all substances—Man. His materials are in truth the lowest and grossest, and most external relations of Man's life.

North. They are.

Talboys. And these he would, with instrumentality of low, gross, outward means, subjugate or subdue under his own most spiritual intuitions.

North. A vain task, my dear Talboys, for an impossible. He must lower his intuition—his aim—to his means and materials. The Philosopher walks in a more etherial region. Compared to the Legislator, he is at advantage. But he has his own difficulties. He must *think feelings!*

Talboys. He might as well try, sir, to trace outline, and measure capacity of a mist which varies its form momently, and, without determinate boundary loses itself in the contiguous air. His work is to define the indefinite.

North. And then he comes from the Schools, which in

qualifying disqualify also—from the Schools of the Senses—of the Physical Arts—of Natural Philosophy—of Logical, Metaphysical, Mathematical Science. These have quickened, strengthened, and sharpened his wit; they have lifted him at last from emotions to notions: but—Love is understood by loving—Hate by hating—and only so! Sensations—notions—EMOTIONS! I say, Talboys, that in all these inferior schools you may understand a part by itself, and ascend by items to the Sum, the All. But in the Philosophy of the Will, you must from the centre look along the radii, and with a sweep command the circumference. You must know as it were Nothing, or All.

Talboys. Ay, indeed, sir; looking at the Doctrines of the Moral Philosophers, you are always dissatisfied—and why?

North Because they contradict your self-experience. Sometimes they speak as you feel. Your self-intelligence answers, and from time to time, acknowledges and avouches a strain or two; but then comes discord. The Sage stands on a radius. If he looks along the radius towards the circumference, he sees in the same direction with him who stands at the centre; but in every other direction, inversely or transversely. Every work of a Philosopher gives you the notion of glimpses caught, snatched in the midst of clouds and of rolling darknesses. The truth is, Talboys, that the Moral Philosopher is in the Moral Universe a schoolboy; he is gaining, from time to time, information by which, if he shall persevere and prosper, he shall at last understand. Hitherto he but prepares to understand. If he knows this, good; but if the schoolboy who has mastered his Greek Alphabet, will forthwith proceed to expound Homer and Plato, what sort of an *ex cathedrâ* may we not expect? Rather, what expectation can approach the burlesque that is in store!

Talboys. All are not such.

North. The Moral sage may be the Schoolboy in the Magisterial Chair. With only this difference, that he of the beard has been installed in form, and the Doctor's hat set on his head by the hand of authority. But the ground of confusion is the same. He will from initial glimpses of information expound the world. He will—and the worst of it is that—he must.

Talboys. A Legislator, a Philosopher, a Poet, all know that the stability and welfare of a man—of a fellowship of men—is Virtue. But see how they deal with it.

North. Don't look to me, Talboys; go on of yourself and for yourself—I am a pupil.

Talboys. The Legislator, sir, can hardly do more than reward Valor in war; and punish overt crime. The Philosopher will have Good either tangible, like an ox, or a tree, or a tower, or a piece of land; or a rigorous and precise rational abstraction, like the quantities of a mathematician. For Good *substantial and impalpable,* go to the Poet. For Good—for Virtue—*concrete,* go to the Poet.

North. The Philosopher separates Virtue from all other motions and states of the human will. The Poet loses or hides Virtue in the other motions and states of the human will. Orestes, obeying the Command of Apollo, avenges his Father, by slaying his Mother, and her murderous and adulterous Paramour. So awfully, solemnly, terribly—with such implication and involution in human affections and passions, works and interests and sufferings, the Poet demonstrates Virtue.

Talboys. And we go along with Orestes, sir; the Greeks did—if our feebler soul cannot.

North. Yes, Talboys, we do go along with Orestes. He does that which he *must* do—which he is under a moral obligation to do—under a moral necessity of doing. Necessity! ay, an Αναγκη—stern, strong, adamantine as that which links the Chain of Causes and Events in the natural universe—which compels the equable and unalterable celestial motions beheld by our eyes—such a bounden, irresistible agency sends on the son of the murdered, with hidden sword, against the bosom that has lulled, fed, *made* him!—HE MUST.

Talboys. Love, hate, horror—the furies of kinned shed blood ready to spring up from the black inscrutable earth wetted by the red drops, and to dog the heels of the new Slayer—of the divinely-appointed Parricide? So a Poet teaches Virtue.

North. Ay, even so; convulsing your soul—convulsing the worlds, he shows you LAW—the archaic, the primal, sprung, ere Time, from the bosom of Jupiter—LAW the bond of the worlds, LAW the inviolate violated, and avenging her Violation, vindicating her own everlasting stability, purity, divinity.

Talboys. Divine Law and humble, faithful, acquiescent human Obedience! Obedience self-sacrificing, blind to the consequences, hearing the God, hearing the Ghost, deaf to all other Voices—deaf to fear, deaf to pity!

North. Now call in the Philosopher, and hear what he has to preach. Something exquisite and unintelligible about the Middle between two Extremes!

Talboys. Shade of the Staygrite!

North. The pure Earth shakes crime from herself, and the pure stars follow their eternal courses. The Mother slays the children of a brother for the father's repast. And the sun, stopt in the heavens, veils his resplendent face. So a Poet inculcates Law—Law running through all things, and binding all things in unity and in Sympathy—Law entwined in the primal relations of Man with Man. To reconcile Man with Law—to make him its "willing bondsman"—is the great Moral and Political Problem—the first Social need of the day—the innermost craving need of all time since the Fall. The Poet is its greatest teacher—a wily preceptor, who lessons you, unaware, unsuspecting of the supreme benefit purposed you—done you by him, the Hierophant of Harmonia.

Talboys. You ordered me, sir, some few or many hours ago —some Short or Long Time since—to swear that after this Morning's Breakfast I would never more so much as confidentially whisper into a friend's ear the words—Othello! Desdemona! And I swore it. I am now eager to swear it over again; but I begin, sir, to entertain the most serious apprehensions that that time will never arrive.

North. What time?

Talboys. *After* Breakfast. We have been sitting here, sir, *before* Breakfast for ages, in the Wren's Nest. During our incubation, what a succession of changes may there not have been in Europe! Revolution on Revolution—blood poured out like water——Hark, the Tocsin!

North. The Gong.

Talboys. The *Breakfast* Gong! The tremulous thunder meets an answering chord within me. Six o'clock in the Morning—and no victuals have I gorged since Eleven Yestreen. Good-by to the Wren's Nest—the very Cave of Famine. This is Turkey-egg—Goose-egg—Swan-egg—Ostrich-egg day. I see Buller eyeing open-mouthed, with premeditating mastication, my pile of muffins. Gormandizing sans Grace. Take care you don't trip, sir, over the precipice—'twould be an ugly fall —into the basin. Now we are out of danger. But don't skip, sir—don't skip—till we emerge—on the open ground—then we may dance among the daisies.

THE MODERN BRITISH ESSAYISTS

At less than Half Price.

The great success that has attended the publication of
THE MODERN ESSAYISTS,
Comprising the Critical and Miscellaneous Writings of the Most Distinguished Authors of Modern Times, has induced the publishers to issue a New, Revised and very Cheap Edition, with Finely Engraved Portraits of the Authors; and while they have *added* to the series the writings of several distinguished authors, they have reduced the price more than

ONE HALF.

The writings of each author will generally be comprised in a single octavo volume, well printed from new type, on fine white paper manufactured expressly for this edition.
The series will contain all the most able papers that have EVER APPEARED IN

THE EDINBURGH REVIEW,

The London Quarterly Review, and Blackwood's Magazine,

and may indeed be called the CREAM of those publications.

It is only necessary to mention the names of the authors whose writings will appear. T. BABINGTON MACAULAY, ARCHIBALD ALISON, REV. SYDNEY SMITH, PROFESSOR WILSON JAMES STEPHEN, ROBERT SOUTHEY, SIR WALTER SCOTT, LORD JEFFREY, SIR JAMES MACKINTOSH, T. NOON TALFOURD, J. G. LOCKHART, REGINALD HEBER.

The popularity of the authors and the extreme moderation of the price, recommend

THE MODERN ESSAYISTS,

To HEADS OF FAMILIES for their Children, as perfect models of style.

To MANAGERS OF BOOK SOCIETIES, Book Clubs, &c.

To SCHOOL INSPECTORS, SCHOOLMASTERS AND TUTORS, as suitable gifts and prizes, or adapted for School Libraries.

TRAVELLERS ON A JOURNEY will find in these portable and cheap volumes something to read on the road, adapted to fill a corner in a portmanteau or carpet-bag.

To PASSENGERS ON BOARD A SHIP, here are ample materials in a narrow compass for whiling away the monotonous hours of a sea voyage.

To OFFICERS IN THE ARMY AND NAVY, and to all Economists in *space* or *pocket*, who, having limited chambers, and small book-shelves, desire to lay up for themselves a *concentrated Library*, at a moderate expenditure.

To ALL WHO HAVE FRIENDS IN DISTANT COUNTRIES, as an acceptable present to send out to them.

THE MODERN ESSAYISTS will yield to the *Settler* in the Backwoods of America the most valuable and interesting writings of all the most distinguished authors of *our time* at less than one quarter the price they could be obtained in any other form.

THE STUDENT AND LOVER OF LITERATURE at Home, who has hitherto been compelled to wade through volumes of Reviews for a single article, may now become possessed of *every article worth reading* for little more than *the cost of the annual subscription.*

I.

MACAULAY.

CRITICAL AND MISCELLANEOUS WRITINGS OF THOMAS BABINGTON MACAULAY.

In One Volume, with a finely engraved portrait, from an original picture by Henry Inman. Cloth Gilt,
$2 00.

Contents.

Milton, Machiavelli, Dryden, History, Hallam's Constitutional History, Southey's Colloquies on Society, Moore's Life of Byron, Southey's Bunyan's Pilgrim's Progress, Croker's Boswell's Life of Johnson, Lord Nugent's Memoirs of Hampden, Nare's Memoirs of Lord Burghley, Dumont's Recollections of Mirabeau, Lord Mahon's War of the Succession, Walpole's Letters to Sir H. Mann, Thackaray's History of Earl Chatham, Lord Bacon, Mackintosh's History of the Revolution of England, Sir John Malcolm's Life of Lord Clive, Life and Writings of Sir W. Temple, Church and State, Ranke's History of the Popes, Cowley and Milton, Mitford's History of Greece, The Athenian Orators, Comic Dramatists of the Restoration, Lord Holland, Warren Hastings, Frederic the Great, Lays of Ancient Rome, Madame D'Arblay, Addison, Barere's Memoirs, Montgomery's Poems, Civil Disabilities of the Jews, Mill on Government, Bentham's Defence of Mill, Utilitarian Theory of Government, and Earl Chatham, second part, &c.

"It may now be asked by some sapient critics, Why make all this coil about a mere periodical essayist? Of what possible concern is it to any body, whether Mr. Thomas Babington Macaulay be, or be not, overrun with faults, since he is nothing more than one of the three-day immortals who contribute flashy and 'taking' articles to a Quarterly Review? What great work has he written? Such questions as these might be put by the same men who place the Spectator, Tattler and Rambler among the British classics, yet judge of the size of a cotemporary's mind by that of his book, and who can hardly recognize amplitude of comprehension, unless it be spread over the six hundred pages of octavos and quartos.—

Such men would place Bancroft above Webster, and Sparks above Calhoun, Adams and Everett—deny a posterity for Bryant's Thanatopsis, and predict longevity to Pollok's Course of Time. It is singular that the sagacity which can detect thought only in a state of dilution, is not sadly graveled when it thinks of the sententious aphorisms which have survived whole libraries of folios, and the little songs which have outrun, in the race of fame, so many enormous epics.—While it can easily be demonstrated that Macaulay's writings contain a hundred-fold more matter and thought, than an equal number of volumes taken from what are called, *par eminence*, the 'British Essayists,' it is not broaching any literary heresy to predict, that they will sail as far down the stream of time, as those eminent members of the illustrious family of British classics."

II.

ARCHIBALD ALISON.

THE CRITICAL AND MISCELLANEOUS WRITINGS OF ARCHIBALD ALISON,

AUTHOR OF "THE HISTORY OF EUROPE,"

In One Volume, 8vo. with a portrait.

Price $1 25.

CONTENTS.

Chateaubriand, Napoleon, Bossuet, Poland, Madame de Stael, National Monuments, Marshal Ney, Robert Bruce, Paris in 1814, The Louvre in 1814, Tyrol, France in 1833, Italy, Scott, Campbell and Byron, Schools of Design, Lamartine, The Copyright Question, Michelet's France, Military Treason and Civic Soldiers, Arnold's Rome, Mirabeau, Bulwer's Athens, The Reign of Terror, The French Revolution of 1830, The Fall of Turkey, The Spanish Revolution of 1820, Karamsin's Russia, Effects of the French Revolution of 1830, Desertion of Portugal, Wellington, Carlist Struggle in Spain, The Affghanistan Expedition, The Future, &c. &c.

III.

SYDNEY SMITH.

THE WORKS OF THE REV. SYDNEY SMITH.

Fine Edition. In One Volume, with a portrait. Price $1 00.

"Almost every thing he has written is so characteristic that it would be difficult to attribute it to any other man. The marked individual features and the rare combination of power displayed in his works, give them a fascination unconnected with the subject of which he treats or the general correctness of his views. He sometimes hits the mark in the white, he sometimes misses it altogether, for he by no means confines his pen to theories to which he is calculated to do justice; but whether he hits or misses, he is always sparkling and delightful. The charm of his writings is somewhat similar to that of Montaigne or Charles Lamb."—*North American Review.*

IV.

PROFESSOR WILSON.

THE RECREATIONS OF CHRISTOPHER NORTH.

In One Volume 8vo., first American Edition, with a Portrait. Price $1 00.

CONTENTS.

Christopher in his Sporting Jacket—A Tale of Expiation—Morning Monologue—The Field of Flowers—Cottages—An Hour's Talk about Poetry—Inch Cruin—A Day at Windermere—The Moors—Highland Snow-Storm—The Holy Child—Our Parish—May-day—Sacred Poetry—Christopher in his Aviary—Dr. Kitchiner—Soliloquy on the Seasons—A Few Words on Thomson—The Snowball Bicker of Piedmont—Christmas Dreams—Our Winter Quarters—Stroll to Grafsmere—L'Envoy.

Extract from Howitt's "Rural Life."

"And not less for that wonderful series of articles by Wilson, in Blackwood's Magazine—*in their kind as truly amazing and as truly glorious as the romances of Scott or the poetry of Wordsworth.* Far and wide and much as these papers have been admired, wherever the English language is read, I still question whether any one man has a just idea of them as a whole."

V.

Carlyle's Miscellanies.

CRITICAL AND MISCELLANEOUS ESSAYS OF THOMAS CARLYLE.

In one 8vo. volume, with a Portrait.

PRICE $1 75.

CONTENTS.

Jean Paul Friedrich Richter—State of German Literature — Werner — Goethe's Helena—Goethe—Burns—Heyne—German Playwrights—Voltaire—Novalis—Signs of the Times—Jean Paul Friedrich Richter again—On History—Schiller—The Nibelungen Lied—Early German Literature—Taylor's Historic Survey of German Poetry—Characteristics—Johnson—Death of Goethe—Goethe's Works—Diderot—On History again—Count Cagliostro—Corn Law Rhymes—The Diamond Necklace—Mirabeau—French Parliamentary History—Walter Scott, &c. &c.

VI.

TALFOURD & STEPHEN.

THE CRITICAL WRITINGS OF T. NOON TALFOURD AND JAMES STEPHEN

WITH A FINELY ENGRAVED PORTRAIT.

In One Volume, 8vo. Price $1 25.

Contents of "Talfourd."

Essays on British Novels and Romances, introductory to a series of Criticisms on the Living Novelists—Mackenzie, The Author of Waverley, Godwin, Maturin, Rymer on Tragedy, Colley Cibber's Apology for his Life, John Dennis's Works, Modern Periodical Literature, On the Genius and Writings of Wordsworth, North's Life of Lord Guilford, Hazlitt's Lectures on the Drama, Wallace's Prospects of Mankind, Nature and Providence, On Pulpit Oratory, Recollections of Lisbon, Lloyd's Poems, Mr Oldaker on Modern Improvements, A Chapter on Time, On the Profession of the Bar, The Wine Cellar, Destruction of the Brunswick Theatre by Fire, First Appearance of Miss Fanny Kemble, On the Intellectual Character of the late Wm. Hazlitt.

Contents of "Stephen."

Life of Wilberforce, Life of Whitfield and Froude, D'Aubigne's Reformation, Life and Times of Baxter, Physical Theory of Another Life, The Port Royalists, Ignatius Loyola, Taylor's Edwin the Fair.

"His (Talfourd's) Critical writings manifest on every page a sincere, earnest and sympathizing love of intellectual excellence and moral beauty. The kindliness of temper and tenderness of sentiment with which they are animated, are continually suggesting pleasant thoughts of the author." —*North American Review.*

VII.

LORD JEFFREY.

THE CRITICAL WRITINGS

OF

FRANCIS LORD JEFFREY.

In One Volume 8vo., with a Portrait.

From a very able article in the North British Review we extract the following:

"It is a book not to be read only—but studied—it is a vast repository; or rather a system or institute, embracing the whole circle of letters—if we except the exact sciences—and contains within itself, not in a desultory form, but in a well digested scheme, more original conceptions, bold and fearless speculation and just reasoning on all kinds and varieties of subjects than are to be found in any English writer with whom we are acquainted within the present or the last generation. * * * His choice of words is unbounded and his felicity of expression, to the most impalpable shade of discrimination, almost miraculous. Playfu., lively, and full of illustration, no subject is so dull or so dry that he cannot invest it with interest, and none so trifling that it cannot acquire dignity or elegance from his pencil. Independently however, of mere style. and apart from the great variety of subjects embraced by his pen, the distinguishing feature of his writings, and that in which he excels his cotemporary reviewers, is the deep vein of practical thought which runs throughout them all."

VIII

SIR JAMES MACKINTOSH.

SIR JAMES MACKINTOSH'S

CONTRIBUTIONS TO THE EDINBURGH REVIEW.

Collected and Edited by his Son.

In One Volume 8vo., with a Portrait, $1 75.

THE POEMS

OF

FRANCES SARGENT OSGOOD.

Illustrated by the best artists.

In one volume octavo, uniform with Carey & Hart's illustrated Bryant, Willis, &c.

The following exquisitely finished line engravings are from original designs, by our most celebrated painters, and are executed in the highest style of art:—Portrait of the Authoress; Hope; A Child playing with a Watch; The Reaper; Ida; Old Friends; The Child's Portrait; Little Red Riding Hood; The Life Boat; Twilight Hours; The Arab and his Steed; Zuleika.

"There is nothing mechanical about her; all is buoyant, overflowing, irrepressible vivacity, like the bubbling up of a natural fountain. In her almost childish playful ness, she reminds us of that exquisite creation of Fouque, Undine, who knew no law but that of her own waywardness. The great charm of her poetry is its unaffected simplicity. It is the transparent simplicity of truth, reflecting the feeling of the moment like a mirror."—*Rev. Dr. Davidson.*

"In all the poems of Mrs. Osgood, we find occasion to admire the author as well as the works. Her spontaneous and instinctive effusions appear, in a higher degree than any others in our literature, to combine the rarest and highest capacities in art with the sincerest and deepest sentiments and the noblest aspirations. They would convince us, if the beauty of her life were otherwise unknown, that Mrs. Osgood is one of the loveliest characters in the histories of literature or society."—*Pennsylvania Inquirer and Courier.*

"The position of Mrs. Osgood, as a graceful and womanly poetess, is fixed, and will be enduring. To taste of faultless delicacy, a remarkable command of poetical language, great variety of cadence, and a most musical versification, she has added recently the highest qualities of inspiration, imagination, and passion, in a degree rarely equalled in the productions of women.... The reputation which Mrs. Osgood enjoys, as one of the most amiable, true-hearted, and brilliant ladies in American society, will add to the good fortune of a book, the intrinsic excellence and beauty of which will secure for it a place among the standard creations of female genius."—*Home Journal.*

THE

PROSE WRITERS OF AMERICA.

WITH A SURVEY OF THE INTELLECTUAL HISTORY, CONDITION, AND PROSPECTS OF THE COUNTRY.

BY RUFUS WILMOT GRISWOLD.

SECOND EDITION, REVISED.

Illustrated with Portraits from Original Pictures.

Complete in one volume octavo—$3.50.

CONTENTS.

Intellectual History, Condition, and Prospects of the Country—Edwards, Franklin, Jefferson, Madison, Dwight, Marshall, Hamilton, Ames, J. Q. Adams, C. B. Brown, Wirt, Quincy, Allston, Story, Paulding, Flint, Channing, Wheaton, Webster, Audubon, Walsh, Irving, Buckminster, Verplanck, Norton, Sanderson, Dana, Wilde, Cooper, A. H. Everett, Hall, Schoolcraft, Dewey, Sparks, John Neal, Bryant, Edward Everett, Kennedy, Bush, Sedgwick, Wayland, Prescott, Edward Robinson, Leslie, Legare, Ware, Bancroft, Marsh, Hooker, Brownson, Child, Bird, Emerson, Fay, Cheever, Hoffman, Kirkland, Hawthorne, Willis, Longfellow, Simms, Joseph C. Neal, Poe, Tuckerman, Fuller, Headley, Mathews, Thorpe, Whipple.

"Mr. Griswold's book has been executed honestly, ably, and well, and is a valuable contribution to the literature of the country."—*Knickerbocker.*

"We deem the book by all odds the best of its kind that has ever been issued; and we certainly know of no one who could have made it better."—*N. Y. Courier and Inquirer.*

A New and Cheap Edition

OF THE HISTORY OF

THE FRENCH REVOLUTION.

BY M. A. THIERS,

LATE PRIME MINISTER OF FRANCE.

Translated from the French, with Notes and Additions.

The Four Volumes, complete in Two.

***Price only* $1 50.**

The edition of the History of the French Revolution now offered to the public is printed on VERY LARGE TYPE, on good paper, and contains upwards of

Eighteen Hundred Large Octavo Pages,

and is unquestionably the cheapest book ever published. It *forms a necessary introduction* to *THE LIFE OF NAPOLEON*, by M. A. THIERS, *NOW IN COURSE OF PUBLICATION*, and the two works present a complete

HISTORY OF FRANCE

from the commencement of the French Revolution, down to the death of Napoleon.

WASHINGTON

AND THE

GENERALS OF THE AMERICAN REVOLUTION.

COMPLETE IN TWO VOLS. 12MO.

Illustrated by Sixteen beautiful, engraved Portraits.

Containing Biographical Sketches of Generals Washington, Greene, Wayne, Israel Putnam, Gates, Lord Sterling, Schuyler, Sullivan, Mercer, Armstrong, Knox, Arnold, Swallwood, De Haas, St. Clair, Elbert, Irvine, Wieden, Varnum, Woodford, Williams, Moylan, McDougall, Glover, McIntosh, Thompson, Nixon, Gist, Wooster, Spencer, Poor, Moore, Patterson, James Reed, Pomroy, Sumner, Stark, Moultrie, Joseph Reed, Greaton, Morgan, Marion, Lee, Mifflin, Parsons, Lincoln, Montgomery, Whitcomb, Cadwalader, Heath, Thomas, Geo. Clinton, James Clinton, Larned, La Fayette, Deborre, Pulaski, Russell, Ducoudray, La Neuville, Steuben, De Woedtke, Kosciuszko, Tufin, Duportail, De Fernoy, Conway, De Kalb, Gadsden, Hogan, Huger, Hazen, Wilkinson, Sumter, Scott, Pinckney, Howe, Frye, Ward, Rufus, Putnam, Nash, Stephen, Dayton, Hand, Muhlenberg, Lewis, Huntington and Maxwell.

"It is a complete, impartial and well written History of the American Revolution, and at the same time a faithful biography of the most distinguished actors in that great struggle, whose memories are enshrined in our hearts. The typographical execution of the work is excellent, and sixteen portraits on steel are remarkably well done."—*City Item.*

JOHNSON'S FARMERS' CYCLOPEDIA and Dictionary of Rural Affairs, with Engravings, from the last London edition, with numerous additions relative to this country, by Gouverneur Emerson, royal 8vo. 1156 pp., 17 plates, full bound, raised bands, reduced to $4 00.

MISS LESLIE'S

LADY'S RECEIPT BOOK.

A useful companion for large or small families—being a sequel to her work on Cookery—comprising new and improved directions for preparing Soups, Fish, Meats, Vegetables, Poultry, Game, Pies, Puddings, Cakes, Confectionery, Jellies, Breakfast and Tea Cakes, Embroidery, Crotchet work, Braiding, Needle work, Cleaning Furs, Merinos, &c., Washing Laces, Destroying Ants, Bugs and Mice, Cleaning Silver, Preparing Colors, making Artificial Flowers, &c. &c. Complete in one volume, 400 pages, price, bound, $1 00.

ALSO,

MISS LESLIE'S COMPLETE COOKERY, bd., $1 00
MISS LESLIE'S HOUSE BOOK, bound, . 1 00
MISS LESLIE'S FRENCH COOKERY, . 25
MISS LESLIE'S INDIAN MEAL BOOK, . 25

www.ingramcontent.com/pod-product-compliance
Lightning Source LLC
LaVergne TN
LVHW010153110826
845151LV00002B/502
* 9 7 8 1 4 2 5 5 3 8 5 1 4 *